Ann E. Yuill
630 Prospect Drive
Medicine Hat

Red Lights
on the Prairies

The Nose Creek brothels, Calgary, in 1911

Red Lights on the Prairies

James H. Gray

Macmillan of Canada Toronto

ISBN 0-7705-0769-7

Reprinted 1971, 1972, 1974

Printed in Canada
for The Macmillan Company of Canada Limited
70 Bond Street, Toronto

Contents

List of Maps vii
Preface ix

1 The booze-brothel syndrome of urban pioneers 1
2 There was no street like Annabella Street . . . 26
3 . . . except Regina's River Street, which was in Moose Jaw 58
4 Saskatoon — where everything was handy to the station 87
5 The saga of Joe Clarke — radical conservative with socialist leanings 99
6 "To hell with Pearl Harbor — remember Pearl Miller!" 124
7 Lethbridge and Drumheller: something more than a house 155
8 Requiem for an era 182

Appendix 193
Footnotes 195
Index 202

List of Maps

"Social Centres" in downtown Winnipeg in 1910   xii
Winnipeg   45
Regina   71
Saskatoon   93
Edmonton   105
Calgary   131
Lethbridge   161

Preface

The title of this book is a misnomer to this extent — there were no red lights used on the prairies to identify "red-light districts". Research has turned up only a single reference to red lights actually being used, and that in Cranbrook, British Columbia. The term, none the less, has been a universally understood synonym for segregated areas of prostitution since at least 1900, and it was still the well-understood designation in 1971, twenty-five years after the last of the old-time houses of assignation had disappeared. The term itself is an Americanism, so it is probably a verbal importation of the settlers who came north from the United States, which also provided most of the early prairie prostitutes as well as sod-busters and entrepreneurs.

Though the term is a fictitious appellation of dubious origin, the houses themselves were as much a part of the "firsts" of settlement as the railway stations and hotel bars. They were invariably established before the churches and long before the schools. And, if they did not actually lead the railway constructors across the prairies, they were in business long before the first trains were rolling down their new tracks. Indeed, from the early reports of the North West Mounted Police, it is quite easy to establish a correlation between the progress of railway construction and the existence of prostitution. Unfortunately, however, the actual number of women involved is lost to history, for the only records now extant are those of the convictions of keepers and inmates of houses of ill fame. For the handful who appear on these records, there must have been scores, even hundreds, who plied their trade without police molestation. The Mounties, for one thing, were spread so thinly that they could not have kept the settlements under constant surveillance. Also, they followed a policy of taking action only when the activities of the whores* got boisterously out of hand.

The West became overrun with brothels for the same reason that it broke out in a rash of boozeries — the first tides of immigration were composed overwhelmingly of unattached young men in the prime of life. A weakness, an attraction, a natural affinity — call it what you will — of unattached young men for booze and broads has been commonplace since the dawn of history. And for the same length of time this affinity has stirred the guardians of public morality to outraged protest. That is what this book is all about — the interaction of alcohol and prostitution on the mores of the times between the start of prairie settlement and the middle of the 1920s.

The focus is on urban as distinct from rural or agricultural settlement. The trials and tribulations of the prairie homesteaders have been preserved in detail in a hundred personal histories. But the ordeal of the thousands of young men who stormed into the towns that became cities, and went no farther, is almost virgin territory for historical research. It was in the unbelievable congestion of the

*pronounced hoo-er, always.

urban West that the mixed tinder of whisky and prostitution set the prairies ablaze with controversy during the first decades of our century. The great prohibitionist crusade, too, swept everything before it like a prairie grass fire, and, like a prairie grass fire, fizzled into nothingness when it passed.

The churches were an integral part of the social history of western cities but no more so than the bars, the brothels, and the poolrooms. In fact, they were less so, in a population that was overwhelmingly male, young, and single. For his book *My Neighbor*, published in 1911, J.S. Woodsworth prepared a map of North Winnipeg on which all the poolrooms, hotel bars, and brothels were located. He entitled this illustration a map of "social centres". The bars, brothels, and poolrooms were not only the social centres for the unattached males; they were almost the only recreational facilities available to them. In total, they outnumbered the churches by six to one. There were three times as many brothels alone as there were churches.

On the unanimous testimony of those who claimed to know, the young men visited the brothels with the same casualness with which they went into a bar or poolroom, or even to church. It was not something done secretly, or with any semblance of a guilty feeling. It was done both singly and collectively as a matter of offhand choice over gambling or drinking. Whatever stigma became attached to the patronizing of prostitutes was in the eyes of the social reformers.

In many ways the twenty-five-year campaign of the forces of righteousness against the forces of evil was the most exciting chapter in the history of the prairie provinces. In documenting it I have relied heavily on two sources — the back files of the early newspapers and the memories of the pioneers of the cities who had personal knowledge of both the bars and brothels. With both sources some almost insurmountable problems were encountered.

The very early journals were "news" papers in name only. Mostly they were adjuncts of printing plants whose main concern was their advertising columns. In many cases they were subsidized by one political party or the other. Few of them had any real news-gathering staffs and they filled their columns with stories cribbed from other papers and serial material bought by the bale from the United States. Their primary interest was in politics and they made no pretence of covering local news; that was supplied by the secretaries of the fraternal lodges and secret societies, the churches, the Christian

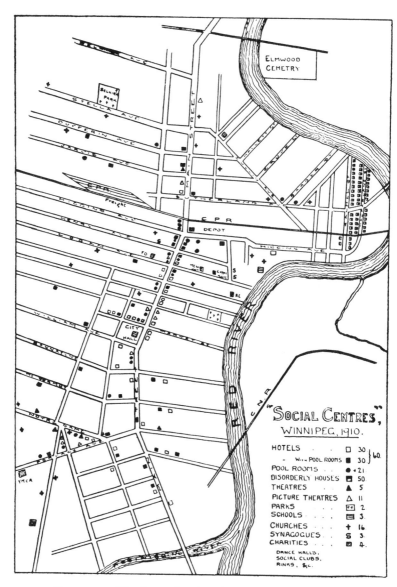

Downtown Winnipeg, showing the centres of social life —
from J.S. Woodsworth, *My Neighbor.*

Endeavor, the Women's Missionary Societies, the Loyal Temperance Legion, the W.C.T.U., and the Boards of Trade. There was no crime news to cover, save infrequent berserk murders and suicides. On the rare occasions in which local prostitutes were hauled into court the item, if reported at all, was usually buried with a miscellany of local items.

In all the cities the combined effect of alcohol and sex on public behaviour periodically so outraged moral sensitivity that the reverend clergy mounted great reform movements aimed at restoring decorum. It was the reportage of these outbreaks that provided the rich veins of factual material around which generalized theories can be woven.

As for first-person-singular testimony, it presented a serious problem. If there are any survivors of the famous raid on Winnipeg's Thomas Street brothels in 1904, they have eluded all efforts to ferret them out. Similarly there are in 1971 few survivors of the young blades who cut such wide swaths through Edmonton, Lethbridge, Calgary, and Moose Jaw in 1910. But some have survived and a number of them were located and interviewed, mostly on the condition that they would not be identified. Only when they could be assured that their confidences would be respected were they willing to help put some flesh on the research bones supplied by the printed word.

Others were prepared to be quoted but their willingness created almost as much of a problem. If some were identified and some not, readers might well attribute to a person quoted on one event what was said by an unidentified person about another related event. I decided that it would be best for all concerned to identify none of the informative old-timers. This leaves readers with only the word of the author that such interviews took place.

Not all the assumptions made and the conclusions drawn are based solely on the foregoing research. During my career as a journalist, I served a stint as a police reporter for the *Winnipeg Free Press*. "Big Bill" Eddy was then head of the Winnipeg Police morality squad and I whiled away many a dog-watch hour listening to the yarns of the morality squad officers who were still, in 1936-7, on a first-name basis with most of the Annabella Street whores. And as a small boy, twenty years previously, I acquired considerable first-hand knowledge of the inside of the Winnipeg saloons and the impact of alcohol on family life.

For enabling me to build upon this knowledge in the creation of this book I owe more than I can say to the magnificent co-operation I have received from the librarians and archivists. I was given free run of the superb facilities of the Glenbow-Alberta Institute in Calgary. The Saskatchewan Archives in both Regina and Saskatoon and the Manitoba Archives in Winnipeg were also most helpful. The public library people in Winnipeg, Regina, Moose Jaw, Lethbridge, Calgary, Edmonton, and Saskatoon were most co-operative and assisted with research suggestions. Above all I am most grateful to the three dozen or so survivors of the brothel era who trusted me with their secret past.

JAMES H. GRAY

Grassmere Farm
Calgary

Red Lights
on the Prairies

The Booze-Brothel Syndrome of Urban Pioneers

Nothing to compare with the great mass migration into western Canada during the first decades of the twentieth century ever happened anywhere in the world before. True, greater numbers of people were transplanted from the Ukraine to Siberia when Stalinist Russia undertook the "liquidation of the Kulaks as a class" during the inter-war years. This, however, was only achieved by force by a tyrannical dictatorship. The 1870 land rushes into the Dakotas and Montana were a lot more frantic. But these human stampedes were

1

evoked by wild rumours of gold strikes, some of which turned out to
be true. Nowhere, however, were more people enticed, cajoled,
persuaded, induced, gulled, and just plain bamboozled into tearing
themselves up by their roots to journey across half a continent, or
halfway round the world, to a land where not a single constructive
step had been taken by anybody to prepare for their arrival.

Between 1900 and 1915, the combined efforts of government,
railways, and free-lance land agents lured more than one million
immigrants to the three prairie provinces.[1] Their coming ushered in
the bawdiest, brawlingest, drunkenest, and back-breakingest era in
prairie history. It was also the most puritanical, law-abiding, Sabbatarian, and pietistic. It was an era in which the forces of self-righ-
teousness collided head-on with the entrenched forces of prostitution. That was a collision which generated uproarious civic turmoil,
made and unmade reputations and political careers, disrupted the
even tenor of law enforcement, and turned Protestant pulpits into
launching pads for morality crusades.

There are, of course, several superficial historic parallels to the
Canadian prairie epoch. At first glance, the great London gin drunk
of 1730 to 1750 seems comparable to the whisky binge on the
prairies from 1900 to 1916. In London, however, everybody seemed
involved — women and children as well as adult males. In the pioneer
Canadian West, debauchery was a male monopoly. Comparable
drunkenness, prostitution, and wide-open gambling also charac-
terized the development of the American cities that burst into existence with the opening of the Great Plains to settlement. In the
United States, however, it was all accompanied by overtones of
violent crime and political corruption for which there was no coun-
terpart in Canada. Aside from sex- and whisky-based enterprises,
frontier Canada was almost unbelievably law-abiding. Nobody held
up trains or stages, or robbed banks, or shot up towns or even
saloons. When a firearm was discharged in drunken anger in Fort
Macleod, for example, the threat by the local editor to print the
name of the peace disturber if he repeated the performance was
enough to restore decorum.[2] Across the border in the neighbouring
states, it was, by legend at least, a poor town that could not boast of
its local bad men or boothill cemetery.

This contrast between behaviour on either side of the border is more than passing strange because roughly the same kind of people settled both areas. The settlement of western Canada and the construction of the Canadian Pacific Railway were undertaken to circumvent the takeover of the Canadian West by the American settlers who were even then pushing northward. The irony of settlement was that once the railway was built the bulk of the first settlers came from the United States anyway.[3] In the first five years of the century, immigrants from the United States outnumbered the British by 147,620 to 126,000, while the famous Slavs in the sheepskin coats trailed far behind at only 61,000.[4] What is more, the Americans kept on coming until, by the outbreak of the First World War, there were better than 500,000 of them on the prairies. So successful were the railways, the land companies, and the government in their sales campaigns in the United States that Minnesota and North Dakota interests fought back by mounting anti-Canadian campaigns.[5]

The generally accepted explanation for the divergence in development patterns between the United States and Canada was the existence of the North West Mounted Police, who enforced rigid laws against gun toting. There is, however, a substantial body of evidence to indicate that, far from being the solution to the problem of law enforcement on the frontier, the Mounties quickly became part of the problem. Once the Force had chased the American whisky traders back across the border and sorted out the Indians its activities diminished to routine. The Force regularly went on long patrols during the summer, but when winter set in its members were confined to their forts for long sieges of inactivity. As Kipling was noticing about British troops in India, "single men in barracks don't grow into plaster saints". The Mounties had as much trouble with booze and sex as any of Kipling's heroes, a fact that is well documented in the diaries of Sergeant S.J. Clarke, who was a member of the Force from 1876 to 1884.[6] During that period he kept track of the high jinks at Fort Macleod and Fort Calgary, and his was a chronicle of non-stop poker games, fist fights, seductions, desertions, and gang-drunks lasting for days.

On New Year's Eve, 1880, Clarke recorded that there were four hundred at the barracks ball and there was lots of drinkable Jamaica ginger. On January 2 more whisky arrived and Clarke noted on January 3 that "C" and "E" Troops were both still drunk.

On January 21 he noted: "Captain Winder, Sergeant Ryan and myself went down to Capt. Jack's house and took Mrs. O'Neil back to her husband. She was in bed with Capt. Jack when we went into the house."

Two weeks later, he reported that the weather was fine and that "Jack O'Neil sued Captain Jack for taking his wife and keeping her. The case was tried before Col. McLeod and the jury fetched in damages of $125. I was a witness. So was Sgt. Ryan. This was the first seduction case that was done in this part of the country." From the size of the judgment Mrs. O'Neil must have been a quite superior type, for the diary had noted previously that one of the Mounties had bought a squaw for three dollars.

Some months later, Clarke reported another barracks party at which Corporal Patterson got into a drunken wrestling match with a squaw in the shoe shop. They knocked over the stove, which set fire to the shoe shop, the harness shop, and the big stable in which all the Mounties' horses were kept. A week later Constables Hannfin and Fogy were each fined three dollars for getting a squaw drunk in the post. This was followed by Constable Robbins' suing Captain Denny for "$1,000 for sleeping with his woman but Denny got off because Robbins could not produce the priest who performed the marriage ceremony".

Composed as it was of a body of inexperienced greenhorns, many of them still in their teens, it was inevitable that the internal troubles of the Mounties would be given a public airing. Questions were frequently raised in Parliament during consideration of the annual estimates of expenditures of the Force. The following is a comment by Sir John A. Macdonald during 1881:

> As regards the habits of the men, I think, on the whole, they are in a very fair state, but there is still a good deal of drinking. As the hon. gentleman knows, some of the force is stationed on the frontier, and there has been, I am afraid, a laxity in granting [liquor] permits. Besides . . . I have reason to believe also that there has been a great use of that most noxious alcoholic drink, Perry Davis' Pain Killer. It contains a great quantity of alcohol, and has not only affected the physical health of the men, but the mental health of some of them. That has been used largely under

the pretence of being medicinal, but, really, I am afraid, as a stimulant. There has been, and there will be hereafter a more rigid discipline preserved among the men.[7]

In their carousing, brawling, and boozing the pioneer Mounties were only imitating the life style that had long prevailed in the Red River Settlement and which was spreading westward wherever a new community was established. These were the opening days of an era when slaking whisky thirsts and satisfying the sexual urges of the settlers combined to put hotel bars on every second corner of all the cities and turned prostitution into a major industry.

Paradoxically, despite its open drunkenness and prostitution, the West in all other ways became the fiefdom of the hard-shell Sabbatarians and morality guardians. Winnipeg suffered through what must have been the most restrictive Sunday on the continent. It took fifteen years of intermittent agitation before the operation of streetcars on Sunday was finally approved in 1906. A suggestion that Sundays might be made less austere by permitting concerts of sacred music was roundly attacked by a Presbyterian zealot.[8] So formidable did the Protestant clergy become when aroused that Manitoba was well into the Jazz Age before its government had the courage to override their opposition to Sunday trains to the Lake Winnipeg beaches. It was almost as if a puritanical Sunday was the weekly revenge the clergymen took on the public for its refusal to join in their crusades against the brothels and bars.

In other western centres Sunday observance was somewhat less rigid but in most things, Winnipeg, from the beginning, seemed to set the fashion for the western cities. It was a style that was an amalgam of a dozen contradictory forces that grew from the attempt to graft a settled agricultural economy onto the fur-trade heritage of the Red River Valley. Though Winnipeg had been the centre of the prairie fur trade for 150 years, it managed a permanent population of barely 100 when Louis Riel struggled to find a way of bringing Manitoba into Confederation.[9] Nevertheless, it was the jumping-off place for the scattered settlements in the West, and the distribution point for the trade goods that came down the Red River or over the plains from St. Paul. The boats and wagon trains that brought the supplies northward carried the furs and the traders back to St. Paul, and St. Paul, as wide open a town as there was in the West, became the model on which early Winnipeg was fashioned. But it was far from the model which satisfied the pious settlers from the rural Bible belts of Ontario who began trickling into Manitoba after the completion of the Winnipeg-to-Pembina railway line in 1878. Not only did the Ontario settlers bring along their Loyal Orange Lodge, and their ingrained piety, but they were shepherded by their Presbyterian, Methodist, and Baptist clergymen of true evangelical zeal. [10] For the next forty years, the West depended in large measure on the theological schools of Ontario for its spiritual advisers, coupled, of course, with the steady infusion of men of the faith from Scotland and the United States.

The strength of organized Protestantism can be gauged in part from the fact that the Orange Lodge forced the Government of Ontario to put a $5,000 price on the head of Louis Riel, even after he had been elected to Parliament by the Red River Settlement. [11] The Métis, during the time of Louis Riel, may have constituted a majority in the Red River Settlement, but the Establishment, such as it was, was totally Anglo-Saxon and Protestant. It was reinforced soon afterwards by the arrival of several thousand families from Ontario who took possession of the countryside in the name of the Queen, the Flag, and militant Protestant Christianity. The strength of the churches naturally gives rise to the question of how the brothels and the boozeries managed to become established in the first place. The answer is quite simple. Both were there before the settlers arrived. They not only followed the railroad builders west but often led the way. By the early 1880s, prostitution was so well established in Winnipeg that the existence of segregated brothels was generally accepted by the citizenry.

Despite the steady influx from Ontario, settlement of the West at first was disappointingly slow. The vacant spaces in Manitoba filled gradually but there was little movement of importance into the Northwest Territories until after the completion of the C.P.R. Then settlement was retarded by a decade-long depression and Canada was into the twentieth century before the full flood of newcomers hit the West. [12]

The emphasis of all efforts to people the West, whether conducted by the railway land agencies or by Clifford Sifton's Department of Immigration, was on settlement of the agricultural lands. The railways obtained millions of acres of farm land which they sold directly or through agents on very favourable terms. The government itself offered free homesteads to potential settlers. So attractive was the prospect of free land that thousands of machinists, carpenters, brick-layers, shop clerks, bookkeepers, and tradesmen in infinite variety from the cities of England, Scotland, and Ireland became instant agriculturalists and embarked for western Canada to discover the horrors of homestead life. Thousands of them actually took up homesteads and only retreated to the cities and towns after nature demonstrated the folly of their action. Other thousands got to Winnipeg, or to one of the other booming communities, and went no farther. After the turn of the century, the flow of immigrants became a veritable stampede for which the country was completely unprepared. The urban settlement pattern which was established at Winnipeg with the arrival of the railway proved hopelessly inade-quate to cope with the influx.

The Winnipeg pattern was the quintessence of logical simplicity. The first railway station became the centre around which everything else developed. It provided the railway with a place to deposit train-loads of immigrants and freight cars full of equipment and supplies. To cater to the immediate needs of the settlers, local enterprisers surrounded the station with jerry-built hotels and stores. The frantic tempo of the construction boom provided immediate employment for all the skilled tradesmen who decided to end their journey in Winnipeg. As long as the good weather remained, the construction crews worked from daylight to dark on urgently needed railway shops, wholesale warehouses, and retail stores, and in tearing down the hotels and rebuilding them on an even grander scale.

Whether the newcomer detrained at Winnipeg, Regina, Calgary, or Saskatoon, the view from the station platform was remarkably similar. Hotels and bars caught his eye in any direction. Beyond the hotels were wholesale warehouses and retail stores, and in the dis-tance houses for the citizens were being frantically carpentered into existence.

Elsewhere the coming of the railways brought a new phenomenon to the prairies — the instant towns which came into existence over-night. When the builders of the Canadian Northern Railway reached the vicinity of Battleford in 1905 they discovered that they were on the wrong side of the Saskatchewan River. The town hugged the south bank, while the railway was on the uninhabited north side. A surveyor picked up a peg and drove it into the prairie sod as the site for North Battleford. By that fall this vacant spot on the prairie had grown into a town of 500, complete with a chamber of commerce, a town council, and a volunteer fire department. Essentially the same story was repeated at several other points that summer as the railway raced toward Edmonton. [13]

There was one notable difference between the settlers who came before the immigration flood and those who came with it. The earlier arrivals were mainly farm families who went directly to their Manitoba homesteads. Those who came later were mostly single men, either bachelors or husbands who had left their wives and families at home until they could get established in the new country. For most of them, getting suitable jobs was easy; finding suitable lodgings they could afford was impossible. Not only did the building boom fail dismally to keep pace with the demand for homes for those already married, but there was such a shortage of marriageable women that the unwed settlers were condemned to single blessedness by simple arithmetic as much as by the housing famine. Mass migration had knocked normal male-female ratios completely out of balance. When the big influx began in 1901 the male population of the prairie region already outnumbered the female by 228,554 to 198,700. By 1911 there were 769,000 males but only 559,000 females, or more than 200,000 males for whom there were no female partners available.

The numerical disparity between the sexes was most strikingly apparent in the statistics for the cities. Thus in 1911 Edmonton's single males outnumbered females by 8,550 to 5,920; in Calgary the comparison was 17,337 to 8,979; in Regina it was 13,616 to 6,020; in Winnipeg, 43,000 to 32,000; and in Saskatoon, 4,309 to 2,581. [14] These figures, however, do not begin to tell the full story because they leave out of account all the officially married but temporarily separated husbands. Thrown *en masse* into the company of single men, the separated husbands naturally reverted to type. They too went searching for female company in competition with the single men and not infrequently they married all over again. During the peak years of settlement, requests for assistance in tracing missing immigrants poured into Ottawa at the rate of 5,000 a year. [15] The existence of this large floating single male population created an environment in which prostitution could flourish, and flourish it did everywhere.

Not only was there an overwhelming surplus of males, but they were hived together in housing congestion that was soon beyond belief and far beyond the ability of any tabulation of population figures to describe. Between 1901 and 1911, for example, Calgary grew from 4,398 to 43,704, and Edmonton from 4,176 to 30,479. During that decade a couple of international financial panics added to the growing pains of the cities by cutting off money for local improvements at critical moments. Even without these financial crises it would have been difficult enough for any city to keep pace with the normal demand for schools, sidewalks, sewers, water mains, and hospitals for a growing population. The population implosion made orderly development utterly impossible. In all the cities houses were built before sewer or water connections were possible. So they became cities of back-yard privies which filled the surrounding countryside with nauseous odours on the hot summer nights. Around the periphery of the cities shack towns were thrown up to bedevil civic governments further, since the city boundaries were continually being expanded.

Over the years Edmonton wrestled with a problem that did not appear to have become quite as acute in any other cities except Calgary and Saskatoon — the tent dwellers. In 1907 a tent count showed that there were 1,550 people living in 575 tents in Edmonton. With the winter coming on concern was expressed for the health of the tenters but the health officer reported that it was much healthier living in tents than in the slum rooming houses. [16]

In 1912 Edmonton had a severe outbreak of typhoid fever which the health inspector traced to rooming-house congestion. In one house on Namayo Street he found fourteen men sleeping in an attic over a two-storey rooming house, in a room ventilated by a single small window. In one Queen Street rooming house there were seven rooms containing thirty-one single beds on the first floor and twelve rooms holding twenty-nine single beds on the second floor. On Jasper Avenue a former store twenty-four feet by sixty feet was cut into two rooms. One side contained nineteen double beds and the other five bunks for ten men. Neither of these dwellings contained sanitary facilities of any kind.

In Calgary the General Hospital decided to ease its overcrowded wards by creating a tent village for its tuberculosis patients near the Bow River. [17] The experiment worked so well that it was continued almost until the outbreak of the First World War. Immigrants by the hundreds, who balked at the high cost of room rent, seized upon the tent idea and devised a combination tent and shiplap shell which provided year-round accommodation. Often two or three settlers shared this accommodation, cooking their meals on a cast-iron stove in the centre of the room and sleeping in bunks surrounding the stove.

The Methodist Church in 1913 had the Reverend J.S. Woodsworth conduct in-depth studies of social conditions in several cities in the West. He found appalling overcrowding in the older Winnipeg slums; yet in Regina, which was too new to have developed slums, conditions were almost as bad. [18] In his earlier book, *My Neighbor*, Woodsworth quoted several newspaper reports as examples of congestion. [19] The following is from the *Winnipeg Telegram* for October 15, 1909:

> The health inspector rudely paid a midnight visit to the place at 47 Austin Street the other night, the place being where Mrs. Chudek runs her boarding-house.
>
> There he found thirty-two men living, where there should be seven, according to the laws of health.
>
> In handling this case the magistrate said that "people are supposed to live like human beings and not like hogs. In your house there was not space for a dog let alone a man."
>
> Another case just as bad was that of M. and P. Kozuchar, who conduct a boarding-house at 37 Austin Street where men and girls were sleeping in the same room and that the cellar was occupied as a living-room. In all there were twenty-five people where there should be only seven.

In his survey of Regina, Woodsworth paid particular attention to an area six blocks square in the east end of the city known as Germantown. It contained 599 dwellings, a few fully modern cottages and the remainder little better than shacks. In one two-roomed house there was a family of seven, including teen-aged boys and girls; in a four-roomed house a family kept six lodgers, and a flock of chickens in the kitchen. In the 599 houses there was plumbing in only forty-eight and baths in only fifteen. The city was laying water and sewer mains in the area but Woodsworth estimated that sixty per cent of the dwellings were too poorly built to make connections possible. In this district the residents were permitted to keep one cow per family and many of them kept chickens as well. When it rained the whole area became a sea of mud and manure.

Within this area, serving the needs of 1,800 persons, there were five hotels with bars, seven poolrooms, eight barber-shop/pool-rooms, and three dance halls. At any hour of the day Woodsworth reported that the bars contained, in the aggregate, an average of 115 drinkers. Aside from the single movie, the bars, poolrooms, and dance halls constituted the only social and recreational activities in the area.

In addition to being overwhelmingly male, the immigrants who caused such congestion were also predominantly young, predominantly single, and predominantly robust. In the age of the railroad builders, all the heavy work was done by strong young backs. They dug, gravelled, tied, and graded the rights of way with pick, shovel, and wheelbarrow. On construction jobs the men sometimes worked a sixteen-hour day, manhandling the foundation stone, bricks, mortar, and steel onto the sites and into place. They excavated the city ditches, built the city streets, dug the sewers, laid the water mains, and mixed the concrete by hand. Only when heavy lifting reached a point beyond the limits of block and tackle and human muscle was horse-power called into play.

Here, in short, was a male population in the prime of life, glowing with the virility of youth, and in the superb physical condition which a steady diet of hard work produced. If they were not driven by sheer animal exuberance to seek the female companionship of the brothels, they would have been driven to do so by the stinking atmosphere of their overcrowded rooming houses. Of this there cannot be the slightest doubt. When the young settlers downed their tools on payday, sampling the delights awaiting them in their favourite bordellos was close to the top of their evening's cultural agenda.

The social upheaval engendered by the booze and the broads was surely of greater continuing interest to the pioneer communities than all the other issues put together. Yet historians have managed to create the illusion that the West was settled by monks, eunuchs, and vestal virgins, interested only in debating such ethereal issues as free trade, the Manitoba Schools question, and discriminatory freight rates.

No such society could ever have turned prostitution into a major industry, as it clearly was in Winnipeg where 200 women were employed in the forty-eight McFarlane Street and Annabella Street brothels, [20] in Calgary which once boasted three segregated areas, and in Edmonton where the brothels spilled over from Kinistino Street in all directions. How many girls plied their profession on the prairies can hardly be estimated. In Winnipeg police magistrate Daly once complained that there were hundreds of streetwalkers there. [21] One Edmonton madam, in 1914, put the number of practising prostitutes at between 400 and 500. Another regarded this as a gross exaggeration and said there were hardly more than forty or fifty brothels in town. Both figures may well have been accurate, for in one raid in 1909 the Edmonton police picked up 28 girls and 64 men in one house of ill fame where sex and gambling were provided as a joint enterprise. Regina, Moose Jaw, and Lethbridge all had their segregated areas although they functioned on more modest scales than those in the larger centres.

It would be incorrect, however, to attribute the flowering of prostitution on the prairies only to the predominantly male population, even when it was coupled with wide-open boozing and housing congestion. Prostitution as a physiological functional necessity and recreational facility had existed since the earliest days of the fur trade. The large half-breed population at the dawn of settlement was the product of liaison between the fur traders and Indian women. As settlement followed the fur trade, sexual exploitation of the Indian women became commonplace among tribes that came into contact with the white men. The practice of Indians' squatting with their families around trading posts and selling the services of their wives and daughters for pennies with which to buy booze is a well-documented fact of American history. [22] What is not so well known is that the practice persisted in southern Alberta long after the whisky traders were driven from the country. The reports of the North West Mounted Police noted that Indians brought their women to the river flats below Lethbridge for the purposes of prostitution. In 1886, traffic in Indian women became a national scandal which involved employees of the Indian Affairs Department.

The Reverend Samuel Trivett, a missionary on the Blood Indian

Reserve near Fort Macleod, charged that Indian girls were being sold into slavery by their parents.[23] White men came onto the reserve, he said, bought the girls, and, when they grew tired of them, turned them out as prostitutes onto the streets of Macleod. The investigation into the Trivett charges was inconclusive, but the answer to them published by the *Macleod Gazette* provides an interesting insight into the public attitudes of the times (see appendix).

Prostitution was by no means confined to the cities. It flourished in the hinterland as well.[24] Sometimes the girls worked the passenger trains from Winnipeg to the Pacific coast. Sometimes they travelled from town to town with pool sharks. The girl would ply her trade quietly while he beat the yokels out of their money playing pea-pool, and if he sometimes lost he would direct the attention of the winners to the wares offered by his girl friend. Still other whores travelled a regular circuit, like the reverend clergy. The railway news agents could always tell when there was a new girl in town by the number of local blades who sidled up to them on the station platforms to buy contraceptives. Many newsies on the branch lines made more money selling such supplies than they did from their fruit and magazines.[25]

Occasionally, a woman would find a town to her liking and settle into it permanently. This, as happened in Big Valley, Alberta, could lead to disaster. An enterprising young prostitute once bought a lot in Big Valley, put up a house, and settled into the business of serving the neighbourhood. Her presence naturally came to the attention of the ladies of the town, who took it as an affront and demanded that she be run out of town. When the Big Valley men refused to cooperate, the women took matters into their own hands. Late one night they set her house afire, and it burned to the ground. The woman got the message and left town.[26]

Whether they practised their profession in town or country, in segregated areas or scattered around the cities, the very existence of the prostitutes was regarded as a challenge to be met head on by the dominant Anglo-Saxon Protestant churches. They thundered against law-enforcement laxity which permitted fallen women to solicit on the streets. But when the police cracked down on streetwalkers, and confined the prostitutes within segregated areas, the moral reformers became even angrier. Yet whether the reverend clergy were dedicated to the complete destruction of prostitution as an institution, or only objected to the whores' plying their trade in the public view, was never quite clear. In some instances they mounted crusades to wipe out the traffic; in others they demanded only that the women be driven out of town. In any event, the interest of the clergy in illicit sex was intermittent, whereas combating the evils of alcohol became their whole existence. Because tarrying in the bars was associated with prostitution, the coupling of prostitution and drunkenness as targets of the moral crusades was inevitable. It was this coupling which led to the formation of the powerful Temperance and Moral Reform Society.

The Roman Catholics took a far more tolerant view of booze and prostitution than did the Baptists, Presbyterians, and Methodists. The Anglicans were somewhere in between. The Baptists laid their angry lash on both vices with equal enthusiasm, and shared with the Presbyterians a passionate dedication to strict Sabbatarianism. The Methodists were less rigid about Sunday observance and were much more concerned with the social implications of the liquor trade and prostitution than with the religious aspects that tormented their allies. As time passed, however, booze became the dominant issue with them all, while prostitution faded somewhat into the background, though by no means was it ever ignored. The explanation was simple enough. More families were adversely affected by booze than were harmed by the ladies of ill repute. The bars were everywhere, and so were the drunks, and so, most of all, was the impact of booze consumption on the lives of the people. [27]

The curious neglect by historians of the important part played by the ladies of ill repute in the settlement of the West might well be attributed to an over-fastidious reluctance to become involved with what was generally regarded as a "nasty" business. This was the zenith of the scruffy age of bowdlerism when nothing sexual was ever identified by an Anglo-Saxon noun. It had reached a stage where even the word "prostitute" was too gamy for the public prints or even the police records. There were no such things as "whores", "whorehouses", or even "brothels" or "bordellos". There were only "inmates" of "houses of ill fame", and even these terms fell into disuse once they gained wide acceptance. Thus the *Calgary Herald*, on May 25, 1907, carried this item from the police beat:

Two sisters, Helen and Marie Stuart, one a manufactured blond and the other a thorough brunette, members of the elite sorority of sisters from across the Langevin Bridge were charged with not complying with the law applied to them and were fined $15 each.

A couple of weeks later, the same paper got carried away even further with the following example of pioneer prose:

Hattie Rodgers and Maud Copeland, two languid ladies of the red glim variety were fined $25 and costs for keeping a disreputable house. Four ladyettes, Eva Hall, Blanche Palmer, Martha Saunders and C. Thomas paid $15. They were unable to appear themselves because the hour of 10:30 was very, very early and they were very, very tired. So they sent Lawyer Ballachey to plead guilty for them.

By 1911 the *Herald* was referring to the women as "demimondaines", and the low of something or other was reached by the *Edmonton Journal* on January 13, 1914, when it reported that one A.J. Clark had been "fined $100 for vagrancy and inducing a married woman to become disorderly".

Such reports as these, however, appeared but rarely in the public prints since months could pass in any western city without a prostitute's being arrested; and this was a condition which prevailed from the arrival of the first N.W.M.P. contingent. It was the Mounties who established what became the general police attitude toward prostitution on the prairies — live and let live. The N.W.M.P., and the municipal police when they came into the picture, were as tolerant toward the oldest profession as the reverend clergy were intolerant. It was only after the women involved themselves in extraneous lawbreaking that they were ever charged with prostitution. It was perhaps inevitable that such an attitude would develop from the nature of pioneer police departments.

None of the emerging metropolises evinced any real interest in the suppression of prostitution. In all the more important towns the attention of the civic leaders was elsewhere — on growing bigger, on putting pressure on the railway for better service, on the interminable politicking of the partisans of the Grits and the Tories. Most of all, the townspeople were worried about fire. Even the best places were little more than tinder-dry shack towns. In the period before the First World War perhaps one hundred towns were severely damaged by fires that destroyed entire business blocks. So usually the first public servant appointed was a fire chief, who also functioned as licence inspector and sanitary inspector. If the town drunks got out of hand, he was expected to handle the situation by locking them in a livery stable box-stall until they slept off their belligerence.

Not until the communities passed the 2,000 mark in population did they consider it necessary to appoint a full-time town constable. When they did appoint one, he became mainly responsible for running off unlicensed peddlers seeking to compete with local merchants, for forcing Chinese laundrymen to shut down on Sundays, and for hauling owners of wandering pig herds before the justice of the peace. Even when the communities reached city status, it was usually some years before they developed all-round law-enforcement agencies. Before that happened policemen were expected to earn their keep by taking in at least enough money in licence fees to balance police expenditures.[28] A combination fire hall and town hall was a prime requisite; a jail was a frill few towns thought they could afford.

Even after a jail was provided, the cities had to develop substantially before accommodation was provided for women prisoners. For the first twenty years of its existence, the Mounted Police used its guardrooms as jail accommodation for female offenders. In the cities, the cells for women shared common corridors with those for men. In Medicine Hat, Police Chief G.H. Markwick devised the easiest method of all for handling women. When he had to lay the strong arm of the law on a female form, he simply called a livery rig and sent her home. If her conduct was such that a charge against her was laid, the chief would send word when she was to appear in court. It was the summons system before the system was invented.[29]

It might be inferred from the lack of police cells for women that this led to the toleration of prostitution in the towns and cities. Arresting streetwalkers when there was no place to put them could be regarded by policemen as unnecessarily complicating their duties. A far more important factor, however, was the nearly universal acceptance by constituted authority that prostitution was something that had to be tolerated because it could not be eradicated. The casual way in which the subject is mentioned by the N.W.M.P. is proof enough of that.

Superintendent R.B. Deane noted in his report of 1890 that prostitution among Indians was a troublesome problem in the Lethbridge area. The police put what pressure they could on the Indians to make them stay on the reserves. But they could not prevent an Indian from moving to town and getting a job. It had become a common practice for Indians to bring their families to the flats below Lethbridge, go into town under the guise of looking for work, and return with "all manner of men" to their tents. Fortunately Lethbridge was soon to be incorporated as a town and Deane hoped that would help solve the problem.

> Incorporation [he wrote] will also enable the town to provide for the "social evil" and it is hoped that the authorities will not allow themselves to be persuaded by the fanatics into going too far. As I say elsewhere in my report I have devoted a great deal of time and trouble to checking the prostitution of Indian women, but the evil cannot be abated altogether. The next best thing to abating it is to have it under control.

The Mounted Police were never "persuaded by the fanatics into going too far". On the rare occasions when they took action against prostitutes, it was for some more important reason than mere prostitution. In Superintendent Deane's case, it was because the "social evil" was having a damaging effect on the Indians. In the years of the railway building booms, the Mounted Police were called on to act as protectors of the work in progress. The presence of either booze or prostitutes around the work gangs became a threat to the construction project. To remove that threat, the Mounties raided the tent brothels and charged the women with being inmates of houses of ill fame. After being assessed a nominal fine, the women were ordered to move on.

Moral indignation was not a quality much esteemed in city policemen, who were hired primarily because they were big enough and strong enough to maintain order. Given physical soundness, it was generally conceded that anybody with good feet could make a policeman. George Gammie, for example, was hired for the Calgary police force in 1911 because he was 6'1" and weighed 200 pounds. His training in the science of criminology consisted of being escorted around his beat once by another constable, shown how to try store entrances to make sure they were locked, and instructed to get to know the residents of the area and to keep a lookout for stolen property. That was it. The next day Gammie was on his own. In the unlikely event that he was called upon to take anybody in charge, he was shown how to complete a complaint form and book his prisoner into custody. If the accused had run afoul of the criminal code, a clerk would dig out the code and copy the appropriate section onto the information being laid. No ordinary policeman was expected to know anything about either the criminal code or the city by-laws. The latter were enforced only when instructions to do so were passed down to him from above.

As for enforcement of the law against prostitution, it was non-existent. Gammie's instructions were to keep order on his streets and not to permit excessive loitering. His contacts with prostitutes were few and far between. The women of the streets could spot a cop a block away by his towering height so it was a simple matter for them to keep out of sight of the law. If they occasionally failed to do so the law could always look the other way. [30]

The casual toleration of illicit sex undoubtedly reached its fullest flower in Police Chief Markwick of Medicine Hat, who owned the house in which the town's main brothel ran without interference for four years. Neither the Chief nor Medicine Hat saw anything wrong with that. He had rented the house to a third party, who leased it to the madam, who paid the rent to the Chief. When Medicine Hat decided to fire the Chief, his ownership of the brothel was not a relevant cause for the action. He had sued the mayor for libel after the mayor criticized him in the city council. The city council felt that, in launching and losing the libel suit, he had created an inharmonious situation that could not be tolerated within the civic administration. So they fired him for that. [31]

Elsewhere across the prairies, the local police followed Mounted Police policy and rousted the brothels only when something worse than illicit sex was brought to their attention. [32] When pressure from the moral uplifters became too great to ignore, they staged token raids and ran the inmates through the courts, which levied minimal fines. This never satisfied the reverend clergy, but the police dug in their heels for very practical reasons. As long as minimum fines were imposed and raids were infrequent, the women accepted them as tantamount to licensing. They willingly pleaded guilty. But if the police became serious about driving them out of business they retaliated by pleading not guilty and forcing the police to convict them in court.

As the uplifters continually pointed out, everybody knew where the brothels were. But a wide gulf divided knowledge of locations and obtaining evidence which would stand up in court. If there was one thing about which the police were all but unanimous it was that the uplifters' solution would not work. Driving the women out of town was no long-range solution. They simply set up shop outside the town limits, or rented apartments in respectable districts. So the police tried to live with what they could not abolish, and collided head on with the moral reformers in city after city.

As for the central figures in the drama, they were by all accounts a very ordinary lot, neither harridans nor courtesans, neither especially attractive nor notably unattractive. They were devoid, in a word, of memorably distinctive qualities of body, mind, or personality. When not practising their craft, they could be as ordinary as housewives with both the time and the inclination to sit down for a cup of coffee with the milkman and talk about baseball or the weather. They talked about their pasts with varying degrees of dishonesty.

"I guess at one time or another all their regular customers would ask them how they happened to get into that business," a policeman recalled. "My guess is that they did it mainly for money but I have my suspicions that most of them liked to build up their background when they talked about it. You know, they made it a lot worse or a lot better than it was. Like saying they hated their fathers and had to run away from home to avoid being raped. Or that they had come into the business to get money to send their mother to a sanitarium, or to Arizona or somewhere. You don't hear about people getting sent to Arizona for their health any more, but you sure used to in my day. Mostly, I think, they said they had financial motives, but they'd dress up the stories to make them sound good."[33]

The closest any Canadian ever came to making a scientific study of the motivation of women to become prostitutes was the survey undertaken by Adjutant McElhaney of the Salvation Army in Winnipeg in 1909 and 1910.[34] His statement that fifty-five per cent of the prostitutes in Winnipeg had been forced into the trade conjured up visions of white slavers gathering up girls bodily and imprisoning them in brothels. The adjutant later made it quite clear that this was far from his meaning. The force, as he defined it, was circumstance — poverty, desertion by or death of husbands leaving children to support, being seduced under promise of marriage and then cast aside, being disgraced by illegitimate pregnancy and unable to find another way of making a living.

And what about the other forty-five per cent? The adjutant would probably have agreed with a widely held police theory that many girls drifted into prostitution from a sub-marginal home environment and once established were not easily reached by reformers.

The classic case of resistance to rescue occurred in Calgary in 1911. On April 11 a young Calgarian went to the office of the *Herald* with a copy of a letter he had written to the chief of police and the Reverend Dr. G.W. Kerby. He claimed he had been beaten up and robbed of $100 when he had tried to persuade a girl to leave a brothel and marry him. The next day three of Calgary's most prominent women reform leaders went to the brothel to see the girl. The madam insisted the girl would have to pay a debt of $75 before she could leave. The women offered to put up the money. The girl, after thinking about it, decided she preferred the life she was leading to theirs. She stayed in the brothel.

Many of the madams are remembered more as den mothers than as exploiters of the "basest of human weaknesses". Their houses, in the main, were ill kept and poorly furnished, and generally bore little resemblance to the satin-draped bordellos of Paris into which the Canadian officers on leave stormed during the First World War. Prostitutes by reputation were disinclined to look with favour on housework. Thus when a donna prospered to a point where she was running a house of four or five girls she improved the surroundings by hiring a Chinese houseboy. He did the cleaning and often the cooking, served the drinks, and ran all the errands.

For the most part, the smaller enterprises dealt with casual as distinct from steady customers. They drifted in on payday from the mines, the railway shops and yards, the construction jobs, etc., usually by way of a lengthy sojourn in the bars. With such a bois-terous clientele, the wear and tear on even the sturdiest furniture was considerable. On the other hand, the women who tried to upgrade their custom by improving their environment often did quite well.

"Pearl Miller was easily the most successful whore Calgary ever had," one of her frequent customers recalled. "I think her secret of success was that she ran a clean and happy joint. There was never much rowdiness, even though her Turner Siding place was often full of Turner Valley roughnecks. She really acted more like a hostess than a whore. You know, she'd visit with you, have a drink with you though I never saw her drunk. She kept her eye on her girls and tried to run a real nice place where you liked to return to. If you didn't think where you were, you could easily get over what kind of a house it was. In that case you could imagine you were in a boarding house parlor with ordinary lodgers, with Pearl being the landlady looking after things."[35]

As for pimps, some of the prostitutes seemed to need them and others wouldn't have a man around. The madams who concentrated on building up a steady clientele had little need to have anybody out on the street soliciting for them. Only the inexperienced newcomers, the aging alcoholics, and the drug addicts, who were never more than a minority in the trade on the prairies, found pimps to be a necessity. Those who catered to the slum and underworld trade often kept a burly handyman around to intimidate the drunks or anybody who had ideas of strong-arming madam out of her earnings or jewellery. In a segregated area like Annabella Street in Winnipeg one bouncer could look after three or four houses.[36] Operating as they did beyond the law, it might be assumed they would have been fair game for other outlaws. But preying on prostitutes was seldom a profit-able caper. The established whores all kept avenues of communica-tion open with the police and co-operated in searches for major criminals. Underworld customers who antagonized the women quickly found the police breathing down their necks for all kinds of offences, some of which they had not committed. Similarly, it was common for a prostitute to get police assistance when she wanted to shed a pimp who had started to knock her around.

"We'd get a call from one of the girls and usually when we went around she'd be rather badly bruised up," a veteran policeman re-called. "She'd say that she'd testify the guy was living off the avails if we would pick him up, and that as you know could be a penitentiary offence. Whether she would have gone through with it was often doubtful, but we would pull him in and she'd come down to the station and tell him what she was going to do. Most of the time we'd put him on a train out of town and that solved everybody's problem, including the taxpayers'."[37]

There was seldom anything even remotely attractive about the houses themselves. In most of the western cities they were located in the near-downtown areas hard by the railway stations or yards. And as settlement boomed these were the districts which deteriorated quickest and furthest. The earliest construction always tended to be jerry-built, and the Anglo-Saxon families who were the first settlers soon vacated their substandard accommodation to build bigger and better houses in the new subdivisions. The real estate market for most of the early years was such that the owners could usually sell their downtown property for enough to pay for their newer accommodation. Much of the downtown property moved into the hands of the commercial developers, and what was left was rented to the late-arriving immigrants and held as speculation. It was in these areas that the prostitutes settled: first, because they were handy to the hotels and bars from which much of their custom was drawn; secondly, because if they behaved with circumspection the police left them alone; and thirdly, because they had no difficulty renting slum houses or rooms because they were preferred tenants with most slum landlords. In his annual report for 1909 Superintendent R. Burton Deane of the N.W.M.P. Calgary Detachment noted:

> The most extravagant rents are charged, as much as $100 to $150 a month in advance. The landlords are little better than sharks . . . In my opinion the most effective way of dealing with this troublesome problem would be to make it unlawful to rent a house for purposes of prostitution.

When the chief of police in Winnipeg in 1909 organized a segregated area, it was hardly an accident that the two streets selected were on the edge of what was Winnipeg's oldest settled area, and a two-iron shot from the Austin Street houses previously cited. In

Edmonton, in 1914, a royal commission received a list of the owners of one hundred houses of prostitution and most of the names on the list were eminently respectable citizens and corporations.

The existence of the houses of ill fame on the fringes of the immigrant areas became an awkward and bothersome threat to the morals of immigrant families. Because the economic pressure on the immigrant families was so severe, many young girls were nudged into the labour market before they were halfway through school. They worked for low wages and most of their pay went to help support their families. In their going and coming between home and work it was not long before they discovered the wide gulf that separated them from the other half of the population. They became conscious of fine clothes and easier living, and the further discovery that both could be theirs with employment in the brothels was hardly calculated to reconcile them to their own deprived existence. Paradoxically, while living conditions turned their attention toward a life of sin, it was often the brothel madam who turned them away. Woodsworth reported the case of an American who brought two sisters from North Dakota to Winnipeg with the idea of putting them to work in brothels. The elder he lured north with the promise of marriage and her young sister was brought along to be the bridesmaid. The brothel owners were happy to recruit the older girl but they refused to permit the sixteen-year-old on the premises. On the other hand, a Broad Street brothel owner in Regina recruited two Polish immigrant girls aged fourteen and seventeen under the guise of hiring them for housework. He was sentenced to four years in the penitentiary at hard labour.[38] Procuring juveniles for prostitution was one criminal offence for which no leniency could be expected.

As for the boys growing up in the slums, it is almost impossible to put enough evidence together on which any kind of a generalization can be based. Woodsworth reported the existence of one house in Winnipeg which was a regular hangout for public school drop-outs, newsboys, and messengers. In Calgary, some Italian boys grew up around the corner from brothels yet recalled nothing of their existence. Others, from more remote neighbourhoods, tell hilarious tales of turning the brothels into objectives of hide-and-seek games. Here's one recollection:

We used to hide down the street until we saw some guy going into one of those houses. Then we would wait for a while until we saw a light go on in the bedroom at the back of the house. There was this house on Fifth Avenue with a vacant lot on the side next to the bedroom and it had a rip in the bottom of the blind. If the women didn't pull it down quite hard enough one side would curl up a little and we could peek into the room. That's how us kids learned about sex — through that crack in the blind in that house on Fifth Avenue. Sometimes when the blind was pulled right down and we couldn't see in we'd stand by the window and listen. Then when we'd stop hearing voices inside we'd rap loudly on the window and run like hell. We never got caught but there was one girl in that house who could also run like hell! She'd have caught us for sure if she hadn't had to hold her skirts up when she was tearing after us! [39]

Important as the economic and sociological explanations were for women's turning to prostitution, the impression will not down that many women were born with a predisposition toward the trade. The ease with which they were recruited seems to indicate an all-pervading gullibility that beggars belief. One reason why the Y.W.C.A. established its Traveller's Aid desks in railway stations was to protect the incoming women travellers from the clutches of the predatory recruiting agents for the brothels who haunted the stations. In Edmonton, for example, a group of six Scandinavian girls turned up in the station en route to jobs as domestic servants. A total stranger accosted them and sweet-talked all six of them into a life of prostitution. [40] Other cases kept coming to light of girls who were conned by promises of marriage from strangers after single dates. Others seemingly drifted in quite casually after being seduced and dropped by their lovers. Clearly entry was easy, but convincing the girls that they should return to the respectable world took a great deal of persuasion. Rescue missions were established by the moral reformers in most of the prairie cities. But on the meagre records that are left, their batting average was hardly impressive. Only if they caught the girls after a pregnancy, a severe illness, or coming out of jail did they seem to have much luck. Yet leave the profession they obviously did. What became of the untold thousands of women who catered to the sexual needs of the single settlers who poured into our country between 1900 and 1920 is wrapped in mystery. Most of them, like the single settlers themselves, eventually must have drifted back into respectability, marriage, and a family, with the secret of their past buried so deeply that no male historian is ever likely to unearth a trace of it.

There was no Street like Annabella Street...

Winnipeg was the first prairie city, so the study of the urban mores of western Canada naturally begins there. The city was incorporated on January 1, 1874, long before any of the other centres was more than a minor gleam in a cartographer's eye. That act of incorporation was perhaps as characteristic of the place as anything that ever happened there. With a scant 2,000 population, Winnipeg in 1873 would hardly have qualified as a good small town. Yet it scorned town status and opted for becoming a city. When its bill of incorporation was delayed by a procedural wrangle in the Manitoba legislature, a mob of indignant citizens seized the Speaker of the house, dragged him from the building, and treated him to a tarring and feathering.[1] That surely was an indication of the depth of the Winnipeg conviction that, whatever its momentary population deficiency, it was manifestly destined to become the great metropolis of the northwest. It was right, of course; Calgary did not achieve city status until twenty years later, while Edmonton, Regina, and Saskatoon were unable to shed their small-town limitations for still another decade. When Winnipeg reached its silver anniversary, at the tail end of the Victorian era, its population outnumbered that of all these other embryo cities combined, and by at least three to one.[2]

Because it was first, Winnipeg tended to become the pattern, if not the accepted trend setter, for the cities that came after. The Winnipeg tycoons, whose interests were eastward, might live and die without ever getting to Calgary or Edmonton. But leaders of the other cities had to pass through Winnipeg en route to the business centres of eastern Canada, or to check in periodically with the western headquarters of eastern firms located there. Thus Calgarians and Edmontonians could hardly avoid being aware of what was going on in Winnipeg. When they watched Winnipeggers frantically planting trees all over the place, they carried the idea home, just as they copied its experiments with publicly owned utilities, its school designs, its street layouts, even its streetcar heating system. Most of all, they adopted Winnipeg's casual enthusiasm for uninhibited boozing, and its toleration of prostitution, preferably within a specially segregated community of its own. Like Winnipeg the other cities, which began as wide-open boom towns, were eventually overrun by legions of reformers dedicated to turning the great northwest into a latter-day Massachusetts. Because it was the first and largest, Winnipeg also became the inspiration centre for the prohibition crusade that kept the prairies on fire from 1880 until 1916. In Winnipeg, however, things tended to go to extremes, and in all directions. The history of morals kept repeating itself elsewhere, but seldom with the same explosiveness that was the Winnipeg hallmark.

In later years it was Calgary which sought to identify with the two-fisted, he-mannishness of the western frontier. In fact it was only in Winnipeg where such a posture could claim a semblance of legitimacy. Winnipeg began as a scattered collection of shacks in which men casually took the law into their own hands. There was, for example, the notorious case of the Reverend Griffith Owen Corbett, the Anglican priest who was jugged in 1864 for attempting an abortion on a housemaid he had seduced. When he was hauled before a justice of the peace and ordered confined to the jail at Fort Garry pending trial, his friends stormed into the post and threatened violence unless Corbett was released on bail. After a lot of shouting and threatening and coming and going, bail was eventually granted. When Corbett was brought to trial, a jury convicted him and he was sentenced to six months in jail. From his cell he bombarded the *Nor' Wester* with denunciations of his accusers and professions of his own innocence. After some days a local schoolteacher named James Stewart organized a posse, knocked the jailer unconscious, and released Corbett, who returned to the bosom of his family at Headingly. The authorities then arrested Stewart, who was promptly rescued from jail by another mob. No attempt was ever made to re-arrest either man. Corbett eventually deserted his family and returned to England, the seduced housemaid died a few years later, and the schoolteacher went on to achieve a large measure of local fame as a leader of the "Canadian Party".[3]

What part booze played in the monkeyshines of 1864 is, of course, conjectural, but is was probably substantial. Winnipeg at the time boasted two hotel saloons. The first was owned by George Emmering and was known far and wide as "The Dutchman's". The Royal Hotel was built by Henry McKenney, a half brother of the notorious Dr. John Schultz. "The Dutchman's" was a favourite watering hole for the American mule-skinners, teamsters, traders, and sundry roughnecks who were then forcing the Hudson's Bay Company to tolerate the free-traders and to switch to St. Paul as its major supply route. At "The Dutchman's" bar the Americans toasted the impending doom of the Hudson's Bay Company and agitated loudly for annexation of the Territory to the United States. At the Royal, Schultz's followers toasted the demise of the Company with equal fervour, but agitated loudly for the annexation of the Territory to Canada.[4]

After Manitoba joined the Canadian Confederation, Winnipeg held firmly to its original development blueprint. It went on such a binge of hotel-saloon building that in 1876 the Y.M.C.A. was able to couple it with Barrie, Ontario, as the two wickedest communities in Canada.[5] The blocks of hotel-bars which had sprung up on Main Street made such a reputation easy to acquire, and the proliferation of such establishments during the next two decades made it an easy reputation to sustain.

There is no evidence, moreover, that the city took more than the mildest umbrage at the Y.M.C.A.'s broadside. Its sense of the fitness of things had been demonstrated the previous year when J.S. Ingram, the boozing, brawling chief of police, was taken *in flagrante delicto* in a Colony Creek whorehouse.[6] The city fired the chief for being stupid enough to be caught and let the brothels continue to operate. They did so without hindrance from Ingram's successor until 1883 when the first morality crusade blew them clear off the Creek to a more remote location on the town's far western outskirts.

This crisis developed from the construction of the Manitoba College a couple of hundred yards from the brothels near what became the corner of Portage Avenue and Colony Street. Based on priority rights, the brothels clearly had a better claim to the general area than the College. They had been in business along the Creek since Winnipeg had become a city. The College did not get into operation on its new campus until five years later. Soon after it opened, however, its corridors buzzed with stories of pupils tarrying in the houses of ill repute en route to and from school. In the end the stories travelled far afield and early in the winter of 1882-3 the *Winnipeg Times* made the juxtaposition of the College and the whorehouses the subject of a front-page exposé. The city council then nudged the police department into closing the establishments. Nothing happened, however, until a new fire-eating Congregationalist minister arrived in town to join the *Times* in an all-out campaign to rescue the Winnipeg teen-age students from the clutches of the scarlet women.[7]

At other times and in other places, clarion calls for action to suppress brothels seemed the prerogative of the Baptists and the Presbyterians. This time it was the rafters of the Congregational Church which rattled to the thunderous oratory of the Reverend J.B. Silcox.

"The Bible is not silent on the sins of unchastity and the pulpit ought not to be either," he declaimed. The tour de force that followed was one that Dwight L. Moody or Billy Sunday might have envied. There were passages that could have been set to music as a battle hymn for morality crusades. For example:

"On the outskirts of Ephesus were the infamous Groves of Daphne where crowds of licentious votaries held a perpetual festival of vice. So on the western outskirts of our city stands in unblushing impudence the same monstrous iniquity throwing its blighting shade over our fair city. There in these abodes of vice are the depths of immorality, debauchery and death. In their swinish precincts the youth of our land are beguiled and ruined, body and soul.

"Let us," he implored, "drive out these leprous libertines who out-Judas Judas!"

That surely must be one of the fanciest definitions ever coined for what the criminal code was content to call common prostitutes. But Dr. Silcox did not stop there. He went on to call down malediction on the sinning customers of the brothels. "Do not," he pleaded, "be content to hypocritically condemn the sinning women and acquit the sinning men." He urged the newspapers to publish the names of the male sinners who frequented the houses side by side with those of the inmates. He reminded his listeners that they were proud members of the Anglo-Saxon race, which ruled the world. It had been able to achieve that lofty pinnacle because of the strength it derived from maintaining its racial purity. Only by recapturing the respect for womanly virtues that prevailed when knighthood was in flower could the present generation rise above and overcome the social evil.

Twenty years later the chief of police of Medicine Hat echoed Dr. Silcox's sentiments, though somewhat less elegantly.[8]

"A skirt is a skirt," he said, "and must be respected as such."

What impact the combined onslaught of Dr. Silcox and the newspaper had on Winnipeg public opinion, or on the business being done by the brothels, is difficult to assess. The *Times* reported that business was so good the brothel operators could afford to pay rents of up to $125 a month, an unheard-of sum when a good wage was $15 a week. The paper also reported that one madam had recently retired and left town with between $30,000 and $40,000 in savings. There was no evidence from the paper, however, that the public was really much aroused. There was no support at all from that usually reliable bellwether of public interest, the writer of letters to the editor. By that criterion the really important question agitating Winnipeg was home rule in Ireland. Nevertheless, the *Times* kept hammering away at the story for the next week with reports of interviews which were also inconclusive. One doctor argued that segregation of the brothels in one area made medical inspection possible. Another was just as sure that medical inspection did not work. A third cynically opined that all such campaigns as Dr. Silcox's were bound to accomplish nothing. Prostitution had begun with the beginning of the human race and would end only with the ending of the human race. Some confirmation of this belief was provided by a fourth member of the medical profession. In the short period since the newspaper had become interested in exposing the social evil, he had noticed a dozen women soliciting within a stone's throw of his office. And there were many others in the hotels of the city, he said.

Dr. Silcox, however, was not one to be put aside by any such negative attitudes as these. He returned to the fray on April 6 to recall the fine example which Mr. Justice Wood had set in sending a prostitute to jail for two years at hard labour. In passing sentence, the judge had severely criticized the Winnipeg system of levying small fines periodically on the women as a licence of sorts. Such a system was a disgrace to the city. Dr. Silcox agreed and insisted that all that was needed to rid the city of prostitutes was for the police to drive them out and keep them out.

"The heart of this young city," Dr. Silcox contended, "beats on the side of purity and right. The police can drive these women out of the city and keep them out by enforcing the law. There is no city in Canada where the law is defied as it is in Winnipeg."

The police all the while were quietly closing down the Colony Creek houses, but they were being reasonable about it, as the *Times* reported in an interview with one of the madams. The operators of the houses were acquiring property farther west outside the city limits. But, as they would be unable to build until the weather improved, the police had extended their deadline from April 1 to June 1. Once they had their new houses (on what would one day become Thomas Street) they would be glad to get out of the city. Anyway, this madam said, the coming of the college had created more problems for the brothels than the brothels did for the college.

"We are forever being pestered by kids," she said. "Just a while ago I had to chase a bunch of them away. 'We don't operate no Saturday matinee for kids here,' I told them."

The June deadline came and went without notice. The brothels moved out to Thomas Street and the question of Winnipeg's sexual morality lapsed more or less into limbo for the next twenty years.

When the dawn of the twentieth century broke over Winnipeg it caught the fastest-growing city in Canada in its rays. Here were 40,000 people where there had been barely 8,000 twenty years before.[9] Crude statistics can be misleading, however. The fact was that Winnipeg was just beginning to break out of a decade-long depression which resulted from the collapse of wheat prices in 1887-8. During the hard times immigration slowed down, and while Winnipeg continued to grow, it did so at a much slower pace. Not only was the Winnipeg of the new century a city poised to take off on the greatest boom in history, it was also a city struggling to extricate itself from the crudities of frontier life; but it would be frustrated at every turn by the succeeding waves of immigrants that were soon to engulf it. The migratory waves were by no means made up only of unlettered peasants and the disinherited of the earth. Each incoming train brought a generous complement of senior managers, junior executives, and white-collar workers for the banks, insurance companies, railways, and the mercantile trade, as well as skilled mechanics for the railway shops and the building trades. But the migratory tides likewise washed in equal proportions of un-skilled labourers, drifters, boomers, ne'er-do-wells, gamblers, prostitutes, and an infinite variety of other human flotsam.

What there was about the Red River Settlement that attracted so many militant Orange Protestants from Ontario and so few French Catholics from Quebec is a question around which many theories can be embroidered. Attract the Protestants it certainly did, not only those from Ontario directly but also many thousands of former Ontario residents who had gone to settle in the United States. By 1881 almost half of Winnipeg's population — 3,397 out of 7,985 — was Ontario-born. Twenty years later, Winnipeg had a population of 42,340, of which 13,322 were Manitoba-born and 10,419 were natives of Ontario. Only 1,365 came from Quebec and 1,405 were born in the United States. The inflow from Europe was already under way in 1901 as England sent 5,223, Ireland 1,218, and

Scotland 1,671. Of the 7,546 foreign-born Iceland accounted for 1,500, Austria-Hungary for 1,343, Germany for 699, and Russia for 1,398. By religion the populace broke down into 10,172 Presbyterians, 10,170 Anglicans, 6,741 Methodists, 5,143 Roman Catholics, 4,253 Lutherans, 1,145 Jews, and segments of a dozen other sects. In summary the city was a good three-quarters Anglo-Saxon and just as solidly Protestant if the Anglicans are included.[10]

So much for quantity. More important was what might be called the hard-shell quality of Winnipeg Protestantism. A measure of its militancy was the fact that Winnipeg enjoyed the most tightly closed Sunday tolerated anywhere in Christendom since the days of the New England Puritans. No wheel of industry turned, no store opened, no streetcar clattered down the streets, no bread or milk was delivered, no game of any kind was played. On Sunday there were only church services. The Protestant sermons were reported fully by all the newspapers, as they also reported the activities of the Christian Endeavor, the Royal Templars of Temperance, the Loyal Orange Lodge, the Masonic order, and the missionary societies beyond numbering. Roman Catholic news was reported when a pope died or a new bishop was appointed. As the clergymen laboured for the souls of their adherents, their communicants worked overtime getting rich and improving their city. Getting rich must have been comparatively easy, judging from the numbers who succeeded; the city itself, however, was something that could stand an immense amount of improvement.

Making anything of a city on the Winnipeg site challenged both the imagination and the financial genius of its early leaders. It was located on the edge of a treeless plain that stretched unbroken to the Rocky Mountains. In the summer its shadeless mud streets baked hard in a blistering sun. In the spring and fall the same streets became impassable bogs of the stickiest, clingingest gumbo known to man. In years of extreme drought, it was plagued with grasshoppers; in wet years, by myriads of mosquitoes which bred by the billions on the flood plains of the Assiniboine. Flies swarmed in all seasons and the annual August outbreaks of typhoid fever kept the city's hospitals filled to capacity. In the late fall, it was likely to be swept by blizzards which continued intermittently throughout the winter and often came back for a final assault after spring had settled in. Yet this was the environment that somehow managed to attract and retain a population that had grown up in the incomparable natural beauty of Ontario and British countrysides.

The dominant segment of the Winnipeg business community was the real estate interest, and in some measure it was the periodic confrontations between the real estate promoters and the brothel operators which caused the moral eruptions. Residential development was beginning to move westward at the time of the first rumblings against Colony Creek in 1883. The existence of brothel concentrations undoubtedly adversely affected property values, so when the reverend clergy began agitating against the prostitutes they could always call on the realtors to exercise some political muscle. And there was undoubtedly a real estate salesman in the background when the Colony Creek women decided to move to Thomas Street, a mile to the west. There, smack in the middle of nowhere, they erected six large frame whorehouses in a cluster about 250 yards north of Portage Avenue. There was not another building within half a mile and, with their white paint glistening in the sun, they became a Winnipeg landmark for the next twenty years. Then they too fell before the western march of the real estate promoters.

Thomas Street might have been an ideal spot for a red-light district when Portage Avenue was the westward trail for the Red River carts, settlers in covered wagons, and teamsters en route to the Saskatchewan settlements. It may even have derived a profit from that traffic. But as the Winnipeg boom developed along Main Street with the arrival of the C.P.R. it was the unhandiest location imaginable. The nearest bars were over a mile to the east, and the C.P.R. station was almost two miles away. However, the streetcar service on Portage Avenue was good, and despite its location the settlement prospered with Winnipeg. At the height of its busy season as many as a hundred girls might be working there, not counting domestic servants and Chinese houseboys. Moreover, for almost twenty years it existed without attracting more than passing notice from the reformers. Until the turn of the century they concentrated their main fire upon the liquor traffic and lobbied for the enactment of stiffer and stiffer penalties for violations of the Sunday observance laws. The Establishment seemed to go along with the clergy as far as the Sunday observance was concerned, though there is no record of any law being passed to restrict the Sunday trade of the brothels. The *modus vivendi* which the bordellos had with the police excluded the enforcement of the Winnipeg by-laws in the settlement. They operated round the clock as the demand warranted, and the demand on weekends consistently did so.

The building boom of the 1880s carried within it the seeds of destruction for Thomas Street. Each year the housebuilders crept a little farther westward and closer to the red-light district. By 1900 houses were being built within two or three blocks of the brothels and the rowdiness of the drunken customers returning from the houses so enlivened the nights for the new residents that they began complaining to their pastors. To their voices were added the complaints of the real estate interests. As the years passed the agitation against Thomas Street increased and was reaching its peak in 1902 when the Reverend Dr. Frederick B. DuVal was elected chairman of the Winnipeg Ministerial Association.

Frederick B. DuVal was born in Maryland, and graduated from Princeton with gold medals for oratory and debate and a first prize for Biblical scholarship. After graduation from the Theological Seminary in 1875 he served churches in Delaware and Ohio before being offered the pulpit at Knox Presbyterian church in Winnipeg. A pint-sized zealot with a hard glinting eye and luxuriant chin whiskers, he arrived in 1888 and served the church for more than twenty years, eventually becoming the moderator of the Presbyterian Church of Canada. His reputation as an outstanding orator, theologian, and moral reformer preceded him to Winnipeg. He not only became quickly embroiled in local controversy, he became the leader of it. Certainly he was a prime mover in the campaign to drive the Roman Catholic parochial schools out of the public schools system. In the struggle for prohibition in the 1890s, he was both the leading agitator and the recognized spokesman before legislative tribunals. [11]

Frederick DuVal was a one-man gang, and when he took over the direction of the ministerial association he soon had all his fellow preachers breathing fire and brimstone from the pulpits. In the fall of 1903 they turned their attention from booze to brothels and launched an all-out campaign to close down the Thomas Street establishments. They collided with Mayor John Arbuthnot and the city police department.

From the day Chief John McRae had first joined the Winnipeg police department in 1882, regulated prostitution had been the accepted policy of the city. As chief of police he had managed to confine most of the prostitutes to the Thomas Street area and the women who tried to work the hotels and railway station were given short shrift. McRae was convinced that segregated prostitution was about as effective a way of treating with the oldest profession as had been devised. So were Mayor Arbuthnot and the police commission. So were most Winnipeggers. When the first oratorical thunder clapped, the chief, the mayor, and the police commissioners took to the storm cellars to wait for the storm to blow over, as it always had before. They woefully misread the character of Frederick B. DuVal.

When the sermons failed to accomplish anything DuVal spurred the ministers to mass action. In the largest churches on November 15, 1903, the ministers asked the male members of their congregations to stay after the services for special meetings "on the social evil". They stayed by the hundreds. [12]

In his after-sermon sermon, Dr. DuVal quoted the recently published report of a commission which had investigated prostitution in New York City. "This most experienced commission ever appointed in the civilized world," he thundered, "has found that segregation does not segregate and regulation does not regulate. It is inevitable that segregated areas become nests of crime."

The Reverend A.W. Wickson told the newspapers that 700 people had stayed for the meeting at the Central Congregational church and voted overwhelmingly to close the Thomas Street houses.

E.D. Martin, a prominent businessman and spokesman for the laity, called the houses a threat to the morals of the children because houses and schools were going up within sight of Thomas Street.

The following night the clergy hired the Winnipeg Theatre and treated a capacity audience to three hours of denunciations of conditions in the city. Of the 1,500 in attendance, only about 15, the newspapers reported, appeared opposed to the stand taken by the ministerial association. Two days later the organized clergy descended on the police commission and demanded action to enforce the law against houses of ill fame. Surprisingly enough, when Dr. DuVal polled the commissioners he found they all claimed to be against their own policy of allowing segregated prostitution.

All this uproar, probably from design, blew up while the 1903 civic election campaign was in full swing. Within hours after the ministers had bearded the police commission the subject got a thorough airing at a stormy election rally at the Winnipeg Theatre. Mayor Arbuthnot, who was running for a fourth term as mayor, lashed out at the clergy for blackening the fair name of Winnipeg. "If this is such a great evil, why have they never complained about it before?" he demanded and added, "Nobody has ever come to me about it!"

One clergyman quickly contradicted the mayor from the floor. They had so complained, he said, and the mayor had sarcastically replied that a better alternative might be to locate the segregated area in Armstrong's Point among the wealthy Winnipeggers.

The mayor veered away from that charge with one of his own. He blamed Dr. DuVal for the uproar. "As a man thinketh so is he!" the mayor thundered. "The man chiefly responsible for all this agitation has by his own admission been thinking about this for twenty years and is now so saturated with the subject that it has to belch out of him somewhere!"

And so the argument raged until Mayor Arbuthnot called it quits and retired from the mayoralty race. The DuVal candidate for mayor was Thomas Sharpe, a wealthy contractor. He was elected almost by default and the reformers took over City Hall. While the morality issue did stir the populace momentarily, it becomes clear in retrospect that it was by no means the main issue of the election.

Several other questions were causing much greater concern to a population just becoming conscious of the great potential of their city and of the practical problems that beset it. There were the thorny questions of municipal versus private ownership of power, municipal operation of the streetcars, the need for more bridges, lower water rates, and a better water supply. Above all there were recurrent municipal financial crises about which all the candidates talked. Prostitution may have been the main issue for the clergy, but none of the candidates paid much attention to it in their speeches. And, except for those who had become thoroughly aroused by the DuVal crusade against vice, the electors paid little attention to the candidates. The turnout at the polls was one of the poorest in years. Nevertheless, Dr. DuVal succeeded in putting most of the civic administration on record as favouring the shut-down of Thomas Street, and the matter got quick attention from the new police commission. [13]

Chief John McRae clearly regarded the DuValites as meddling

busybodies who would provide his morality squad with an impossible task. The new boom was taking hold and Winnipeg's population was rising at the rate of 1,000 people a month. In addition, the prairie farms were at last beginning to realize their potential and in 1903 more than 50,000,000 bushels of wheat were marketed through the Winnipeg Grain Exchange. That Winnipeg had at last become the financial centre of the West was indicated by the erection of no less than thirteen bank buildings along Main Street and Portage Avenue. On several of the corners brand new brick and stone banks replaced some of the city's earliest hotels. The surplus warehouse space that had resulted from the optimism of previous decades was now filled to capacity and additional floors were being added to several of the largest buildings. Bank clearings were rising at such a rate that the town boosters were forecasting that a billion dollars a year would soon be reached; by 1913 the clearings exceeded $1.5 billion.

All that anyone had to do to dispel all doubt of Winnipeg's future was to be on hand when the harvester specials arrived at the C.P.R. station during late July and August. [14] So jam-packed were these trains that the men coming west to cut and thresh the grain crops could not be accommodated on the platform. From the station platform those who were detraining in Winnipeg were herded along the tracks to branch line trains which would distribute them to the country towns where they would find farmers eager to hire them at rates that sometimes got as high as three dollars a day, for an eighteen-hour day.

After being cooped up on the board-hard seats of the excursion trains for three or four days, an irresistible desire to interrupt their journey to the harvest field seized many of the youthful newcomers when they stretched their muscles on the Winnipeg station platform. Away from parental control for the first time, many of them developed an urge to explore the flesh-pots of Winnipeg. Wherever they looked from the C.P.R. platform the hotel bars and poolrooms beckoned. They could count half a dozen within a stone's throw of the station north on Main Street. To the south, Main Street was dotted with hotels and poolrooms as far as they could see. Between the harvesters and the hotels, however, lurked an awesome assortment of con men, sneak thieves, pickpockets, and pimps all waiting to separate the newcomers from whatever small sums of cash they possessed. In midsummer the incoming harvesters, who were usually short of cash, were far from the favourite targets of the petty criminals. Then they much preferred permanent settlers or construction workers intent on a spree. Only after the harvesters came back in the fall with their summer earnings unsafely stowed in pockets and purses did they merit special attention. Nevertheless, the malefactors had specially developed senses that enabled them to ferret out harvesters with a thirst for booze and broads, and they quickly latched onto their prey and steered them, first to the bars and later to the Thomas Street brothels.

Keeping minor crime under control occupied most of the waking hours of the police department. It was a task that was continually complicated by the steady inflow of petty crooks and prostitutes from the United States. As the number of permanent immigrants increased, so did the floating population, which sooner or later came to roost in the bars and brothels. Chief McRae had been adding to his force a dozen men at a time as finances permitted, but he continually lost ground in the race to keep up with Winnipeg's growth. Clearly his job was difficult enough without having the Thomas Street Jezebels scattered all over town where they could not be kept under a watchful eye. He was completely out of sympathy with the DuVal campaign.

Like all Winnipeg policemen, Chief John McRae was an imposing figure. Over six feet in height, he habitually wore the peak of his cap well down over his eyes, whose colour matched the steely grey of his moustache. That there was steel in his personality as well as in his mien can be assumed from the fact that he survived for more than twenty years as head of the Winnipeg police department and built it into one of the best in the country. But he was also a man who knew how to obey orders as well as give them. On January 7, 1904, the new police commission gave the Chief his orders — raid the Thomas Street brothels and drive the prostitutes out of business. [15]

It did him no good to argue that this would spread the women all over the city. Orders were orders, and the chief laid his plans to carry them out. To prevent a leak to the district, no one on the force was taken into his confidence. When the night shift arrived for duty the following Saturday, he gathered the entire force together and issued his instructions. They were to proceed at once to the Thomas Street houses, arrest all the women keepers and their employees, and transport them bodily to the police station in the conveyances provided. For the occasion the Chief called in a dozen hired hacks to supplement his own horse-drawn paddy wagon, and assembled them in front of the James Avenue station.

The long procession moved down Main Street and out Portage Avenue at a leisurely pace. By the time they got to Thomas Street the houses were beginning to jump with the usually brisk Saturday trade. The raid went off without a hitch, accompanied by considerable confusion and shouted protests from the customers. Individual houses had been raided before, for unseemly conduct or on suspicion of harbouring fugitives from the law. But a raid on the entire settlement violated everybody's sense of the fitness of things, including, if truth were known, that of most of the raiding policemen.

It quickly became apparent that the transport facilities were inadequate. While they waited for the arrival of more hacks, the raiding party sorted out its catch. The madams were all identified, as were the working prostitutes. The names of the customers were taken and then they were ordered on their way. But it was not a particularly cold night so they gathered in front of the houses and awaited further excitement. As the police emerged from the houses with their prisoners in tow the crowd jeered loudly and followed the parade of prostitutes and escorts all the way to the police station. There, according to the *Manitoba Free Press*, they stood ten deep in front of the station and hooted at the police in the late-arriving hacks. The paper also reported that the police bag for the night included twelve keepers of bawdy-houses, seventy-two women inmates, and four male porters. While the arraignments were taking place, the Chief thoughtfully ordered a guard to be posted against looting in all the houses which the raid left vacant. The women who ran the joints were all fined forty dollars when they pleaded guilty, while their employees were each assessed twenty dollars. All were warned by the magistrate that the era of segregated prostitution was over for Winnipeg and that they must either reform, leave town, or face much stiffer penalties if they ever again appeared in court.

Little attention was paid to the warning from the bench. The women paid their fines, disposed of their houses, and moved to better locations closer to their customers. Doris Vennette, for example, moved several times before landing permanently on

Annabella Street, where she remained for the next twenty years. Minnie Woods, who enjoyed a thirty-year reign as queen of the brothels, moved from Thomas Street to James Avenue, where she lived until the Annabella-McFarlane district was opened in 1909.[16]

The name of Thomas Street itself disappeared from Winnipeg annals under circumstances which clearly indicate that somebody at City Hall had a most ribald sense of humour. The Earl of Minto, Canada's most colourful governor general, made a vice-regal tour of the West in 1904 after the Thomas Street raid and the street's restoration to respectability. To mark the visit Winnipeg decided to do for Lord Minto what it had done for many other ornaments of British aristocracy — name a street after him. And what street was chosen to forever carry the name of Minto for future generations of Winnipeggers? Thomas Street. Then in 1912 Ottawa decided it needed an armoury in Winnipeg. It was also named for Lord Minto and was located across the street from the long-vacated Thomas Street whorehouses.

Having achieved total victory, the reverend clergy retired from the field of battle, though they returned to the fallen-woman theme occasionally in their sermons. The Reverend Charles W. Gordon of St. Stephen's church managed a series of three discourses in which he developed the idea that women themselves were mainly to blame for prostitution. He went on to describe the men who patronized the houses of ill fame as moral lepers and urged that action be taken to identify them publicly so that respectable women could quarantine their homes against them. Dr. Gordon felt respectable women would scratch them from their social invitation lists if the men's sins were publicized. But for the most part the clergy concentrated their attention on booze and the blue laws whenever they wandered from biblical texts, and left the enforcement of laws against houses of ill fame to the police.

After scattering the inmates from Thomas Street, the police encountered heavy going. When there was an understanding between the police and the brothel keepers it was fairly easy to keep the traffic under control. The police staged periodic raids; the operators pleaded guilty and paid small fines, and went about their business. When the crackdown came, however, and the police tried to suppress the houses permanently, co-operation ended.

It was not enough for the police to prove that houses under inves-

tigation had an unusually large number of people wandering in and
out. As long as the occupants behaved with reasonable decorum they
could not be convicted of operating disorderly houses. To get a
conviction on a charge of operating a house of ill fame necessitated
testimony from somebody who had visited the house and paid for
the service. While the Chief was prepared to have his newly formed
morality squad keep watch on the houses from the outside, he
categorically refused to send his men into the houses to become
accessories to the commission of an offence. Yet if the police refused
to fabricate evidence how could the law be enforced? By stool
pigeons who would visit the prostitutes, pay them with marked
money, and testify in court. In July 1905 the city acceded to a
request from the police commission and put up a $250 "secret
service fund" which Chief McRae could spend buying testimony. [17]

Unhappily for the moral reformers, after the brothels were closed
on Thomas Street the problem broke out in a new place. Now the
prostitutes took to the streets to sell their charms while they worked
up a clientele which would come to their houses. Soon it seemed to
the Winnipeg gentlefolk that Portage Avenue and Main Street were
being overrun with doxies. Naturally, the gay blades in search of
female accommodation frequently took to accosting the wrong
women and there were complaints to the police.

There was no way in which city policemen on patrol duty could
cope with the streetwalkers, for the policemen could be spotted a
block away by their height alone, to say nothing of the London-
bobby type of headgear they wore. A year after the Thomas Street
dispersal, an indignant citizen wrote to the *Manitoba Free Press* to
charge that the growing number of attacks on women on the city
streets was the direct result of scattering prostitutes all over the
city. [18] Winnipeg's recent experience, he contended, was proof of
the soundness of a statement by a Montreal preacher that segregation was the best way to handle the social evil. The ever-alert Dr.
DuVal rushed an immediate reply to the paper. While the hotbeds of
vice had existed on Thomas Street, he wrote, ladies of the best
families of Winnipeg had been assaulted on Broadway and Donald
streets. What Winnipeg needed, he contended, was not segregated
prostitution but more zealous law enforcement by the city police.
With this the city council seemed to agree. In January 1906 it raised
the Chief's secret service appropriation to $5,000, surely an

immense sum in the context of the times.[19]   For the next three years, save for casual references, the controversy over sex faded from the public view.

One reason for the decline in interest in moral issues may have been the emergence of an overabundance of other news concerning the great economic boom that was developing on the wings of mass immigration. A second transcontinental rail link with the east was under construction, and vast new railway shops began to go up in south Winnipeg and in Transcona. Between the City Hall and Portage Avenue, new banks and insurance buildings were beginning to give Winnipeg its first hint of a skyline. Building permits were being issued amounting to $10,000,000 a year, while the city's manufacturing centres were turning out products worth more than $18,000,000 annually. With only a rough sketch of a plan scratched on a piece of wrapping paper, building contractors were throwing up whole streets full of identical houses, both within the city proper and in the dozens of suburban municipalities that were coming into existence around its periphery. The city voted to embark on its own hydro-electric system, and construction of its first generating plant on the Winnipeg River was begun.

Thomas Sharpe served three terms as mayor and was succeeded by James Ashdown, Winnipeg's richest merchant and a great pillar of the church. C.P. Walker came in from New York to build the finest theatre in Canada outside Toronto. The C.P.R. was planning the construction of the Royal Alexandra hotel, which would exceed the luxurious proportions of anything Toronto or Montreal had to offer and would raise Winnipeg's hotel total to 69. When the lieutenant-governor held his formal ball on January 21, 1907, it boasted a guest list of 600, all of whom got their names in the papers along with descriptions of the gowns worn by the ladies.[20]   The city government itself had to struggle frantically to keep pace with private development. But it had crews out from dawn to dark gravelling some streets and paving others with creosoted wooden blocks, installing sewer and water lines, and building schools and hospitals. By the end of 1906 it had even managed to cut the number of outdoor privies in the city from 4,900 to 3,600.

It became abundantly clear with the passing years that closing the Thomas Street houses had failed to solve Winnipeg's "problem with social vice". During 1907 the police managed to convict the keepers of 71 bawdy-houses and 101 prostitutes. The following year the figures doubled and as they did so Magistrate T. Mayne Daly became increasingly provoked at the moral reformers and delivered periodic homilies on the folly of their actions. In 1908 he kept track of the number of young girls coming before him on morals charges and when it reached sixteen he decided that enough was enough.

Ordinarily Daly, who had been a Conservative Minister of the Interior in a post-Macdonald cabinet, presided in a perpetual pique that made him the terror of the underworld. In the winter of 1905 a pair of strong-arm American footpads created panic in the streets and alleys of the town as they waylaid and robbed drunken wayfarers. At last they were caught and hauled before Magistrate Daly. He sent John Sandercock to prison for fifteen years at hard labour plus seventy-five strokes of the lash. Frank Macdonald got ten years and fifty lashes. Soon after that Daly established a Canadian record by sending a mere burglar to prison for fourteen years.

Yet when it came to prostitution, T. Mayne Daly was the image of tolerance and understanding. The system which turned prostitutes into streetwalkers, and not the streetwalkers themselves, was always on trial in his court. On April 20, 1909, he committed his convictions to paper which he took with him to the meeting of the Winnipeg Police Commission. The gist of his letter was that since 1904 things had gone from bad to worse. He produced a list of over 400 convicted prostitutes over the five-year period. In the end he moved that the 1904 resolution be repealed and that "all matters relating to houses of ill fame and immoral women be left to the chief of police, he to act in accordance with his discretion and best judgment". His motion won unanimous approval from the commission.[21]

Chief McRae's best judgment was that a red-light district under his control should be re-established forthwith. As a first step, the houses would have to be concentrated in one area. He sent a messenger for Minnie Woods, who was then running a bordello on James Street, a hundred yards east of the police station. Minnie was a former operator of one of the largest houses on Thomas Street and was recognized as the leading madam of her day, though Lulu Thornton, who was somewhat younger, was probably better known among the frequenters of the brothels. The Chief broke the news of the commission decision to Minnie and asked her to pass the word along to the sisterhood. The Chief and the madam undoubtedly discussed

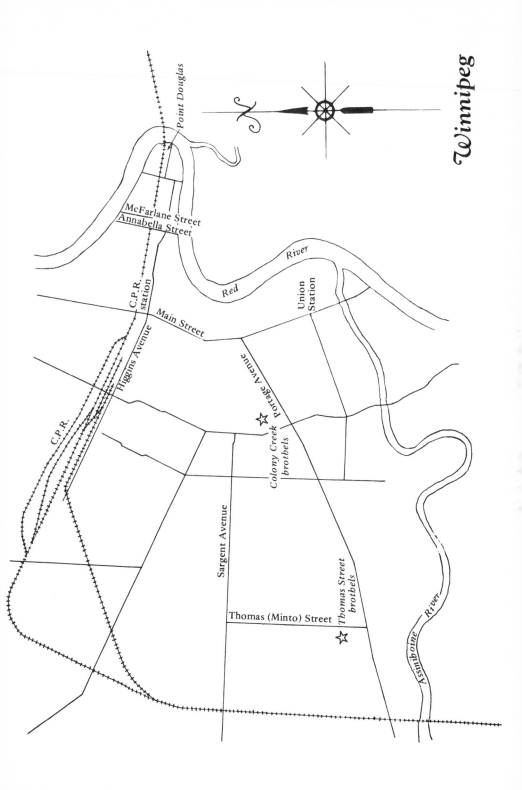

Winnipeg

Point Douglas

McFarlane Street
Annabella Street

Red River

C.P.R. Station

Main Street

Higgins Avenue

Union Station

C.P.R.

Portage Avenue

Colony Creek brothels

Sargent Avenue

Thomas Street brothels

Thomas (Minto) Street

Assiniboine River

possible locations for the new district, though the evidence on this point is clouded by disclaimers. In any event, the upshot of the conversation was that an isolated area in Point Douglas was selected.[22]

Until it got well north of Winnipeg, the course of the Red River was almost as serpentine as that of the Assiniboine. At the foot of Market Street the Red River veered sharply eastward for half of a mile and then swung sharply to the northwest. It thus created the long narrow triangle of land which was named for a Scottish noble-man — Point Douglas. The main line of the C.P.R. entered Winnipeg over a bridge roughly at the apex of the Point Douglas triangle. Two streets paralleled the railway from the river to Main Street — Higgins Avenue on the south and Sutherland Avenue on the north. The railway was flanked most of the way by a succession of warehouses and factories, a flour mill, a lumberyard, and an iron works. To provide access from the Sutherland side to the Higgins side of the tracks, the city had recently completed a subway which joined Annabella Street on the west with Rachel Street on the east. Eventually it was given the name of Annabella Street for the entire length and was selected as the locale for the new red-light district.

In all Winnipeg no other site could have been discovered which would have served that purpose so well. It was far out of range of sight or sound of the pulpits of the moral reformers, it was well insulated from the downtown business section, and it was easily one of the city's least attractive residential areas. One side of Annabella Street from Sutherland to the Red River was given over completely to the coking ovens, coal piles, cinder piles, and gas tanks of the Winnipeg Gas Company. Facing the gas plant were a dozen modest houses and several shacks.

Winnipeg harlotry had kept pace numerically with the growth of the population so that it now far outnumbered the housing capacity of Annabella Street between Higgins Avenue and the river. However, immediately to the east was McFarlane Street, which ran from the C.P.R. tracks to the river, a distance of less than 300 yards. By adding McFarlane Street to Annabella, the new red-light area would contain fifty houses. As that total was more than the estimated needs for the moment, it was decided to incorporate only the west side of McFarlane Street into the segregated area. Neither Minnie Woods nor Chief McRae seems to have considered the interests of the hard-working residents of either street, or the result of permitting a row of brothels to operate opposite respectable homes on the east side of McFarlane Street.

Minnie went off to spread the word among the girls, and shortly afterward she was visited by one John Beaman, a real estate agent who had been sent around by Chief McRae. Beaman took Minnie for a walk down Annabella Street to inspect the houses. As queen of the whores, she naturally got first choice and selected No. 157, the largest house on the street, located midway between Sutherland and the river. It contained seven smallish rooms and had a broad verandah along the front. Beaman then conducted other women on similar tours and when he had a solid deal he approached the owners with purchase offers. He succeeded in buying most of the houses on Annabella for prices ranging from $2,500 to $5,000 which he resold to the women for up to $8,000. When word got around that a mysterious stranger was buying up property, prices stiffened on both Annabella and McFarlane streets. The late-comers, *ergo*, had to pay the stiffest prices. The highest price was apparently that paid by Lila Anderson, who was charged $12,000 for a double house at 113 McFarlane Street, which she claimed had probably cost $2,000 to build. Like all the other madams, she financed her purchase with a small down payment of $500 and whopping instalment payments of $225 a month. Rented to ordinary tenants the double house might have brought $30 a month. [23]

By the middle of July 1909, Annabella Street was completely converted to brothels and McFarlane Street was perhaps a quarter occupied. But if the authorities had trouble from complaining citizens before the policy was changed, it was multiplied tenfold by the uproar that the invasion of the whores created in the Annabella-McFarlane enclave. Instead of the red lights in the windows which the Barbary Coast of San Francisco affected, Annabella Street went in for the largest electric porch lights obtainable and foot-high, brightly painted house numbers. Within a matter of weeks the new district was the most brightly lit area in the city. Soon the respectable McFarlane Street residents were being solicited as they passed back and forth from work. Their children were accosted en route to school. After the west side of McFarlane Street was filled with brothels, they began to spread to the east side. [24]

Early in the fall of 1909 the police commission seemed to realize that the existence of the April resolution on its books might lead to embarrassment if the complaints of the residents got out of hand, so it repealed that motion and thus left the problem of coping with prostitution up to Chief McRae on a completely informal basis.

The morality squad by then had put the houses under regular surveillance. The inmates were required to have a medical examination every two weeks and to produce medical certificates when required. In response to early complaints, Chief McRae decided that the brothel keepers were becoming a bit carried away with the light-burning. He ordered the porch lights removed and the house numbers reduced to normal proportions. Indeed, the morality department put a whole set of rules into force for the houses. The houses must not permit rowdy conduct on the premises. The women were not to go streetwalking, or embark on shopping excursions uptown without prior notification to the police, who sent a policeman along as an escort. There was even a rule that white women were not to be employed as cooks in the houses. [25]

None of these rules prevented the behaviour of the inmates of the houses and their customers from getting completely out of hand. The residents of McFarlane Street became particularly vocal in their protests. As the opposition mounted, the police decided to back off a little by evicting the inmates and closing the houses that had become established on the east side of McFarlane Street.

On July 12 a Thomas Street type of raid was organized.[26] The street was blocked off at both ends and the women were swept from one house to the next and then on to the next until they had better than thirty of them cooped up in the fourth house. The paddy wagon spent the rest of the afternoon hauling them to the police station, where the women cried foul at the top of their lungs. They had paid exorbitant prices for these houses on the understanding that they would be allowed to operate with impunity. They had good reason to accuse the authorities of double-crossing them. In any event, they pleaded not guilty and were released on bail. They were acquitted in the end and their return to McFarlane Street signalled the complete takeover of the street by the brothels.

During the winter of 1909-10 relative calm prevailed and it began to appear that the city had solved its prostitution problem to the extent of hiding it away out of sight. But a wave of umbrage soon broke out louder than ever. When spring came, customers by the thousands swarmed into the new district. And not only customers. Winnipeg Sunday being what it was, the only available recreation for the populace was going for a stroll. Annabella and McFarlane streets became the mecca for Winnipeg sightseers on a Sunday afternoon. The women of the houses sunned themselves on their front steps, clad only in flimsy kimonos, and exchanged obscenities with such passers-by as spurned their proffered wares. As often as not, both streets were choked with hacks, taxis, and the hundreds of rubbernecks who milled about. They not only milled about the streets, they also patronized the brothels, as openly and casually as if they had been going in for a package of gum. A private detective hired later by the moral reformers swore that on one occasion fourteen Annabella Street brothels put through 292 customers in two and a half hours.[27]

Not only was sex for sale but it is clear from the record that the brothels did a thriving business in bootleg liquor in competition with the Main Street saloons. The delivery rigs of the wholesale liquor vendors hauled in Scotch and gin by the case and often by the wagonload. The brothels quickly became popular with under-age drinkers who had difficulty getting served in the licensed bars, which were under more or less regular inspection by the provincial liquor police. A recurrent complaint of the residents was about the number of under-age patrons seen emerging drunk from the houses of ill repute. The liquor laws of the province were enforced by inspectors employed by the provincial government, into whose jurisdiction the city police never intruded. The houses were all raided periodically by the provincial police, and the keepers pleaded guilty to violations of the liquor act and were fined $100 and costs. This was the minimum penalty for the offence and was never varied, although the same women appeared in court every three months.[28]

After the abortive raid of July 12 the city police continued to make token raids on the houses when things became too boisterous. But the outer limits on rowdiness were quite elastic and the raids were probably undertaken more to show City Hall the police were on the job than as a serious effort to eradicate the nuisance. There was, however, a fatal public-relations defect built into the Annabella-McFarlane complex that did not show up until well into the summer of 1910. By then the whores had taken over the whole of McFarlane Street, and most of the residents who could not sell out to the prostitutes newly arriving from the United States rented their houses for brothels for $200 a month. So the cries of anguish emanating from inside the area diminished. It was then that the police and the brothel keepers discovered that the segregated area had stopped one block too soon.

Adjoining McFarlane Street to the east was Syndicate Street, and the houses on the west side of Syndicate shared a back alley with the brothels on the east side of McFarlane. In the spring and summer of 1910, living on the west side of Syndicate Street was like having a front seat at a huge outdoor peep show. Blinds were seldom drawn on the McFarlane Street houses, so that the services being provided were easily viewed from the houses on the next street. The nude men and women who were seen cavorting in the houses occasionally spilled out into the back yards. The Syndicate Street citizens joined the odd holdout still on McFarlane Street to carry their protests to the City Hall. They got brushed off by the mayor, who pointed out that the police were under the control of the police commission, not the city council.

It seemed to the residents that their police protection had all but disappeared. In actual fact the uniformed policemen who patrolled Sutherland Avenue were instructed to stay out of the brothel area. When the citizens sought advice from the patrolmen they were ridiculed with the reply that the city could hardly afford to station policemen permanently in their front or back yards. Yet one of the residents swore that while he and his neighbours were talking to a policeman on Sutherland Avenue, they heard a sound they thought was a police whistle being blown on Annabella Street. The policeman took off like a shot and when the citizens followed they found him clubbing into submission a belligerent drunk who had been disturbing a brothel. [29]

By the summer of 1910 the Winnipeg red-light district had degenerated into a massive orgiastic obscenity. The sky-rocketing Winnipeg population, coupled with the tremendous floating population, kept the district on a twenty-four-hour shift all through the summer. Though it was isolated from the main part of the city, it was only five minutes by streetcar or ten minutes on foot from the C.P.R. station. As many of the customers had already tarried in the Main Street saloons, it was only to be expected that they would arrive in the district somewhat foggy about precise addresses. So it was common for householders some distance removed from the brothels to have their meals and their sleep interrupted by ruffians bursting in looking for prostitutes. Men exposing themselves to women and children on the streets was an almost continual occurrence. Citizens who sought to protect their women from abuse were often painfully assaulted by the drunks who ranged through the district in groups. A woman testified that one afternoon three men entered her home on Higgins Avenue (some distance from the red-light district) and, assuming she was a prostitute, threw some money on the table and started tearing off her clothes. She escaped to the street and a nearby factory where her husband worked. Another resident complained of being awakened at five o'clock in the morning by the whooping and hollering of a couple of whores who were chasing each other around the block on horseback, naked, as he said, from knees to hips.[30]

The district that summer was living proof that there was nothing glamorous or exciting about commercial sex. The area was drenched continually with dense smoke and acrid fumes from the gas plant which, in combination with the dust from the streets and cinders from the trains, coated everything in grime. The houses were mainly the product of spare-time workmanship of rough carpenters, who built their own houses and expanded them as their families grew. Inside, the brothels were furnished mainly with whisky-stained chairs and tables, beds sometimes two to a room, and footworn linoleum. They were decorated with brewery calendars and, not infrequently, framed religious mottoes.[31] As for the women, the reformers who tried to rescue them from their lives of shame wrote most of them off as hardened beyond redemption.

Eventually the complaints of the citizenry reached the ears of the reverend clergy and things began to happen. The Salvation Army brought in Adjutant McElhaney and his wife from Toronto and in 1910 put him to work in the district. The women from Annabella and McFarlane streets occasionally became hospitalized, and when they turned up in the new Grace Hospital the Salvation Army workers tried to talk them into returning to the respectable world. Both the reformers and their quarry were faced with an impossible problem. The respectable world, Christian or secular, wanted no part of the converted female sinners. Even where the spirit was willing, and it was occasionally when the girls were hospitalized, there was no place for the flesh. There was no women's rescue mission, aside from the Margaret Scott home, where the girls could go en route to respectability. Occasionally the Salvation Army leaders took women into their own homes while making preparations to return them to their families.

The contacts that McElhaney established with the prostitutes did yield a lot of factual information. From the seriously ill, he obtained names of other women who might be amenable to reason. Unhappily, when the Sally Ann girls went calling on the brothels they seldom had much luck. The adjutant was convinced that there was a well-organized white slave ring operating. He encountered one girl who had been shipped to Winnipeg from Kenora, then out to Saskatchewan, and back to Winnipeg. He started collecting data on drug addiction, alcoholism, and a system which kept the girls so deeply in debt to the keepers of the houses that they could not escape. Once he had his material he intended to launch a publicity campaign. In the interim he encountered representatives of the Temperance and Moral Reform Council who were also making the rounds. They had already decided to hire a pair of detectives to conduct an in-depth investigation and Adjutant McElhaney joined forces with them.

When the two detectives delivered their report it triggered a double-barrel blast that rocked Winnipeg for days. While McElhaney was delivering a summary of the report to a businessmen's club on November 12, the Reverend J.G. Shearer, national secretary of the Temperance and Moral Reform Council, was being interviewed in Toronto by the *Globe.* In that and subsequent statements, the Reverend Shearer went a lot further than Adjutant McElhaney. By the time the newspaper headline writers got through with him, Dr. Shearer was accusing Winnipeg of permitting the wide-open operation of brothels under police protection. He stated flatly: "They have the rottenest condition of things in Winnipeg in connection with the question of social vice to be found in any City in Canada."

Dr. Shearer went on to detail circumstances which he believed to be strongly suggestive of graft. Not the least telling of his points against segregated areas was the fact that they offered a ready market for the white slave trade. He gave instances of this:

Speaking of the white slave traffic, Dr. Shearer said:

"Some half a dozen of white slave victims have been marketed within the past year in the vice district of Winnipeg. Four of these have recently been deported, two being sent to Scandinavia and two to the United States. One is waiting deportation to England. Two of these cases were discovered through the efforts of our Federation and its detectives while in Winnipeg."

.   .   .

"In the first place I reiterate the statement I previously made, and affirm that it was a moderate statement of conditions that I know to prevail in Winnipeg. The Winnipeg City Hall officials will not deny that they have a segregated vice district, in which is permitted the carrying on of the criminal business of social vice — criminal, because expressly prohibited by the Code of Canada. There are in round numbers 50 of these dens of vice. Every one of the fifty keepers, every one of the 250, or thereabouts, inmates, and every male frequenter, whether he be a prominent citizen of Winnipeg or not, is a criminal in the terms of the code. In addition to this, every one of these 50 dens of vice is also an illicit liquor dive in spite of the license law of Manitoba, every day of the week and at all hours of the day or night. The officials moreover, will not deny that no serious attempt is made to close up these dens of vice or to put a stop to the running of these liquor dives.

It is not easy to believe that such an utterly disgraceful condition of things is permitted day after day, week after week, and month after month, either for love of vice and crime or on any high moral principle. What then is the motive? Members of the City Council and City Hall officials are said to complain bitterly that I have been guilty of blackening the fair name of Winnipeg. I have only said what is the truth, and moreover, by no means all of the wretched truth. The true blackeners of the fair name of Winnipeg are those that are responsible for this criminal, disgraceful and debasing condition of things. The vice area has become one of the great show places of Winnipeg. The real vilifiers of the good name of Winnipeg are those that are responsible for the permission, if not the careful protection, of this moral cesspool, the stench of which is making itself felt to the discredit of Winnipeg throughout the Dominion and elsewhere."

The next day the city council unanimously asked the Manitoba government to appoint a royal commission to investigate. The government immediately named Mr. Justice H.A. Robson of the Court of King's Bench to head the inquiry and within a week he had his investigation under way. Before him came not only Adjutant McElhaney and Dr. Shearer but representative citizens from the area, representative prostitutes, the mysterious real estate agents, the chief of police, and enough other witnesses to titillate the interest of even the most blasé of Winnipeggers for the next ten days.

Lila Anderson told the commission she was in business with her sister and had come from Ohio. Together they employed four girls at 113 McFarlane Street and guessed that their average patronage was from ten to fifteen customers per night. Amy Norris, who had operated at 549 Logan Avenue for six years, did a lot better at 173 Annabella. According to an official from the Manitoba Telephone System, who reported on the money taken from the pay phones which were installed in most of the houses, Amy Norris's pay phone was always full of nickels. One month her customers had deposited $39 in the telephone. Mostly, she explained, the customers used the phone to call for hacks or taxis, an indication that almost 800 calls a month went out for transportation from Amy's place. As the customers seemed usually to arrive in groups of two, three, or four, it could reasonably be assumed there were nights when Amy's place must have accommodated at least 100 customers. Amy, moreover, was one of the earliest settlers in the area and picked up her house for $4,250 compared with the $8,000 Alice Penchant paid for the house across the lane on McFarlane Street.

From the testimony before the commission, it became apparent that the new segregated area had not attracted all the prostitutes from downtown residential districts. Among the exhibits tabled was a list of 490 keepers and inmates the police had identified in the city. While the police claimed they had reduced the number of houses operating outside the district from 63 to 7 or 8, they also admitted they still received complaints about 80 houses allegedly operating outside the area.

As the Robson Commission hurried its hearings to a conclusion the civic election campaign of 1910 moved into high gear. It was one of the bitterest ever held in Winnipeg. Mayor Sanford Evans, then completing his second year in office, was about to drop out of civic politics when the brothel scandal broke. In order to vindicate his position and, in the process, to put the issue of segregated versus proliferating prostitution squarely up to the electors, he decided to run for a third term. The reformers welcomed his challenge and nominated E.D. Martin, a lay leader of the Presbyterian Church. The Martin supporters leaned heavily on the testimony of the Robson Commission witnesses and demanded that the laws against prostitution be enforced and that wide-open bootlegging be ended. Evans ran on his record, which he defended as best he could. To the astonishment of everybody concerned, the electors went to the polls on December 13 and re-elected Evans by a vote of 7,250 to 5,660 for Martin. It was a decisive majority, yet the reformers refused to accept it and went to court in an effort to upset the election. That attempt failed; Evans served out his term and then returned as full-time editor of the *Winnipeg Telegram*, the raucous organ of Toryism in Manitoba. He ultimately became leader of the Manitoba Conservative party.

In January 1911 Judge Robson brought in his verdict. His findings were:

1. That the charges as to vice in Winnipeg appearing as headings to the newspaper items in question are not true.
2. As to the charge made by Dr. Shearer, so far as it condemns the condition of things in Winnipeg in regard to the question of social vice, I have to report that a policy of toleration of the offence in question in a limited area, with regulations as to conduct, was adopted by the Police Commissioners, that such an area was accordingly established by immoral women; that since October 1909 there was no attempt to restrict the increase of houses of vice in the area, and the number of houses of this class grew from 29 to 50.
3. That the result of the above state of affairs has been the disturbance of peace and good order in the locality, a menace to morals and great depreciation in value of property of the neighbouring residents.
4. That the above conditions were not brought about by the corruption of any police authority, and that the occupants of the houses referred to do not pay for police protection.

Winnipeg, however, had beaten Judge Robson to the punch when it had gone to the polls. It had opted for tolerated prostitution although it also indicated to the police commission that there was strong opposition to the wide-open variety that had developed in the last eighteen months. The morality squad became more severe in its repression of drunkenness and rowdyism. As it did so the district began slowly to shrink back to its original size. The houses on McFarlane Street were gradually vacated, perhaps more than anything else because the business had been vastly over-expanded during 1910. For the real estate interests that had been gouging the whores for all the rent traffic would stand, the party ended too soon. Those who had helped push prices to ridiculous heights found themselves with unrentable houses on their hands. Gradually the street re-assumed its working-class image, but with a difference. So notorious had it become as a result of the Robson Commission that only unwary foreigners could be lured into renting the vacant houses even at a tenth of the rate the whores had paid.

In the months following the vindication of Mayor Evans the denizens of the district undoubtedly began to take too much for granted as far as law enforcement was concerned. There was a series of violent outbreaks on the street. An angry pimp waylaid his woman and tried to shoot her full of holes. Strong-armed gangsters attempted to move into the brothels. A messy murder brought the street back to the front pages of the newspapers. The police commission decided a crackdown was called for. Mayor R.D. Waugh, who had succeeded Evans, started enforcing the criminal code. A series of raids was ordered which eventually restored a measure of tranquillity.

But Annabella Street was proof against vice crusades, wars, booms, and busts. The madams from Thomas Street who had taken root on Annabella Street survived the Great War with ease, as well as prohibition and the changing mores of the 1920s. Minnie Woods celebrated her thirtieth anniversary in the oldest profession in her house on Annabella Street. Gertie Curney, who took over the house at the corner of Annabella and Sutherland streets in 1909, survived three marriages and other disasters, and in the process became a legendary figure among western prostitutes. She, almost alone in Winnipeg, was a whore with style and finesse. She converted her brothel into a fair imitation of a classic Parisian bordello. She hung her walls with tapestries, draped her windows with velvet hangings, hired a French cook for her kitchen, and laid in a stock of French wines; as late as 1929 her Chinese houseboy was still sporting a queue and answering the door dressed in brocaded silk. Of all the Annabella Street madams, she had the least trouble with the police, probably because she had a commanding view of Sutherland Street from her front door and of Annabella Street from an adjacent side window. Hers was not a place, moreover, for the callow farm boys, or for the crude and rude harvesters who flocked to Annabella Street from all over western Canada in the 1920s. Gertie sought and got the carriage trade. When the leaders of the Establishment wanted a secret hideaway in which to conspire, a dinner at Gertie's was a frequent choice.[32] But the high and the low alike suffered economic disaster in the 1930s and Gertie was no exception. Long before the war, the girls on Annabella Street were reduced to spending hours sitting at windows, prepared to cut prices for any prospective customer who came along, and prospects were few and far between. The patrons who once phoned to make reservations for all-night appointments were long gone. The prospects who did appear on the street came on foot, halting at each window-rapping to haggle over a two dollar fee. Yet the street itself survived well into the war years, when it quietly lapsed into respectability. The oldest profession, as a segregated and regulated institution, faded from Winnipeg as it was already disappearing elsewhere from the West.

... Except Regina's River Street, which was in Moose Jaw

The word for Regina was "typical". In the beginning it was no different from a score of other towns that grew up along the railways as they built westward from Winnipeg; except that it might have been muddier than most when it rained, and dirtier than most when it did not. A sad-sack of a shack town on Pile of Bones Creek, it had nothing to recommend it but Lieutenant-Governor Edward Dewdney of the Northwest Territories, a part-time real estate speculator who had an interest in a huge tract of the best land in the area.

Dewdney lobbied mightily not only to have the C.P.R. locate its station in the original shack town, but to have the town made the capital of the Territories.[1] He missed on the first objective, and saw a fortune melt before his eyes. The C.P.R. located its station a mile to the north, and would have gone even farther away without Governor Dewdney's lobbying. The result of the station's location was to provide the village with an excuse to abandon the name of Pile of Bones and adopt the grandiose title of Regina. It was a preposterous name for a preposterous townsite, centred as it was in a treeless plain, devoid of the prime requisites for survival — wood for fuel and wood for lumber. It also lacked an adequate water supply and was sadly deficient in natural drainage.

Yet not only did Regina survive, it became a living testament to the efficacy of pioneer political lobbying. First it euchred Battleford out of being the capital of the Northwest Territories. Then it managed to supersede Fort Macleod as the headquarters of the North West Mounted Police. Finally, it became the capital of Saskatchewan.

No prairie community ever went farther with less going for it than Regina. In the beginning it differed from places like Virden, Moosomin, Sintaluta, and Broadview only in the number of hotels which went up overnight in a cluster around the C.P.R. station. Six months after the station was built there were eight hotels within a five-minute walk, including several "tent hotels", with wooden floors and sides and canvas roofs. The hotels were all grandly enough named — the Grand Union, Queen's Royal, Criterion, Dominion, etc. — but without exception they were crudely built, minimal in size, and supplied only rudimentary creature comforts.[2] None had sewers or water; the largest probably had fewer than a dozen rooms but all soon had bars over which liquor was sold illegally.

The sale of alcoholic beverages was still prohibited in the Territories in 1882 and the citizens were allowed to have liquor in their possession only if it was imported under permit from the lieutenant-governor. As the latter dispensed permits with a free hand, imbibing citizens seldom had any difficulty getting supplies. The general practice was for the urban drinkers to deposit their permits with their favourite bar. This enabled the barkeeps to have permits in the drawer to cover any liquor they had in stock if the Mounties tried to charge them with having it in their possession illegally. The hotels could thus import booze by the barrel, hide it carefully, and refill their bottles as they were emptied at the bar. In addition to being available at the bars for those who lacked permits, liquor was also supplied by druggists on doctors' prescriptions. Sibbald and Lindsay, Regina's first druggists, regularly advertised that they carried stocks of whisky, wine, and beer for medicinal purposes.[3]

With a force of 500 scattered all over the Northwest Territories the Mounted Police could not have enforced prohibition if they had tried, and their efforts were desultory at best. Liquor was freely available in neighbouring Manitoba and it was brought into the Territories in shipments of every conceivable commodity from lumber to furniture to flour to pickles. Mrs. Annie Habourg, a Regina woman identified only as a "notorious character", was reported to have devised a rubber attachment for her corsets which she filled with several gallons of whiskey in Brandon and wore back to Regina.[4]

Regina, like all the other mainline towns, was a classic example of a free-enterprise system in operation. As the track-layers moved westward, a small army of adventurous artisans followed with their eyes peeled for the main chance. It included carpenters, tinsmiths, blacksmiths, bakers, butchers, doctors, lawyers, printers, plasterers, and others. Often they would begin prospecting as the trains pulled into the stations west of Winnipeg. While the train was loading and unloading way-freight, express, and passengers, they inquired around about the local prospects for their trade. If their skills were in short supply, that would be the end of their journey. If not, they would keep going till they found a favourable place in which to go to work.

In the summer of 1882 Regina was as favourable a place to stop as there was in the West. Carpenters earned up to five dollars a day, teamsters with horses ten dollars. Lumber was hammered into stores and houses as fast as it could be unloaded, but the method of construction could only be described as jerry-building at its worst. There was neither time nor inclination to bother with foundations. The crude clapboard buildings were erected on wooden beams laid on surface footings. Most of the structures were a single storey high, the stores differing from the houses only in having square-topped false fronts that gave illusions of height and size. Few of the buildings were painted and, as the occupants would discover to their sorrow, even fewer were weather-tight to the cold. Despite the change of

name from Pile of Bones to Regina, the settlement was still very
much a shack town like all the other villages between Winnipeg and
the end of steel. The tempo of the Regina building boom of 1882, as
a correspondent of the *Manitoba Free Press* reported it, could well
have been as accurate a description of any of the others.

> The town has not yet assumed any degree of regularity.
> Tents and houses alike have been put down without any
> regard to geometrical precision. It is now for the most part
> directly south of the C.P.R. station. Six weeks ago the
> town was established on the open prairie. Today it
> contains 8 hotels, 12 stores, 2 blacksmith shops, 2 liveries,
> 2 laundries, 3 billiard rooms, 2 bakeries, 1 drug store, 1
> jewelry, 2 doctors, 6 lawyers, 4 lumber yards and a popu-
> lation of 800-900.[5]

Included in that population were perhaps 150 men attached to the
newly built Mounted Police headquarters at "The Barracks" on the
outskirts of the town. Included, too, was Nicholas Flood Davin, a
40-year-old lawyer who became Regina's most vociferous champion.
Scholar, poet, bon vivant, editor and journalistic termagant, past
master of invective, and an up-and-down politician, Davin lived and
died a Conservative voice in a Liberal wilderness. It is to Davin that
we can look for a key to the curiously inverted pietistic attitude
which Regina turned outward to the world. Earl Drake's *Regina, The
Queen City* contains this paragraph:

> Reginans in 1891 had not favored the idea of appointing a
> constable to combat crime; they preferred to hold their
> noses piously and pretend the stench did not exist. When a
> zealous new minister preached a very earthy and specific
> sermon on Regina's sins, many citizens were annoyed. One
> man summed up their indignation when he wrote, with
> becoming modesty, "Regina is one of the most moral,
> religious and law-abiding towns in the Dominion."

It was not, of course. It only dedicated itself to keeping the
seamier side of its social life out of the public prints and the public
view. It was a process which curiously enough began with Davin
himself. As founder in 1883 of Regina's first newspaper, the *Leader*,
Davin set off at once to do battle with the Winnipeg papers which

were then engaged in a campaign of derogation against Regina. At issue was the location of the capital of the Northwest Territories for which Winnipeg and Regina were competing and in which Regina was successful. Once the row started between the newspapers, it quickly expanded to take in everything in sight, including personalities.

This early trading of insults reveals that the first prostitutes arrived in Regina and were in business before the roof was on the station. Certainly there were whorehouses in Regina months before there was a single church. The Presbyterians began holding meetings, first in a large tent, and then in the loft above the blacksmith shop. The Methodists were also organized informally in 1883, but without a church or permanent pastor. The first Presbyterian church was erected in 1885, a year after the Anglicans got their church under construction. It was long before that, however, that the *Winnipeg Sun* in one of its dispatches chided Davin with closing his eyes to the streetwalkers that were infesting Regina during the winter of 1882-3. He vigorously denied the charge in an open letter to the *Winnipeg Sun* which he published in the May 10, 1883, issue of the *Leader*:

> Your correspondent wrote that not a word has appeared in The Leader about a house of ill-fame. He is wrong on that head. But I have not made the matter a prominent subject of discussion because I hope to have The Leader go into families. *The less families read of that unsavory subject the better. I never saw any good follow the discussion of it except to the newspapers. Any prurient subject tends to swell their circulation.* [Italics added.] I spoke to Major Walsh and told him if painted prostitutes were allowed to walk the streets I should have to attack the Mounted Police. I told him he must rid Regina of so great a curse. He went, as he told me, and warned these persons but they defied him. My opinion as a lawyer, whatever it may be worth, is that he had the power to get rid of the nuisance. The streets, however, have not been disfigured by the presence of these persons since.

From Davin's day onward, keeping news of "that unsavory subject" out of the columns of the *Leader* was the settled policy of the paper. The extent to which it was prepared to go is well illustrated by its handling of a fire which burned a prominent bagnio to the ground on a bitter January morning in 1897. Within a matter of minutes the fire incinerated two never-identified inmates in their sleep and burned Gertie Underwood, the madam, so badly she died three weeks later. It was Regina's worst fire but the *Leader* refused to run a story on it, presumably because it involved a notorious north-side brothel. The rival *Regina Standard* gave it full play, however, on January 29 and the story fuelled the indignation of the Reverend J.A. Carmichael of Knox Presbyterian church. Using the fire as a text he heaped oratorical coals on the heads of his pew holders.

Where, he demanded, were they when such houses could operate so openly on the north side of their town? Why did the business men in his and other Christian congregations do nothing about the social evil on their doorsteps? Why were the newspapers keeping silent when such an evil was running rampant? Five years before, he reminded them, the ministers of the gospel had themselves led a campaign to drive the prostitutes out of town. Where were the ministers that they permitted the evil to exist without rising in protest?

Not content with a mere barrage of pulpit pounding, the Reverend Carmichael stormed into the office of the *Leader* and demanded action. The *Leader* ran his sermon almost verbatim on February 5. But so far as can be discovered it drew not an atom of response from anybody. A week after her death, the *Leader* noted that "Gertie Underwood who had been burned in the fire, died at the Salvation Army barracks." The following week the Women's Association said it was soliciting donations to recover the fifteen dollars which had been spent caring for Miss Underwood in her fatal illness.[6]

In its desire to attract no public attention to the existence of prostitution, the *Leader* was far from alone. The Mounted Police never regarded it as a major concern. Although it was the headquarters for the Force, Regina was just another example of the standard Mounted Police attitude toward the "social evil" — to ignore it completely until public clamour forced some kind of token action to be taken. The location of the police headquarters at Regina, how-ever, may have inhibited the prostitutes from moving into that city with the force of numbers common elsewhere. In any event, there is no record of any mass migration of moonlight madonnas into Regina comparable to the periodic influxes which flooded Winnipeg, Brandon, and Moose Jaw. On the other hand, there is no reason to assume that the burghers of Regina were any less interested in sex than their brothers elsewhere. It was simply that the town managed to keep its struggle with the social evil better hidden. Nevertheless, in the years that followed, public discussion of the prostitution problem would erupt periodically to enable fate to paint mustaches on the city's holier-than-thou self-image.

Davin himself was impelled to speak out soon after the publication of his aforementioned letter to the *Sun.* He was a lawyer first and a publisher second. Like many other lawyers, he had a sense of fair play which was outraged by the complainant-arrester-prosecutor-judge-jury-jailer role of the Mounted Police in the Territories. His indignation boiled to the surface in the Stanton case, about which the facts are by no means clear but seem to be as follows.

Stanton was a young clerk who got a job with the Bank of Montreal, the first bank with a branch in the Territories. He became involved with a local whore and got the bank's money mixed up with his own, with the inevitable result. Instead of being speedily brought to trial after his arrest, Stanton was charged and remanded repeatedly while his friends were frantically scrounging around to collect enough money to make up the deficit. When they succeeded, the charge was dropped and Stanton was turned loose, after the Mounties billed the bank for Stanton's board and room at sixty cents per day. That was only the first verse. As Davin wrote on July 26, 1883:

"But while he was held in jail, with the connivance of the Mounted Police, the wretched woman who was responsible for Stanton's plight was brought to his cell and left alone with him. She then spent the rest of the night in the barracks." "Such misconduct," thundered Davin, "must cease."[7]

Davin's earlier letter to the *Winnipeg Sun* could hardly have convinced the Manitoba critics of Regina's moral purity. But, coupled with his outburst in the Stanton case, it convinced the Mounties they had a viper in the nest. They wanted no self-appointed guardian of Regina's morality heckling their law enforcement team from the sidelines. The summer of 1883 saw the start of one of the longest running feuds in western history. Nicholas Flood Davin, clearly, was a self-important individual pre-ordained to get on badly with the

British army types who were running the Mounted Police. He was also a two-fisted drinker of legendary capacity. Soon after the exchange with the *Sun* he was travelling back to Regina from Winnipeg. A Mounted Police sergeant boarded the train at Moosomin as it crossed from wide-open Manitoba into the whisky-prohibited Northwest Territories. Spotting Davin, he made directly for him, searched him, and found a half-empty flask on his hip. Davin naturally admitted illegal possession and said to the policeman, "Okay, spill it out."

As he explained later in court, this was the standard practice when the police found travellers with liquor in their possession on the trains coming into the Territories; they spilled the liquor on the floor and dropped the matter. But not with Davin. They summoned him to court, where he was convicted and fined fifty dollars and costs. This set off a vendetta between Davin and the Mounties that lasted as long as he retained control of the *Leader*. The editorial clubs he used to chastise the police serve as evidence of the mores of early Regina. On August 16, 1883, for example, the *Leader* carried this note:

> On the day on which Mr. Davin was fined for having a partially empty flask in his possession at Moosomin, one J.F. Burns, notorious as a brothel keeper and who moves about the police barracks as a master of the scene, appeared at the Commerical Hotel and said: "We have downed Davin at last!" Whom did he mean "we"? Whether he associated himself with the whole Mounted Police, or only with a few of the select members, or only with Colonel Herchimer, we do not know.

A month later, the *Leader* attacked the police force itself:

> What a stupendous farce! A Mounted Police constable goes up to the Barracks a little shakey and smelling of whisky and is made to disclose the name of the person who gave him the glass. Forthwith a sergeant major comes down to know whether the man had a permit. But the officer in charge can have any number of Bacchanals at the Barracks, and they can make the moonlight air hideous with curses and ribaldry and there is no sergeant major to ride into the officers' quarters to ask him if he has a permit.

On the first page of the same edition the *Leader* reported on a drunken brawl that had broken out at the Barracks among visiting members of the Manitoba legislature who were guests of the inspector. The members had been poured back into their train by the Mounties, still hurling fists and obscenities at each other.

Unfortunately for Regina, the early hopes which Davin and the other boosters held for its future tended to be blighted by one disaster or another. Its population zoomed from nothing to 1,000 within a matter of months, then it took the better part of the next twenty years to reach 2,000. The Riel Rebellion gave the town a temporary lift, but a decade of disastrous crop failures interspersed by half-crops threatened to destroy not only Regina but also the Territories with it. Regina hung on, however, mainly by the regular infusion of the wages of the Mounted Police and the civil service.[8] By the time of the 1901 census, its population had managed to reach only 2,246. Then it took off, to double and redouble and redouble to 30,233 during the next decade, to become Exhibit "C" in J.S. Woodsworth's catalogue of the social disasters that resulted from unplanned and disorderly population explosions.[9]

In the years that followed the calamities of the 1880s the people of Regina understandably could only with difficulty restrain an impulse to keep looking back over their shoulders for signs of the next catastrophe. Thus it was fated to be a town which would never become infected with the ebullience of Winnipeg, Brandon, Calgary, Lethbridge, or even Moose Jaw. It tended to drag its feet on local improvements which other localities pushed to the limit of their credit. Thus, when the immigrant armies detrained on its platform, it was hopelessly ill-equipped to accommodate them and struggled with an impossible backlog in such things as sewers, water, sidewalks, and streets that took two generations to overcome. Similar patterns of overcrowding occurred in all the other prairie cities. The problem just seemed to be worse in Regina, perhaps because the plate-flat site on which it was located seriously increased its sewer and drainage problems. In any event, in a matter of a very few months the near-downtown east side developed into the slum described in Chapter 1.

The centre of the Regina booze and brothel area was the corner of Ottawa Street and Tenth Avenue where the Kaiser Hotel was located. Though it quickly degenerated into a notorious dive, the Kaiser in appearance was one of Regina's most imposing hotels at the turn of the century. Unlike the Waverley, the Paris, and the Commercial hotels, which were located in the general area, it was a substantial-looking structure of imitation stone. With the first rush of immigrants, the area became known as Germantown, perhaps more by reason of the Kaiser Hotel than because of the ethnic cast of the population, which was decidedly mixed. Prior to the population explosion, Germantown had gone downhill like the rest of Regina, and the prostitutes and liquor trade undoubtedly shared the long economic drought with the other residents. In 1904, for example, when the Regina hotels sent in their applications for licence renewal to the Territorial Government, just one out of the eleven was granted.[10] Only the Alexandra Hotel, the government said, had a standard of accommodation equal to that offered by the Ontario dollar-a-day hotels. As they were then charging $2.50 a day, or $3 with bath, the other Regina hotels were ordered to make substantial improvements in their premises before their licences would be renewed. In an environment where even the saloons were going broke it could well be assumed that the prostitutes who could get out of town, did.

Regina was well into the twentieth century before it got around to hiring a proper police force. During the city's first decade, the fire chief seems to have been in charge of the town for, like all other settlements, Regina was desperately concerned with fire hazards. Eventually when the town council did decide in 1891 to appoint a single policeman, it did so largely to abate obvious public nuisances. Protecting persons and property from any criminal activity was very low in the scale of arguments on behalf of a police force.

Some time during the next decade, Inspector R.J. Harwood became Chief of Police Harwood and when the city itself was incorporated in 1903 he had a staff of four. Not until 1909, when Theodore Zeats was imported from Scotland, did the city get a regular police department. On the morals front, Harwood and Zeats had one major concern — drunkenness. Anything more serious than that was left to the Mounties, perhaps because the city itself had no jail. All it had was a makeshift collection of cells which functioned mainly as a drunk tank in the basement of the City Hall. Indeed, it was the riotous clamour of the drunks in the tank, which interrupted a temperance rally being held upstairs in the council chambers, that led eventually to the construction of a new city hall and a proper jail. On that occasion, the Temperance and Moral Reform Society was meeting to prepare its submission to the first session of the Saskatchewan legislature. Because that presentation was concerned exclusively with liquor law enforcement, it can be taken as an indication that the Regina moralists did not regard their "social evil" problem as worth worrying about. Wherever else the reverend clergy gathered in those years, booze and the "social evil" were usually joined as the twin scourges of the population.

The absence of ecclesiastical ferment in Regina over the activities of the scarlet women set the town apart from other cities on the prairies. Could the explanation have been that it was so overwhelmingly a farm-supply centre that it did not have the floating urban population needed to sustain a red-light district? That there were not enough farmers coming to town often enough during the long winter months to make a red-light district economically viable? Any such explanation is demolished simply by bringing in the city of Brandon as a case in rebuttal. Brandon was even more farm-oriented than Regina, as bucolic a bailiwick as existed on the Great Plains. Yet Brandon struggled with a king-sized prostitution problem for years without coming up with a satisfactory solution.

In 1905 Brandon was about the same size as Regina, both having a population of around 6,000. On May 14, the largest delegation that ever crowded into the Brandon City Hall appeared to demand the total eradication of prostitution from the town. It was spearheaded by delegates from the Christian Temperance Union, the Board of Deacons of the Baptist Church, the Deaconate of the Congregational Church, the Department of Social and Moral Reform of the Methodist Church, the Session of the Presbyterian Church, and the Catholic Church. They were supported by a crowd that filled the city council chamber and overflowed the hallway and stairs to the street.

Principal McDiarmid described the situation in Brandon as the worst in Canada. (In all such confrontations, moral reform spokesmen always claimed their city was the worst in Canada.) The Reverend Finlay said that no city of its size was worse than Brandon. He said the operators of the brothels boasted that their trade was mainly with married men, that without the married men they could not exist. He urged the council to publish the names of all married men found in brothels. If the wives of Brandon knew what was going on, there would be twenty divorces a week. Finally, he estimated that 200 boys between fourteen and seventeen had been led astray by the Brandon brothels. [11]

There was a sharp undercurrent of urgency to the demands of the clergy because the big holiday on May 24 was approaching. The previous year, they charged, the brothel operators had imported 60 prostitutes who had turned a Victoria Day celebration into an unprecedented sexual debauch. If the city council was unwilling or unable to exterminate the evil, then, the delegation warned, it was prepared to take matters into its own hands. The Brandon City Council was intimidated to the extent of setting up a committee to negotiate with the denizens of the east-side houses of which, the mayor insisted, there were only five.

When the call went out for the madams to come to City Hall for a meeting the next day, ten showed up. They were assured that there would be no harsh action against them but they were also told to get out of town. Mrs. Simmons, who acted as spokesman for the assembled madams, objected strongly to the order and after a lengthy discussion the committee decided the women would have one week in which to obey the eviction order. Despite the bold front, the mayor and the council clearly doubted the wisdom of trying to suppress prostitution in Brandon.

"Personally," said Mayor J.W. Fleming, "I am opposed to the system of licensing prostitution by regularly fining the keepers of these houses. They operate quite openly and sell liquor illegally, also quite openly. But we must admit there is a great difference of opinion in Brandon about this problem. Will the citizens stand behind council if it takes the kind of action the clergymen demand? That is the question."

To all of which his colleagues on council echoed agreement. Alderman Harcourt wondered aloud whether it was really better to disperse the prostitutes than to segregate them. Alderman Caldwell noted that vice was universal and difficult to suppress. In Winnipeg, he said, things were much worse since they closed Thomas Street and scattered the women around the city. He recalled that Brandon had closed down all its brothels several years previously and one had opened up near the Langberry Hotel on Twelfth Street and had run for a year. He voted to leave the brothels where they were. Alderman McEachern agreed with the object of the moral reformers but doubted their remedy. He had made personal inquiries in Winnipeg and been told that matters were now very much worse. Why, even the newsboys now earned commissions by directing strangers to Winnipeg brothels. He noted several former aldermen in the delegation that had come before the city council. What had they ever done about the problem? Why were they now coming forward to demand action when they had done nothing when they were in power? With such doubt-plagued members of council, it can be assumed that the uproar accomplished very little and that the "social evil" continued as a fact of everyday life in Brandon. Undoubtedly there were excursions and alarums periodically, but it was not until 1912 that the brothels got so completely out of hand that a royal commission was set up to look into rampant vice.

How could Regina escape from a condition which seemed endemic everywhere else? The answer is, in part, that it did not. Prostitution in Regina in those years was, as previously noted, centred in Germantown, in a dozen blocks bounded by Montreal and Wallace streets, the railway tracks, Arcola Street, and Twelfth Avenue. To the west of this area the older houses were being rapidly replaced with warehouses and commercial buildings. Wealthier Reginans were moving across the Wascana Creek to the vicinity of the Legislature. It was in that area, and southward from Victoria Avenue, where the housing boom developed after Regina became the capital of newly created Saskatchewan in 1905. Germantown was a sort of backwater down by the tracks, comparable in many ways to Winnipeg's Annabella Street. It was out of sight and, save for payday celebrants on a spree, out of mind for upper-class Regina.

There were times, of course, when the uproar in Germantown spilled over into the respectable residential areas, but a few words from the *Leader* were usually all that was needed to dampen down the disturbance.

> It is high time [the paper observed in May 1904] that council took steps to stop disturbances on the street which are now an almost nightly occurrence. Hardly a night passes without some intoxicated persons . . . parading the

Regina

Wallace Street
Winnipeg Street
Quebec Street
Montreal Street
Toronto Street
Ottawa Street

Osler Street
Broad Street

Arcola Street

Tenth Avenue

Railway
station

Eleventh Avenue

Twelfth Avenue

Victoria Avenue

Thirteenth Avenue

Waskana
Lake

streets making the night and especially the early morning
hours hideous with disputes, song and uproar. Regina has
grown beyond the stage where one policeman in the town
station can look after the whole city.

An insight into the highly moralistic tone of the *Leader*'s editorial
policy may be gained from the fact that on March 30, 1904, it
published a long editorial deploring the growing tendency of small
boys to play marbles for keeps. This, it allowed, destroyed the
innocence of childhood games and directed the steps of the children
into unhealthy growth patterns.

That Regina had a rather imposing red-light district was demonstrated by Chief Zeats with the only substantial raid he ever made,
on February 14, 1911. Late that afternoon Chief Zeats dropped into
the Mulligan Livery Stable and hired a fleet of buggies. Then with the
assistance of a couple of Mounties he organized two task forces to
raid the Germantown brothels. The first call was at Jack Webster's
"Nigger Club" [the *Leader*'s appellation] at 1660 Osler Street,
where they took three of the six gamblers there into custody. Then
raids followed at 1776 Quebec, 1802 Quebec, 1932 Toronto, and
1400 Rae Street. There was also a raid on the Regina Café at Osler
and Eleventh. In each house the tenant was a Negro and most of the
dozen prostitutes arrested were Negroes. When they appeared in
court the following day and pleaded guilty, jail sentences without
the option of a fine were imposed. William Taylor and his wife, who
were white and ran the Regina Café, got six months and four months
respectively. Jack Reynolds and his wife, Louise Maxwell, and
Josephine Turner, all black people, got three months each. Emelia
Webster, who pleaded guilty to keeping a house of ill fame, got five
months. Her husband, however, pleaded not guilty and was
defended by C.A. Wood.

Wood raised what was probably the first public outcry in Regina
against racial discrimination. He charged that the police had raided
the houses not because they were brothels but because they were
Negro brothels. Police witnesses testified they had raided the houses
because the neighbours complained about heavy traffic and boisterous behaviour. The constable who had kept score on the Webster
house counted seven men entering one evening, eleven the next, and
eight the next. It transpired during the hearing that one of the

women had four previous convictions for prostitution in Regina. No word of the previous raids on the whorehouses had been published in the *Leader*; it remained true to the code established by Nicholas Flood Davin — the less a newspaper permitted families to read about unsavoury subjects the better. After this brief lifting of the curtain, the *Leader* reverted to type, and the social evil resumed its clandestine existence.

All the while, Chief Ted Zeats was doing what he could with what he had. He expanded his police force as Regina grew, but in the end the task of keeping the lid on Germantown proved to be too much for him. His patrolmen seemed to quickly develop blind eyes where vice was concerned. On one occasion a new girl became established in one of the hotels and developed such a wide demand for her services that the lobby was crowded with customers waiting to be served. It was only when disturbances arose among those waiting in line that the police discovered what was going on. When action was taken the raiding policemen somehow managed to let just about everyone concerned escape the dragnet.

For Chief Zeats, events started to come to a head in the summer of 1912 when Magistrate William Trant gave the city a general blistering from the bench. Where, he asked, was the Social and Moral Reform Society? Where were all the guardians of Regina morality? Did they not know that vice was rampant in Regina, that respectable apartment blocks were being turned into premises for licentious debauchery? Had they not seen young women going into these blocks and staying with young men until all hours? [12]

What Chief Zeats knew, but did not say, was that Magistrate Trant was making enforcement of the law against the prostitutes almost impossible. Trant liked sending the girls to jail without an option of a fine. For months thereafter it was impossible to get the women to plead guilty, and getting convictions without such a plea was all but impossible. And even when he carried off his raids successfully, Chief Zeats seldom managed to harvest much credit for his efforts. Thus he raided a large Negro brothel on Osler Street and hauled in not only the whores but some Negro women and children. It turned out that most of the inhabitants of the house were respectable working people who had been unable to locate any vacant housing in Regina which the landlords were prepared to rent to Negroes. [13]

Regina drifted along under Chief Zeats until the early winter of

1914, when a series of misadventures in trying to bring the brothels under control moved the city council to order an investigation into its police department. However, before the inquiry could get started, Zeats decided big-city police work was not for him. He quit and got a job as town constable at Yorkton. His successor was E.G. Berry, who tripled the size of the force, ran into a crime wave, and was fired within a year. Then Regina reached out to Edmonton in 1915 for Martin Bruton, who ruled the city with an iron hand for the next thirty years. But not even Bruton could keep everything under complete control. The underside of Regina life was given another brief exposure when, in September 1920, John McCarthy walked into the Regina courthouse and started filing libel suits against just about everybody in sight. He filed one against the mayor and the city council, another against the chief of police, another against the licence inspector, and another against the editor and publishers of the *Leader*. The suits added up to $50,000 in damages which McCarthy wanted for the besmirching of his character by the defendants, jointly and severally. It had all begun innocently enough at a hearing of the city's licence committee. McCarthy, who might have been described as Germantown's Conrad Hilton, had applied for a licence transfer of the Waverley Hotel to himself. He had been the licence holder of the Commercial Hotel and had recently been granted a licence for the Paris Hotel. All the hotels were within a couple of blocks of each other on Broad Street and Osler Street and within the same distance of the Kaiser. To McCarthy's surprise, the licence committee refused his request for a licence transfer after the police department and the licence inspector reported on the unsavoury character of McCarthy's other operations.

By 1920 prohibition had been in force long enough for slum-area hotel owners to have learned how to survive marginally without a legally operated bar. They turned to bootlegging, and McCarthy's Commercial Hotel had run up no less than sixteen convictions for various licence and liquor violations between May and August 1919. The hotel, the officials testified, was a notorious dive and a hangout for drunks and vagrants. When a *Leader* reporter got hold of the statement and included a short summary in his story, McCarthy sued for libel.

The case was a year coming to trial and McCarthy served as his own counsel. He lost the case when the Regina officials pleaded they had only spoken the truth and the *Leader* claimed fair comment and the publication of an official statement believed to be true. The police said that McCarthy had proved completely uncooperative when they went to his hotels looking for wanted malefactors. On the other hand, he was forever pestering them to come to the hotels and evict troublesome drunks and brawlers. His hotels kept only rudimentary registers of guests and a clerk testified that he often was unaware who was occupying the rooms. Frequently strangers came in through the back doors or the windows, and the management would only discover they had a full house when the maids did a bed check in the mornings. In their searches, the police often found the rooms occupied by well-known prostitutes.[14]

It is clear from the libel suit testimony that, despite the sharp drop in drunkenness that resulted from the closing of the bars, conditions within Germantown remained pretty much what they had been in 1913 when Woodsworth made his report on slum conditions. With the loss of their booze revenue, the Germantown hotels became little more than flophouses for doxies, alcoholics, and sundry vagrants. Though its sale was legally forbidden, whisky was still available from the same sources that were turning medicinal alcohol into branded lines of Bourbon and Scotch for export via the rumrunner to the United States. But booze was no longer a bonanza for its retail dispensers and neither, from all indications, was the operation of brothels. The city suffered through a prolonged depression after the First World War as the western wheat-growers were caught in an inflationary squeeze between rising costs and depressed farm prices. As one veteran morality-squad officer observed, the prostitutes were usually the first to suffer with the onset of hard times. Price competition became more pronounced and the wages of sin dropped almost to the starvation point, in part by reason of the intrusion of a lot of new entries into the business.

The decline and fall of prostitution in Regina, however, was attributable neither to the Great War, to prohibition, nor to the hardness of the times. Prostitution was doomed, it turned out, by the fire that destroyed the new C.P.R. roundhouse in 1883. When that happened the railway changed its divisional headquarters from Regina to Moose Jaw, forty-five miles to the west. Later, when the Soo Line came in from Minneapolis, its terminus was also located at Moose Jaw. The railway made Moose Jaw, and for twenty-five years it kept pace in population with Regina and fought bitterly with Regina and Saskatoon to become the capital of the province. Its failure in that attempt doomed it to inferior status though it managed through the years to acquire a modest industrial base which Regina never matched. And on the morals front, Moose Jaw became everything that Regina was not, a wide-open town from the turn of the century to the Second World War. And that happened in part because Moose Jaw became, in a real sense, Regina's red-light district. A Canadian newspaper editor who learned his trade in Moose Jaw coined this description as he watched three carloads of Regina fun-seekers debouching onto River Street:[15] "Moose Jaw isn't a city or a municipality or even a geographic location! Moose Jaw is a goddam virus that has permanently afflicted Regina and for which there is no known cure!"

From the Regina perspective, a journalist who arrived there just after the First World War described the situation this way:

> You simply can't appreciate what these prairie cities were like for young guys just out of their teens unless you lived through those years. There were no girls. They were just starting to work in offices, they operated the telephones, worked in cafés and in some of the stores. But they disappeared out of circulation at 6 o'clock and you never saw them again until the next day. Talk about a man's world! Regina was certainly it. You know I've seen girls almost cringe in terror if you asked them for a date. I asked a salesgirl in a store for a date and she called the manager in a great fluster.
>
> So after I'd been in Regina about a month I asked one of the guys on payday how about going down the line. He didn't know what I meant and when I explained he gave me the shock of my life. He swore that there wasn't a single brothel in all Regina, except for a couple of dives in Germantown. Since Martin Bruton took over as chief of police in 1916, the girls avoided Regina like a plague spot. I couldn't believe it, for if that had happened to Regina it was the first time anywhere, ever. He swore it was true. So I asked, what did all the young guys around town do for girls? They went to Moose Jaw. There was a cheap round-

trip fare between the two cities on the C.P.R.; I think it cost $1 return.

The contrast between Regina and Moose Jaw was unbelievable. You came out of the Moose Jaw station, turned left on River Street and you could have been in New Orleans. If it was early in the day you could see girls waving from the windows of the hotels across the street. If they caught your eye they'd call you up. There were a couple of poolrooms and on one side of the street was Pipeline Johnson's gambling joint and the Zess brothers had two places across the way. They played a lot of faro and poker but the gambling joints never interested me much. Like the poolrooms they were good places to kill time in between trains.

Everything in Moose Jaw was wide open. By night the streets were really filled with men roaming around, and the traffic down to the whore houses at the other end of the street was something to see. There was nothing attractive about any of the houses or in fact about most of the girls. But they were great places for railroaders, particularly if you happened to hit town on their paydays. Like as not there would be a fight between the Soo-liners and the C.P.R.s, and when that happened a cop would appear out of nowhere and break it up. They got there so fast when trouble started that they must have been stationed inside the houses! Next to the railroaders, the commercial travellers were the best customers of the River Street houses, and of course every Saturday would bring carloads of Reginans into town for the week-end.

It was true what they used to say in Regina: What did Regina need with a Red Light district when it had Moose Jaw? The same was true for gambling, and even the local pool sharks preferred to play at Moose Jaw when they had money to bet on their games. And you know there was one very curious thing about all this. You always felt safe in Moose Jaw. You might have assumed with all the vice there was on tap that your pocket would be picked or you'd be knocked on head on the street. There were always a lot of Americans in town which might have been expected to create crime waves because rum running was just beginning. But nothing like that ever happened to anybody I

knew. Mostly crime in Moose Jaw involved crooked
gambling, opium, and lifting of wallets by the broads in the
hotels. How many women worked on River Street? A lot
more in summer than in winter, by a long shot, but I'd
guess a year round minimum of at least 50 and perhaps
more than 100 when things were really jumping.[16]

From the Great War onward, Moose Jaw became the happy
hunting ground for Regina gamblers, philandering husbands, stag
partyers, unattached tom-catters, drinking preachers, service club
sports, and unclassified scofflaws. During the summer the new gravel
highway between the cities was choked with dust from the weekend traffic. In the winter fun was only an hour away from Regina by
C.P.R. daycoach. As Moose Jaw's fame spread, it became the "in"
place for travellers and those of the commercial variety regularly
arranged their schedules so that they laid over between train connections in Moose Jaw instead of Regina. Moreover, the ending of
prohibition in Saskatchewan in 1924 created an income boom for
scores of Moose Jaw citizens who cashed in on the demand for
Canadian booze in the United States. Recalling the roaring twenties
in Moose Jaw, a native said:[17]

> I can remember as a kid being intrigued with one of our
> neighbours. He must have had the first two-car garage in
> Moose Jaw and he had two cars to go in it, but we never saw
> but one being driven. Occasionally we'd get a squint at the
> other car as we wandered up or down the lane. Then
> regularly about once a week very late at night we'd hear
> him warming up the car in the garage. We'd peek out our
> window and pretty soon the other car would be backed out
> of the garage and roar down the lane. It made a hell of a
> racket, more like a truck than a car. When we went out in
> the morning and checked the car was always back in the
> garage. It was as clear as it could be, the guy had a regular
> booze run down into the badlands of Montana. But it
> wasn't something we thought too much about. Some of
> the kids at school used to talk about older brothers taking
> cars to the border. There was almost no chance of them
> getting caught. The Mounties' cars could never keep up
> with them, and besides the Mounties never really had a
> tenth of the cars they needed to patrol the main roads,

never mind the back roads. So the risk was small and there was no highjacking around Moose Jaw that I recall.

As the booze and brothel centre of Moose Jaw, River Street became as notorious all over Saskatchewan as Annabella Street was in Manitoba. And not only in Saskatchewan. Under the benign regime of Chief of Police W.P. Johnson and Tony Townsend, his deputy, it reportedly became the hide-out for American gangsters on the lam and the headquarters of well-organized rumrunning rings to the United States. Johnson was the West's most famous lawman, around whom a hundred legends have been woven — all of them libellous. Certainly Johnson was the wealthiest policeman in the West, for he owned and operated a 1,000 acre showplace farm north of Moose Jaw[18] and had a fine home across the street from the police station. His favourite occupation, according to one of the telephone operators, was to stand at the door of the police station and ogle the girls on their way to and from work at the telephone company. He ran Moose Jaw as a pocket fiefdom from 1905 until 1927. He was, indeed, Moose Jaw's first chief of police, since his predecessors had all functioned primarily as licence inspectors. He owed his appointment largely to the fact that the city had outgrown its rudimentary law enforcement department and there were recurring demands from the residents for a cleaning out of the lawless element. Thus in the civic election in 1903, one of the main concerns of the electorate was to "get rid of the houses of ill fame in the parks". W.D. Sanders, who was elected mayor by acclamation, promised to carry out the clean-up.

Chief Johnson was his answer and the Johnson regime began with a mild wave of arrests that established a pattern for the future. Merely to consult the record, without the leavening testimony of residents who recalled the way in which the city operated, can give a distorted picture of a vigorous police department in action. Certainly Johnson was strong on raids and it is doubtful if any other Saskatchewan police departments could have approached his record of arrests if only numbers were considered. But those who were there insist that it was all mainly for show. The first major arrest was perhaps an example. On June 1, 1906, Louise Breckenridge, a local madam, was arrested on the charge of having tried to recruit a thirteen-year-old girl into her brothel. But when the case came to trial some weeks later Mrs. Breckenridge was acquitted when the main witness against her could not be located.[19]

The establishment of the brothels on River Street during the early years of Johnson's rule followed the traditional western pattern of locating them as conveniently to the railway station as possible. The process was helped along by several big fires on Main Street and River Street which wiped out concentrations of jerry-built wooden stores and houses that had been constructed in the 1880s. By 1910 the north side of River Street from Main Street to Fourth Street West was built up solidly with brick hotels, some of which had stores and restaurants on the street level. The south side of the street, however, remained largely untouched and, after the turn of the century, between Main Street and the Plaza Hotel it was given over to Chinese restaurants and small stores. Beyond the hotels as far as the bend in the Moose Jaw Creek, the buildings were mostly individual houses, of which a dozen were brothels. Most of the hotels had women working in their rooms.[20]

The location of the bars and brothels hard by the main business street of the town naturally caused occasional outbreaks of moral indignation. As a general rule the Moose Jaw police seemed to keep the drunks and streetwalkers off Main Street. But if the activities of the gamblers and petty crooks on River Street got out of hand and the city police refused to act, the citizens could and did appeal to the R.C.M.P. The Mounties, however, would only act if the criminal code, as distinct from the city by-laws, was involved. Until the Saskatchewan Provincial Police became an active rather than a paper force in 1916, the Mounties also enforced prohibition, but confined their activities to the excise and smuggling aspects rather than to local enforcement in the cities and towns.

In Moose Jaw the three law-enforcement agencies seldom co-operated. This lack of mutual assistance reached its climax in 1920 when the local police gave a Chinese merchant a permit to own a pistol at a time when the Mounties were trying to catch him running an opium den. On another occasion the city police arrested Mah Pow, a secret agent of the Mounted Police drug squad. They charged him with having opium in his possession when they found a package of the stuff in his pocket. He was convicted and heavily fined but the verdict was reversed on appeal. The court suggested that the circumstances of the arrest were so suspicious that the opium could well have been placed in Mah Pow's pocket by somebody trying to destroy his usefulness to the Mounted Police. Whether that was what had happened or not, Mah Pow's usefulness as a police spy was in fact ended.[21]

The only serious threat to Chief Johnson's suzerainty over Moose Jaw resulted from a personal clash with Alderman Caulder. It began in a shouting match between Caulder and the chief over the uninhibited celebrations on River Street at the height of the Stampede weekend in August 1921. It was customary in all western cities for the police to take a more relaxed attitude to law enforcement during the annual Fair Weeks. Games of chance for charity were allowed, and the merchants went all out in promoting full attendance at festivities by the people for miles around. The carnival spirit took over and joy reigned supreme. During the prohibition era it was also customary for the gendarmerie to take a tolerant view of drunks and those who catered to them. But conceding all that, what was happening on River Street that Saturday night was ridiculous, at least in the eyes of Alderman Caulder. Not only was the street jammed with carnival booths and a boundless sea of humanity, but the word was out that real beer was on sale both in the hotels and in the refreshment booths operated by the Ladies Aid. To the alderman's startled eyes it looked like the biggest grand drunk in western history. He rushed around to the police station and demanded that Chief Johnson call up the reserves and get things under control before the drunks tore the town apart. Johnson went around to the hotels, shut down the bars, and went home to bed. The evening passed without incident.

Caulder, however, became increasingly indignant as time passed. "Monte Carlo in its palmiest days had nothing on River Street," he complained to anyone who would listen. Seemingly he got the ear of a couple of disgruntled policemen. They informed him of a sorry catalogue of graft and incompetence in the police department. Caulder demanded and got a public investigation into Chief Johnson's administration.

In the hearings before Commissioner A.F. Bence some incredible examples of bookkeeping legerdemain were revealed, but whether the blame lay with the chief of police or with the police magistrate could not be determined. The magistrate should have been responsible for keeping track of all fines levied, bail escheated, court costs, etc. Unfortunately nobody told the magistrate this was part of his job. So the police department took over the responsibility for collecting and keeping track of the money. An example of Johnson's casual regard for money was the way in which $500 in cash bail was treated. The bail was ordered forfeited. The chief or his deputy simply tossed the money into a seldom-used drawer in a filing case and forgot it. It was only rediscovered months later after the office went through a thorough ransacking following an inquiry from the attorney general for the money. Various other sums were also unaccounted for and when the attorney general got them all added up the total exceeded $1,400. With scarcely a moment's hesitation the chief said if that was what was owed he'd be happy to write a cheque so the books could be balanced. A chief of police who could casually write a cheque for $1,400 was clearly a cut above anything the other prairie cities could boast of in 1921. In addition to his charges of police corruption, Alderman Caulder said that gamblers were being mulcted of large sums in crooked card games and even robbed by faked armed hold-ups of the games in which they participated.[22]

When the gambling charges were first made to Chief Johnson he promised an immediate investigation. He took Constable Simser, the best known and oldest member of the force, out of uniform and turned him into a detective with orders to go out and gather evidence against any gambling joint running games at which a rake-off was taken. When Simser started his tour at the Railwaymen's Club there were a couple of games in operation, but before he could investigate he was ejected from the club by the manager. Policemen, Simser was told, were not allowed in the Railwaymen's Club, which was exclusively for C.P.R. and Soo Line employees. Simser left. Commissioner Bence himself decided to make a tour of the main gambling clubs on River Street. In addition to the Railwaymen's there were the Prairie Club, Bruce Zess's, and Pipeline Johnson's. At none did he find any signs of high-stakes gambling.

Bence's report was a complete vindication of Chief Johnson and it even contained a mild swipe at the hypocrisy of the local business interests represented by Alderman Caulder. He noted that they went overboard to entice as many visitors into the city as possible, and then complained because the visitors snapped up the bait that had been used to bring them to town. That year, the word had been spread far and wide that real beer would be available at all the outdoor stands to be set up on River Street for the Stampede. When these reports got back to the hotel owners, they spread the word that they too would have real beer for sale. Naturally, when the visitors hit Moose Jaw that August they headed directly for the refreshments and were soon gloriously drunk. But when the events of the day were replayed for the Bence commission there was only humiliation and embarrassment for the Moose Jaw beer drinkers. The provincial police had heard the rumours of real beer being sold. They moved in quietly and took samples. Upon analysis it proved to be nothing more than normal two per cent temperance beer dispensed in soft-drink bottles to fool the drinkers into thinking they were getting the real thing. Never before — and probably never since — did so many men get so drunk on temperance beer.[23]

During all the years Johnson and Townsend rode herd on River Street, Moose Jaw was remarkably free of serious crime. The rumours abounding that American gangsters regularly holed up at the Plaza Hotel gained credence from that fact. In return for a safe shelter, the American gangsters were supposed to have made Moose Jaw out of bounds for highjackers and other strong-armed criminals who frequently appeared in eastern Saskatchewan. The unlikeliest story circulated about the era was that Al Capone himself was once a guest of a River Street hotel. No account of any such visits was ever reported in print and no eyewitnesses to the alleged visits survive.

After being exonerated by the Bence commission report, Chief Johnson had no further trouble with the city council. Two years later, however, he was involved in trouble aplenty with his own police force. It began when a local milliner let out a scream of surprise as she stood watching an Orangemen's parade on the Twelfth of July, 1923.

"Look!" she cried to the assembled on-lookers. "Look! That's my hat!"

The hat she pointed to was pinned to the head of one of the lady marchers. Miss Knight, the milliner, did not recognize the lady, so she backed out of her vantage point on the curb and ran down the street to get ahead of the parade and have another look. When she reached a corner several blocks later she encountered an acquaintance who identified the woman in the hat.

"Her husband's a policeman," the woman said.

Had it been a policeman who had broken into her store and stolen half a dozen hats? Miss Knight wondered and for an answer consulted her fellow merchants on Main Street. All the storekeepers recalled the disappearance of stock. Some had even fired clerks they suspected of thefts. Some wrote it off as shoplifting. Still others had had burglaries which they reported to the police. A couple had had burglaries which the police on night patrol had discovered. The merchants themselves tried setting traps for the thieves but caught no one. Eventually they went to Chief Johnson with their suspicions. He put his senior detective on the case and for the next three months the detective kept the night patrolmen under surveillance. When three of them disappeared into the Robinson McBean store together one night the chief decided to take a look inside the homes of his men. Then on February 16, 1924, he sent his day staff out with warrants for the arrest of his night staff. The four men spent that Saturday night in jail and on the basis of the information Johnson and Townsend got from them, three of the daytime constables who had made the arrests were also picked up. That weekend seven out of the nine policemen on the Moose Jaw force were in jail charged with shop-breaking, theft, and possession of stolen goods. Not being absolutely sure of the two still on duty, the chief decided to suspend them too. [24]

The loot recovered following the arrests filled a truck. It included clothing, food, tools, household equipment, and even automobile tires. When the policemen needed new shoes for themselves or their wives or families, they simply went into a shoe store with a skeleton key, or opened the door with a knife, took what they needed, and left. When the cases eventually came before the court some were convicted and some got off. The stiffest sentence was 27 months in the penitentiary to the constable who had taken the largest quantity of goods and confessed to his crime. Several of those who pleaded not guilty and went to trial were acquitted.

Once again Chief Johnson emerged with an unblemished escutcheon, to preside over River Street with benign toleration. As the postwar depression lifted the city prospered with the farmers, and by 1925 River Street was beginning to realize its full potential. That Moose Jaw was generally well satisfied with the way Johnson controlled the River Street brothels can be deduced from the fact that he survived until 1927, at which time he retired to contemplate the operation of the force from his front verandah across the street from the police station. There he sat until 1939. Then at the age of 77 he was inspired with a solution to Moose Jaw's financial problems — cancel half the taxes owed the city if the taxpayers would pay the other half. He ran for mayor on that platform, was elected, and put the plan into operation.

Johnson's successor as chief of police was John Fyvie, a dour Scottish martinet who put the department on a spit-and-polish basis with emphasis on smart saluting. And though he took his best shot at River Street Fyvie was never able to number it among his successes. He put an end to opium smoking, and cleaned out some of the worst dives, but the changes were all on the surface. What really did River Street in was the Great Depression, which was more severe in Moose Jaw than it was in Regina or Saskatoon. The Regina playboys ran out of gas for their cars; the travelling salesmen scurried through town with their order books and kept on going. The Soo Line fell on evil days as did the flour mills and the refinery. The Aquatic Club became a mud hole and River Street became just another slum street where most of the people survived on unemployment relief. A sad end surely for the province's most legendary sin street which had the added distinction of being the place where drive-yourself transportation was invented.

The U-Drive owes its existence to a confrontation between Chief Johnson and a whore named Rosie Dale. Rosie operated a brothel at the west end of River Street before the First World War and her place was a favourite with the Soo Line railroaders, who preferred her accommodation to the C.P.R. bunkhouse. She also built up a thriving clientele among the travelling salesmen who made Moose Jaw a regular stopover as they covered their territory. Her location was ideal, for it was close enough to be within easy walking distance of the C.P.R. station but far enough removed to be away from the disorder and drunkenness of that part of River Street closer to the station.

Something happened to sour relations between Rosie and the law on Moose Jaw Creek. They deteriorated to a point where Chief Johnson ran Rosie out of town. But not far. She bought some property on the hill outside the city limits and was back in business in no time. Now, however, Rosie suffered a locational disadvantage because her place was all uphill from downtown and her short-winded customers had to rely on hansom cabs to get there. This created a minor boom for a couple of River Street livery stables, until the liverymen discovered that it was a boom with a bust attached. To take care of the weekend demand they needed more horses and drivers. During the week the horses ate up the profits and the drivers sat around and did nothing. It was not long before they were passing up requests for rides up to Rosie Dale's. Not only did they have to hire extra help, they had to tie up their rigs at Rosie's — sometimes for the whole night. When the customers emerged full of booze, moreover, they tended to argue with the drivers over the fare and refuse to pay for the waiting time.

Whether it was Rosie or the liveryman who solved the problem is lost to history. Perhaps each contributed to a joint solution. Rosie agreed to let the liveryman erect a horse shelter in her yard into which the horses could be driven. He could also store some feed behind the shed and when the horses arrived her houseboy would halter, feed, and water them. This quickly taught the horses they had a home away from home. The hay and oats would bring them directly to Rosie's when they left the River Street stable.

The liveryman fired all his extra drivers. When the customers for Rosie's wanted a rig he simply hitched the horses to the buggies, headed them in the direction of Rosie's, and handed the customer the reins; the horses did the rest. Whether the customer emerged drunk or sober, early or late, did not matter. Rosie's houseboy simply had to wind the reins around the whip-socket and head the horses back toward River Street and home. Sixty years later, the Avis-Hertz-Tilden computers had still not devised anything with sophisticated efficiency to match the ingenuity of the River Street liveryman.[25]

Saskatoon
– Where Everything
was Handy
to the Station

One of the more intriguing ironies of prairie settlement was the way in which Saskatoon, which was founded by a group of Sabbatarian prohibitionist zealots, became a haven for wandering prostitutes. The appearance of inmates of houses of ill fame in Regina was often explained away by saying they were recent arrivals from Saskatoon. When an Edmonton purity drive put the run on resident whores, they took off for Saskatoon.[1] Winnipeg women seeking a change of venue were shipped out to Saskatoon.[2] Yet on the basis of its origins, no other western community should have been able to match it in high-toned morality. It failed abysmally to reach the heights outlined for it in its prospectus. That was inevitable from the beginning because in the history of prairie settlement there are few examples of ineptitude to match that of the moral reformers who sought to establish a temperance Nirvana on the banks of the South Saskatchewan.

Given reasonable judgment and sound management the Temperance Colonization Society would still have been doomed eventually because of the structural flaws in its land grant. With the kind of management it got, it was an almost instant disaster. The Temperance Colonization Society began as a profit-oriented gleam in the eye of J.A. Livingstone, a Toronto tycoon, who discovered that the federal government in 1881 was selling off homestead land in the West to settlement companies for one dollar an acre.[3] He communicated his discovery to J.N. Lake, a fellow prohibitionist as well as a fellow tycoon. Together they formed a company which immediately subscribed for 100,000 acres and made plans to obtain 2,000,000 acres. Arrangements took time and during the hiatus the two men organized the Temperance Colonization Society and began selling shares and land.

Ontario at that time was on the threshold of its greatest temperance crusade and the two promoters decided they would marry that burgeoning temperance zeal to an increasing interest in settlement in the West. They would get a big enough tract of land so that the settlers could live in a temperance enclave "free forever from the threat of distilled damnation". Not only would settlement be limited to teetotallers; each customer would have to sign a pledge never to permit alcoholic beverages to be brought onto or consumed on his land. With a solid block of 2,000,000 acres covering a rough square 55 miles by 55 miles, they were sure they could insulate themselves from the liquor traffic.

Unhappily the promoters, who knew nothing about prairie land tenure, climate, transportation, or agriculture, had seemingly neglected to read the fine print in their agreement with the Dominion government. The government set aside 2,000,000 acres, all right. But it decreed that the society should take only the odd-numbered sections, and not all of those. The entire prairie was being surveyed into a grid system of sections one mile square, 36 sections to each township, each section numbered from 1 to 36. Within each township, sections 11 and 29 were set aside as reserves for schools. In addition, sections 8 and 26 were Hudson's Bay Company reserves. The Dominion itself retained ownership of all the other even-numbered sections. Thus the 2,000,000-acre tract became a giant checkerboard of one-mile squares in which the society would have the reds and the government the blacks, with the exceptions noted. The over-all effect was that each "dry" section would be bordered by a "wet" section over the entire tract. This destroyed the basic concept of the promoters. Nevertheless they sold off better than 3,000 tracts to gullible Ontario buyers, of whom only a mere handful turned out to have any intention of going west. The majority were land speculators getting in on the ground floor in the hope of quickly unloading their purchases to late-comers, at a profit.

Headed by Lake himself, the directors set off in 1883 for their promised land in the great northwest, armed only with a map of the general area. At Moose Jaw they hired a guide to take them across the prairie in the general direction of what was to become the temperance town of Saskatoon, 150 miles to the north, smack in the middle of nowhere. The journey took the party three weeks, with full stops every seven days for total Sunday observance, including a suitable sermon by Lake to his nine companions. Well satisfied with their land, the directors returned to Toronto to prepare for the departure of the actual settlers the following year.

Somewhere along the line they seemed to get the Saskatchewan River confused with the St. Lawrence. In any event they bought a thirty-five-foot steamboat at Winnipeg and had it shipped by rail to Medicine Hat and launched there into the Saskatchewan River. It was to be used to haul barges of supplies and rafts of lumber to the settlement. Unhappily, it drew five feet of water, which was about as deep as the Saskatchewan was after the spring floods.[4] The *May Queen* fought her way through the mud banks and sand bars to the Saskatoon townsite, pushed along mainly by the river current. There she expired in a mud flat never to move again. The main casualties of her journey were the hopes of her crew — three carpenters, a tinsmith, and a stonemason who were bound for Saskatoon to work on the 200 houses the promoters were supposed to be building there.

Instead of a housebuilding boom, there was a smattering of shacks along the Battleford trail and some surveyors' pegs in the townsite.

The lumber that was floated to the site was so badly waterlogged that it was all but useless for building. When the settlers themselves arrived overland they were scarcely able to catch their breath before the whole countryside was engulfed in prairie fire, the terror of all early homesteaders. In Winnipeg the project was made the subject of editorial attacks in the newspapers, and in Toronto the organization itself became involved in lawsuits by disgruntled shareholders and in squabbles between the directors.[5]

In 1884 the promoters managed to get less than a dozen families onto their land, families whose faith in the venture was deeply undermined long before they finished the trek to Saskatoon. Wherever they stopped they were met with questions: why were they buying land from the Temperance Society when it was available free as homesteads from the government? Why were they going 150 miles from a railway when land was available handy to the C.P.R. right of way? By 1886, settlement had slowed so badly that the Dominion cancelled the whole deal with barely a hundred settlers in the Temperance bloc.

Saskatoon itself was a townsite on which a handful of shacks were built, and was doomed to survive as such for the next fifteen years. With the turn of the century, and the onset of the railway construction boom, Saskatoon at last began to come to life. Railway surveyors discovered that this was as good a place as they could find to bridge the South Saskatchewan River. From a dead-both-ways hamlet of 113 people, Saskatoon became so overrun with railroad builders and real estate promoters that it exploded into town status and then city status with hardly a pause for breath.[7] By 1909 three railway bridges were going up simultaneously across the Saskatchewan River, stations were being built, and warehouses, stores, and office buildings were going up on Second Avenue and Twenty-first Street. On paper, at least, Saskatoon had overnight become the railway hub of the Prairie West as main lines and branch lines radiated from it in all directions. Even Winnipeg in its zaniest promotional excesses could scarcely have exceeded the euphoria of the Saskatoon land boom. A church site bought for $500 in 1904 sold for $42,000 in 1910. A downtown corner bought for $450 in 1904 brought $47,500 in 1911. By 1914 there were 150 real estate agents in a city of 10,000, and over 15,000 acres outside the city limits were subdivided and being sold as 25- and 40-foot residential lots.[8]

And the great Temperance enclave that was to be forever Saskatoon? Gone without a trace of ever having existed, which in fact it never had. Saskatoon's bars were as freely open as any in the West and prostitution was as much a fact of life there as anywhere else. By 1909 there was enough drunkenness and overt prostitution on the streets to attract the wrath of the Protestant clergy, and sermons against rampant boozing and wenching began to be heard.[9] In one respect, the original red-light district of Saskatoon was unique among the brothel clutches in the West, because it alone offered patrons three choices of races, by colour. One of its houses was inhabited exclusively by white whores, a second was all black, and a third was entirely Japanese.[10]

The first brothel area was naturally located in close proximity to the main construction area in the southwest corner of what became Riversdale, where the present city dump is located. It was established in 1907 when the Grand Trunk Pacific began to construct its permanent crossing of the Saskatchewan River at the south end of town. As was frequently the case, the pioneer prostitutes set up shop outside the city or town limits. This took them outside the jurisdiction of the local licence-inspector-cum-policeman and kept them out of sight of the reverend clergy. Within the towns the preachers seemed to be supersensitive at smelling them out and trying to set the law on them. Outside town limits they had only the Mounted Police to contend with, and this of course was never a problem, in Saskatoon or elsewhere, if they stayed reasonably sober and resisted larcenous impulses.

As the west bank of the river was much lower than the east bank, a long dirt-filled embankment had to be built to bring the grade level for the railway tracks to a height even with the east bank. This was a gigantic undertaking and it took hundreds of men, horses, and scrapers the better part of a year to complete the land fill. During construction the workers lived mainly in tents on the north side of the mound they were building. Once they were finished the bridge builders moved in.

"When I first came to Saskatoon after World War I, I kept my horse out in that area and rode over it regularly," a retired Saskatoon horseman recalled. "You know when you are riding along you notice a lot of things you don't see on the ground. Well I kept noticing these three old surface foundations where houses had once stood and there was a well worn path leading to them down the embankment from the railroad tracks. And there was a continuation of the path down the embankment on the north side as well. The puzzling thing was it was a path from nowhere to nowhere, because there were no houses on either side of the railway.

"One day I was riding along with a fellow who had known the area as a boy as he had worked for a farmer herding cows during the summer. He was surprised I had not heard of the brothels that once stood on the site, because he said most old timers in Saskatoon knew them well. The path was made by the railway workers and mound builders who cut across the tracks from their camp to get to the houses. And not only the railway workers. On Saturday nights the area was full of buggies from town and when everybody got whooping it up on paydays, he said, you could hear the singing and shouting for miles."

Once the bridge and railway construction was over, so was the boom for the brothels. There was so much work going on in the city, and so much boozing in the bars, that the south-side brothels were too far from the centre of the action. Already their competitors were getting most of the travelling salesman trade by being located in the hotels and houses around the C.N.R. station. The white madam moved her house into the city while the Negroes moved clear across to the north end of town, leaving Riversdale to the Japanese. They survived there until 1912 when the Mounties in a series of raids put both the Negroes and the Japanese out of business, but only in the suburbs.[11] Thereafter they plied their trade within the city itself, on Twentieth and Twenty-first streets, Avenue D, and Avenue N, and in the hotels and rooming houses.

The best illustration of Saskatoon's basic attitude toward prostitution was the Babe Belanger case, which was heard in superior court in 1910.[12] Babe had run afoul of the Mounties and had been run out of town the previous fall. She went to Regina, found the climate unhealthy, and settled in the town of Broderick, thirty miles south of Saskatoon. She wanted to come back to the city but was worried for fear the Mounties would pick her up on an outstanding sentence and force her to serve a short jail term. So she wrote with a proposition to the Mountie stationed in Saskatoon.

She would like to come back to Saskatoon and go into business in a small way. Perhaps with only one girl working for her so she could

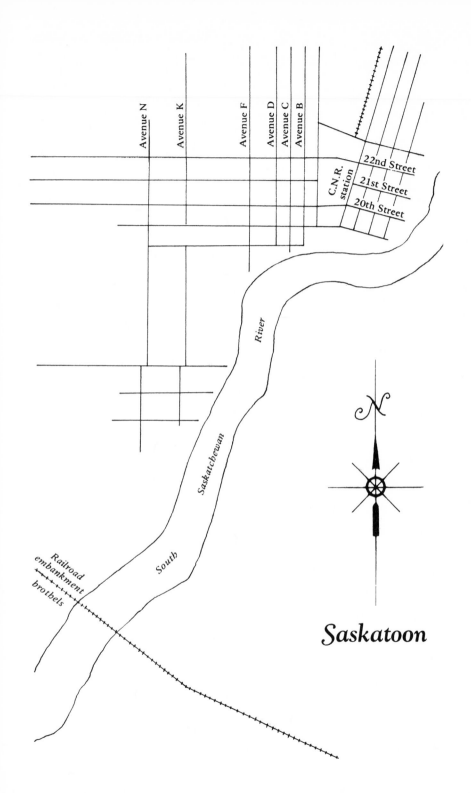

run a nice quiet place. If the Mountie would give her the word that she could run without trouble, she would gladly make it worth his while, say to the tune of $100 every couple of months. With the $2 tariff then in effect, it looked like a reasonable offer. But not to the Mountie. He took the letter to his superior, who signed a warrant for Babe's arrest on the charge of offering bribery to a police officer, a penitentiary offence.

The case became a minor *cause célèbre*. When it came before judge and jury in January 1910, the letter was produced and read. Babe took the stand and explained away the damning epistle by saying she was only trying to play a joke on the policeman. When the jury chose to believe Babe's unlikely story and acquitted her, the judge blew his top. So did the *Saskatoon Phoenix*, whose editor was outraged that any jury could be so wrong-headed as to reject the evidence of the letter.[13] Sending a prostitute to jail was clearly not Saskatoon manhood's idea of how the providers of such an essential service should be treated.

One of the critical problems for the Saskatoon prostitutes was always to find a spot from which to ply their trade. Because the Saskatoon boom was condensed into half a decade, housing congestion was simply beyond description. Even bank tellers and store clerks lived in tents. In the spring of 1912 the situation was so bad that the city council tried to lease downtown churches as dormitories for women and children who were being refused accommodation in the hotels.[14] To make matters even worse, one large downtown rooming house evicted all its regular male tenants and turned the place into hotbed accommodation for streetwalkers.[15]

During the summer of 1912 the Saskatoon police were kept busy running in prostitutes. There were indications, however, that it was more a matter of trying to clear the streets of prostitute congestion than a determination to clean up the city. Thus when plans were being made for a raid on a west-side rooming house, care was taken to raid the place only when all was quiet, rather than when it was fully occupied.[16] A raid that might have collected a dozen women yielded only one white and two Negro girls. A week later the police cracked down on another house on Twentieth Street and rounded up a half-dozen women. All of whom, the *Saskatoon Star* reported, were well dressed and after being fined $20 and costs promised to leave town.[17]

That such raids and departures made scarcely a dint in the Saskatoon prostitute population can be taken for granted. A week later a raid on Second Avenue yielded seven inmates, and similar raids were carried out periodically for the rest of the summer. But even before prohibition came in, the Saskatoon authorities were always more concerned about the peddling of booze in brothels than with sex. Perhaps the licensed liquor dealers in Saskatoon had more influence with the police than their fellow dealers did elsewhere. Thus when Rosie Wilson was arrested on a charge of bootlegging as well as prostitution she was fined fifty dollars and costs on the first but only five dollars on the second. In 1912, when the police were publicly threatening dire punishment for prostitution, the fine imposed was usually only twenty dollars and costs.

The Saskatoon police, during this period, were highly selective in their choice of brothels to raid. Some brothels operated unhindered while others were driven out of business; it all depended on the relationship the girls were able to establish with Chief of Police William Dunning and his senior officers. Instead of co-operating with the R.C.M.P., the Saskatoon force worked in competition with it. By the summer of 1913, conditions were so far out of control that the *Saskatoon Phoenix* ran editorials calling for an investigation into law enforcement in the city. Nothing happened, then or for the next year.

In November 1914, a small-time Saskatoon burglar made a statement in Edmonton that resulted in the laying of criminal charges against Alderman Joe Clarke of that city and set off a royal commission investigation into the Saskatoon police department. The criminal was Frank Heaton, who said that, as a result of a deal made by Alderman Clarke with Detective William Springer of Saskatoon, he and two other thugs had come to Edmonton to launch a crime wave with the objective of making the new chief of police look bad. In making his statement he mentioned that they had an arrangement with Detective Springer in Saskatoon which gave them protection from arrest in Saskatoon provided they confined their burglarizing to other localities. Clarke was able to produce enough witnesses, including two Edmonton detectives and Springer himself, to discredit Heaton's story. In the end Heaton himself repudiated his confession and Clarke was acquitted. It was, Heaton said, all a plot by the new chief of police in Edmonton to destroy Joe Clarke. [18]

Heaton's original charges, however, were enough to move the attorney general of Saskatchewan to set up a court of inquiry under Mr. Justice E.A.C. McLorg. During the winter of 1915 he listened day after day to testimony from prostitutes, policemen, and sundry citizens about police malfeasance and corruption.

Lena O'Connor, who had operated under the benign eye of Detective Reeves, made the mistake of wearing a new set of diamond earrings one night when she had an appointment with the detective. He admired the baubles so much that he appropriated them for himself. He then gave them to a burglar friend to give to another burglar friend so that Reeves could buy them from him and hence have a perfect explanation for having the gems in his possession, should Lena become foolhardy enough to complain about his action.

When the chief detective wanted a new winter coat, he simply passed the word to the burglars, who went shopping for him after-hours in the stores of rural Saskatchewan. When the chief and his detectives discovered that a local woman was acting as an undercover agent for the R.C.M.P. they arrested her as a prostitute and sent her to jail for six months.

Sergeant Stuart of the R.C.M.P. told the McLorg hearing that the west side of Saskatoon was a sea of vice. He ticked off a long list of addresses, including "a green house near the corner of Avenue K and 20th Street, a dance hall behind the St. Thomas Church, Negro joints on Avenues B, C and D and a big house at the corner of Avenue F and 21st Street". Saskatoon, said the sergeant, had a wide reputation as a harbour for criminals. [19]

Patrolmen on the Saskatoon force told the inquiry they were under strict orders to leave morality affairs to the detectives. When they occasionally edged into the detectives' precincts, nothing but trouble happened. Constable Gray reported a complaint from two prostitutes who were being hounded from room to room because they would not pay off Detectives Reeves and Springer. When he tried to chase a disorderly whore off his beat she defied him to touch her because she was a friend of Chief Dunning and Sergeant Springer. He prodded her on her way and the next day was transferred to the windiest, coldest beat in the city.

Chief Dunning resigned while the inquiry was in progress and was found guilty of condoning the fabrication of evidence, and of undue oppression of certain women. The detectives were found guilty on all counts, of harbouring and protecting criminals, inciting criminals to commit theft, taking hush money, fabricating evidence against innocent parties, consorting with bad characters, and general laxity. The upshot of the inquiry was that most of the Saskatoon police force was fired; also, criminal charges were laid against Springer and he wound up in Prince Albert Penitentiary for a three-year stretch. [20]

A new police force was recruited, but there is little evidence it had any more success in the suppression of prostitution than its predecessor. Saskatoon continued to enjoy a reputation as a wide-open fun town. Out of that reputation grew the legend that this was really the way the R.C.M.P. wanted it. Fugitives from serious criminal charges in eastern Canada, fleeing to safe shelter in the Vancouver underworld, would avoid Regina because of the concentration of Mounted Police there. Instead, they would break their journeys in Saskatoon and tarry a while in its friendly brothels, where, however, they might sometimes be quietly arrested by the Mounties on tips from the madams. Certainly there were a dozen brothels within a five-minute walk of the C.N.R. station. Men who have lived in both places have a curious explanation for the contrast between wide-open Saskatoon and sex-suppressed Regina. They say the difference was accounted for by swarms of commercial travellers. [21] As the distribution centre for central and northern Saskatchewan, Saskatoon sent its own salesmen out weekly to beat the parkbelt bushes. In addition the manufacturers of the east had their salesmen calling on all the wholesalers and retailers in Saskatoon. Because of its multiplicity of railway lines, salesmen could get to almost everywhere from Saskatoon. So the town had armies of drummers going and coming all the time, and these men were steady customers of the bordellos and their ladies awaiting.

This, however, was a side of Saskatoon which one of its newspapers, the *Phoenix*, chose to ignore. It was as pristine in its attitude toward news of the underside of city life as the *Christian Science Monitor*. Its rival, the *Saskatoon Star*, had no such inhibitions. So it is perhaps poetic justice that, when the *Phoenix* was absorbed by the *Star*, it became the only newspaper in the West with a brothel for a next-door neighbour. Not only that, but it owned the property on which the brothel stood. As the publisher of the paper explained

when uplifters complained, it was a well-run place and it was no part
of the responsibility of a newspaper to police the morals of its
tenants. Its management did, however, police the morals of its staff
— from the vantage point of an open window in the composing room
which provided a commanding view of the entrance to the brothel.
One of the first things newcomers to the staff learned was to restrain
their libidinous urges when the window was open, which of course it
seldom was during the long Saskatchewan winter. [22]

The Saga of Joe Clarke — Radical Conservative with Socialist Leanings

The earliest documented case of prostitution in Edmonton was that of "Big Nellie" Webb, and it can be taken as an example of both the fundamental connection between booze and illicit sex and the casual, even cavalier, attitude habitually taken by the police toward prostitution. It can also serve as evidence that pioneer prairie prostitutes had few rights that anyone else was bound to respect. The Nellie Webb case begins with a one-line item in the *Annual Report* of the North West Mounted Police for 1888. On October 31 of that

99

year Nellie was convicted and fined fifteen dollars for keeping a house of ill repute in Edmonton. Behind that simple fact was this story:

On October 24, three Mounted Police constables named Thomas, Cairney, and Cudlip left their Fort Saskatchewan headquarters for Calgary by way of Edmonton. At Edmonton they decided to delay their departure while they soaked up enough booze to get thoroughly drunk. When they reached that stage they further decided "to paint the town red" and went prowling around in search of a brothel. In their search they blundered into three private homes and were run off by angry householders. Eventually they got headed in the direction of Nellie Webb's house of ill repute. Nellie saw them coming; being a woman of the world, she knew that roistering drunks spelled TROUBLE and that, of all the customers she could do without, three drunken Mounties headed the list. She locked her doors and hoped they would go away. When she failed to respond to their pounding, they proceeded to break the door in. While this was happening, Nellie got out her gun and fired a shot through the broken door. Her bullet lodged in Cairney's leg and the attack was halted, but only temporarily. The Mounties sobered up enough to arrest Nellie, charge her with wounding with intent, and lug her off to jail. While Nellie was awaiting bail the N.W.M.P. stationed two other Mounties in her house to protect her property against thieves. They got so drunk on Nellie's booze that they passed out and permitted some wayfaring stranger to steal both their guns. The Mounted Police then held an official inquiry, following which one constable was fired and another was suspended for a month. Nellie, meanwhile, pleaded guilty to keeping a house of ill repute, paid her fine, and was released on $2,000 bail to await trial the following spring on the charge of wounding with intent.[1]

The affair excited the attention of Frank Oliver, the editor of the *Edmonton Bulletin*, who let fly at the Mounted Police with both barrels: "This," he thundered, "is one of the most disgraceful affairs that has ever occurred in Edmonton, through a set of men who are supposed to protect the citizens and their property.... The men are not so much to blame for the contempt in which the force is held as those who have charge of it!"[2]

There is one baffling aspect of the Nellie Webb story. Why did the three Mounties from Fort Saskatchewan have to go blundering into three respectable houses before they were given directions to Nellie's place? Everybody in the settlement must have known where Nellie lived. On the odd chance that the first resident was a newcomer, or given to unwonted stuffiness when it came to prostitution, they had only to ask their fellow Mounties. No prostitute could have long remained unidentified in the Edmonton of that era, which had a population of not more than 1,200 in its clutter of frame houses, brick and wooden stores, churches, and hotels on the north side of the Saskatchewan River. Across the river was the settlement of Strathcona which, after the railway spur line from Calgary arrived in 1891, threatened to outgrow Edmonton. But the early start Edmonton got in the days of the fur trade enabled it to keep well ahead until the Canadian Northern Railway arrived in 1905. It then became the capital of Alberta and absorbed Strathcona a few years later. But whether a large city or a small town, Edmonton was not a community in which the police should have had much trouble keeping a casually benign eye on the houses of ill repute. The Mounted Police knew where they were, as they knew in Calgary, Lethbridge, Macleod, Medicine Hat, and Regina.

In Edmonton, as elsewhere, the Mounties let the girls alone as long as the houses were operated with reasonable decorum. Once or twice a year they would raid the houses and haul the inmates before the Mounted Police inspector, who would fine them nominally and send them back to work. The standard fee extracted was ten or fifteen dollars and costs for the madams and five or ten dollars and costs for the inmates. Periodically, when something more than prostitution was involved, such as theft or bootlegging, the tariff might go to twenty dollars and costs for the keepers and fifteen dollars and costs for inmates. Ten years after the Nellie Webb case these rates were still in force in Alberta. It can be assumed from the fifteen-dollar fine that the Police regarded Nellie's case as one of moderate seriousness, far less important, for example, than keeping liquor for sale illegally, which cost fifty or one hundred dollars, but more so than keeping a filthy pigpen, which carried only a five-dollar penalty. In any event, nobody ever bothered Nellie again, which put her a couple of notches above her Lethbridge and Fort Macleod sisters whose names appeared regularly on the Mounted Police dockets.[3]

It seems clear, from the sketchy reports of the times, that the police and the madams mutually accepted a system of fines in lieu of licence fees. The latter invariably pleaded guilty, and that freed the police from the distasteful task of proving their charges by the employment of paid informers. If the police passed the word that they were going to crack down more heavily on repeaters, the girls simply took turns pleading guilty to being keepers and paying the low fines for first offenders. When they were told to move, they moved and accepted the extra-legal rousting around by the police as part of the game.

Most of the hotels in the Territories seem to have allowed a girl or two to occupy a back room on the second floor if there was a second floor. Bartenders frequently functioned as business agents and salesmen for the girls; so did waiters, the livery operators, and later the taxi drivers. It was a natural arrangement because getting tanked up on nickel beer or two-bit Scotch was the usual prelude to an excursion to the sporting palaces.

There is not the slightest doubt that booze and bawdy-houses were a part of the social fabric of the Alberta cities and towns from the earliest days of settlement. Yet there was a widespread conspiracy to keep that fact from being bruited abroad. The urban press confined its crime reporting to crimes of violence, embezzlement, and political monkeyshines. On the rare occasion when there were reports of gambling raids the principals were usually Chinese.

Prosecution of prostitutes, when it was reported, was confined to three-line items buried among the local news briefs. Occasionally, in circumstances where it could not be avoided, there would be an oblique mention about the concern of the clergy over "the social evil" which afflicted certain areas of the paper's particular city. What was meant, of course, was that life was being made intolerable for respectable people by the rowdiness of the segregated areas.[4] Local blades who got tanked up in the saloons drove their buggies, and later their cars, through the streets with much loud harrooing as they headed for the brothels. Instead of complaining to the police, which seldom did much good, many of the indignant householders complained to their clergymen, who stirred things up at vestry meetings or at the regular conclaves of the Temperance and Moral Reform Society. It would all be summarized by the newspaper with a sentence or two. To wit: "There was a discussion of the social evil which has arisen in the east side of the city."

Edmonton, as far back as the days of Nellie Webb and the drunken

Mounties, was already in the hands of the real estate promoters. Like the other regional newspapers, the Edmonton papers habitually trumpeted the virtues of the newest subdivisions and the wealth to be derived from real estate investment. The splendiferousness of the new schools, warehouses, post office, and sawmills being erected were extolled in lyrical prose and pictures. For chasers they gloried in the future heralded for the community by the newest-arriving railroad, packing plant, or brickyard. The worst crime any census taker could commit was to underestimate a town's population. So the Edmonton editorialists confined their critical fire to the evils of the opposition political party. This attitude naturally spilled over into the news columns, where politicians that the papers supported got twice as much space as their opponents, coupled of course with highly coloured and favourable headlines. When the press or civic leaders did criticize anything local, it was usually something of utmost civic importance, like the rutted condition of the streets, the cows-at-large nuisance, the menace of horses and wagons left untied and unattended, the sanitary condition of horse troughs, and the urgent need for additional public latrines in the vicinity of the city markets.[5] Nevertheless, the booze-brothel syndrome was an ever-present problem in Edmonton as elsewhere and it was one that kept erupting despite the general conspiracy to keep it safely hidden.

The first big Edmonton scandal occurred about midway between the arrival of the Canadian Northern Railway in 1905 and the coming of the Grand Trunk Pacific in 1911. The city's struggle to extricate itself from its mud-caked small-town status and blast off toward its projected destiny as the "Edinburgh of the North" was sadly retarded by its lack of a mainline railway connection. About the time that Alberta became a province the new railways ignited a boom that more than made up for lost time. Once they reached Edmonton, the railway construction workers deserted in droves.

The jobs available to strong-backed labourers in the city were no easier than laying railroad tracks, but any town they could settle down in was a vast improvement over the best railroad camp. There was work in abundance in Edmonton for anybody with physical stamina or any kind of skill. There were pick-and-shovel jobs without limit — mining coal, digging up and gravelling the streets, excavating basements, and putting in the miles of sewer and water mains that were dug every year. By 1906 there was no way to keep

up with the building boom. Not only had the new provincial government embarked on a massive construction program, but private
enterprise was putting in warehouses, factories, railway shops, yards,
and office buildings. Topping it all was the housebuilding boom in all
the bright new subdivisions. It got so far out of hand that many of
the new houses went in without even foundations, let alone water or
sewer connections.

Because the labouring jobs were the lowest paid, they went mainly
to the newly arrived immigrants from Central Europe, identified as
"Ruthenians" in most of western Canada regardless of where they
came from. The Ruthenians and the first settlers from the United
Kingdom had one thing in common. Most of them came unencum-
bered by wives and families. Because they were both single and
earning the lowest wages, they sought out the cheapest possible
accommodation in the jam-packed rooming houses in the poorest
section of the city. In Edmonton they hived themselves away in Old
Town along Kinistino, Namayo, Fraser, and McDougall streets from
Jasper clear out to Wilson Avenue. It was an area of cottages
cramped onto twenty-five-foot lots, rooming houses, cheap hotels,
poolrooms, Chinese laundries, bars, odoriferous restaurants, and
small stores. And brothels; an average of at least a brothel a block
throughout the whole area.

As the population was squeezed out of Old Town into the
adjacent newly developing districts, so were the prostitutes. Immediately north of the Old Town slum was the new district of Norwood which, in the early spring of 1908, organized its own vigilantes
to protect the area from streetwalkers and marauding drunks who
made the streets both uncomfortable and unsafe for the residents at
night.[6] Edmonton by this time had grown to between 10,000 and
15,000 people but was still getting along with a small-town police
force of eleven men and a horse. The force was so overworked riding
herd on the drunks on Jasper and Kinistino alone that it decided to
attack the problem at its source by putting its men on duty inside the
bars instead of on the streets. This, unhappily, left the streets open
for the streetwalkers, who proved more than the Norwood vigilantes
could cope with. In the end the Norwood residents put such pressure
on the mayor that he ordered Chief Billy Beale to send a squad out
and raid the brothels that had become established in Norwood.

Beale was undoubtedly a conscientious policeman, but his job had
outgrown him. In addition he had difficulty getting his underlings to

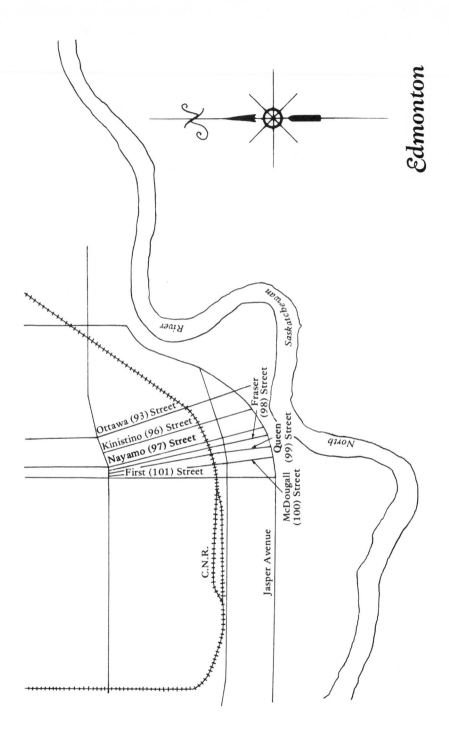

Edmonton

Ottawa (93) Street
Kinistino (96) Street
Nayamo (97) Street
First (101) Street
Fraser (98) Street
Queen
McDougall (100) Street
(99) Street
River
Saskatchewan
North
C.N.R.
Jasper Avenue

obey his orders. Before his raiders could get organized one of his sergeants, according to the sworn testimony of a prostitute, tipped her off that the raid was coming.

"I was in the Grand Central Hotel last March 31 when Sergeant Griffith came in," Dorothy Drake, alias Jeannette Byron, said in her affidavit. "He asked me when I was going home and said I had better get a rig and get home right away and warn the girls to cache their liquor because a raid was coming. He said the chief had ordered Bill Howey to raid the houses in the north end between 10 and 11 that night."

Dorothy Drake did as she was told. The raids were staged but nothing incriminating was found. Some days later, she said, she saw the sergeant again and he asked her what she was doing. She said she had closed up, that the other girls who had been working with her had gone to Vancouver.

"Why don't you move down town?" Griffith asked her. "You're a friend of mine so you know I won't bother you. There are two or three houses in every block and they are all making money. One of my friends saved over $1,000 last winter. It would," he said, "serve the chief and the mayor right if there were houses everywhere."[7]

As the *Edmonton Journal* reported months later, there were rumours of dissension on the force. The story of the tip-off got back to the chief. He investigated and got a couple of independent investigators to go out with Dorothy Drake to interview one of the madams she had warned. The madam's name was Ruby Bauman and she corroborated Dorothy's story. The chief collected affidavits all around, suspended Griffith, and demanded that the mayor fire the sergeant. Instead the mayor named a committee of aldermen to investigate.

Sergeant Griffith denied everything, while Ruby Bauman developed a bad memory for everything that happened that spring. The defence produced other prostitutes who swore that they had not been warned of the raid. The aldermen exonerated the sergeant, and Chief Beale said that when Edmonton reached the stage where the aldermen took the word of prostitutes in preference to that of responsible citizens it needed a new chief of police. He quit. A new chief was hired and he became the next fall guy in the game of musical chairs that was played spasmodically in the police department over the next decade.[8]

Police Chief A.C. Lancey, who took over early in 1909, had flitted from one police job to another during the previous decade. He had served in the N.W.M.P. for a short time, then had worked as a railway detective, and had also worked in Montreal. Like all new brooms, he swept a clean path through Edmonton. He beefed up the police department, cleaned out the incompetents, put the men on twelve-hour shifts, and continued the system of patrolling the Old Town bars from the inside. With a doubled force in his first year of operation Chief Lancey was able to report the arrest of 479 drunks, 39 gamblers, 26 prostitutes, and 60 various and sundry assaulters.

When Chief Lancey arrived in Edmonton the city was in mid-flight from country town to urban metropolis. It was still mainly a community of wooden sidewalks, mud roads, wayward livestock, and horse-drawn vehicles. Yet the forces of citification were running wild. Stone-veneer schools were replacing the frame fire-traps of the Victorian era. The fire department was buying its first motorized equipment. The first upward-poking spikes of a skyline were appearing. A drummer for the Bitulithic Paving Company sold the city on putting in asphalt pavement along Jasper Avenue and Namayo Street. The other main streets were being macadamized and paved with stone or wooden blocks as well as asphalt. The first automobiles had begun to appear in sufficient numbers to justify the establishment of speed limits and other traffic regulations. The horse, however, was still king of the roads. Horses hauled the hundreds of dump wagons that were forever going and coming in all directions. Horses provided the power for the delivery rigs of all kinds and there were livery barns and blacksmith shops handily located throughout the downtown area. Buggies still competed with open touring cars for the taxi business around the hotels and stations. When the police department acquired its first motorized paddy wagon is not clear, but as late as 1909 the patrolmen who arrested drunks still had to walk them to the lock-up, which could take an hour for those with interfering friends. It was mainly to overcome this difficulty that Chief Lancey adopted a system of regional police stations.

Serious crime was never much of a problem in Edmonton and the police department was fortunate that it was not. It had so much other work to do aside from putting the run on the drunks that it couldn't begin to handle the boom in prostitution, let alone an outbreak of bank robberies. Its main concern soon came to be the enforcement of the new traffic by-laws along Jasper Avenue. As one of the city's few smooth surfaced roads it was an open invitation to every new car owner to try out the speed of his vehicle, despite the fifteen-miles-an-hour speed limit. So the policemen on duty in the bars also had to watch for speeding motorists and chase after them on foot once they sighted them. The speeding motorists created a subsidiary hazard. Educating the Edmonton teamsters to tie their horses to the hitching posts while they were in the bars or stores was never a complete success. A backfiring car speeding down the street inevitably frightened the horses into miniature stampedes which left trails of broken wagons, fences, and store fronts in their wake. Offending teamsters were regularly hauled into court and fined ten dollars and costs for leaving a team unattended on a city street.[9] They were assessed the same amount for making U-turns in the middle of a block, or for driving on the wrong side of the road. Clearly, bringing order out of the chaos of early Edmonton traffic took patience, time, and a lot of police man-hours. So it was hardly surprising that, despite Chief Lancey's best efforts, things kept getting out of hand along the Kinistino strand.

The influx of prostitutes kept pace with the growth in the city's population and reached the point where the sheer force of their numbers on Kinistino, Namayo, and First streets drove the girls to carry their sales efforts farther and farther west along Jasper Avenue. When a uniformed policeman spotted one at work, he would simply run her off down a side street. Naturally the city aldermen were bombarded with complaints from the respectable citizens. The complaints filtered down to the police department, which would order the madams to keep their girls off the main streets during business hours. The regular operators of the brothels appear to have co-operated fully with the police; many of them stayed in business for years without police interference. The problem was with the newly arrived girls, who were just trying to become established in the trade or who were being recruited into it. The recruiters were everywhere.

In December of 1909 Mrs. E.E. Marshall, the wife of a prominent Edmonton clergyman, launched a special campaign for assistance for the Y.W.C.A. Travellers' Aid department. Unless the department's booths at the railway stations could be kept occupied, she said, single women arriving in Edmonton would be lured into "lives of shame" in increasing numbers. White slave rings, she claimed, were operating openly under the eyes of the police.[10] There was, at this period, a steady influx of young girls into Edmonton, both from the surrounding farm settlements and from eastern Canada and the United States. Many were simply being crowded out of farm families and sought work as domestics. Others had experience in office, clerical, or restaurant work. Aside altogether from the pimps who infested the railway station, there were other hazards facing the incoming girls. One of the most pressing problems was finding a place to live. There were rooming houses by the score, but most of the legitimate places refused to rent their rooms to single women. Some of them even drew the line at husband and wife for fear the wife was a whore and the husband a pimp. Their reluctance was soundly based. Frequently the newly arrived prostitute got into business simply by getting a room in a respectable lodging house. Then, with a place in which to ply her trade, she took to the streets to round up customers. The landladies knew from past experience that there was nothing to set a well-ordered rooming house for single men on its ear like a prostitute in residence.

The Y.W.C.A. tried to help by providing newcomers with beds for a night or two while they obtained permanent quarters. But the Y quarters became so congested that the institution had to expand into an old barn on the rear of the property, which it renovated into a makeshift dormitory and used for ten years. A young woman on her own in Edmonton would discover that the downtown restaurants were as much a threat to her virtue as the Old Town hotels and rooming houses. Many of the male waiters moonlighted as pimps and one girl told a judicial inquiry that she had been enticed into prostitution by a waiter in the Lewis Brothers' café on First Street who had three girls working for him.

In addition to the incoming innocents, the Edmonton police were also beset with the problem of juvenile delinquents. Magistrates regularly thundered against children running at large, and raids on brothels frequently turned up juvenile girls. In 1911 a total of thirty-seven juvenile girls were turned over to the Children's Aid Society after being arrested for prostitution.[11] But whether all the innocents put together were as numerous as the experienced women who came into Edmonton from outside is indeed doubtful. Once the word got around that Edmonton was a brothel-tolerating town the girls headed for it from Montana and even as far away as Montreal. Whenever they were given "floaters" by the police in other prairie cities, or were invited by old associates, Edmonton became their destination.

The story that Billie Morton told a judicial inquiry could undoubtedly have been told in similar terms by a hundred other girls. She said she had come into Edmonton from Jasper in 1910 and got a room in the Palace Rooming House on Namayo Street. After some weeks she moved to a better room in the Waverley House on Fraser Street. A few months passed and she was able to rent a cottage on Fifth Street. From there she moved to a larger place at 450 Fraser Street and had two girls working for her. The next moves were to houses on Ottawa Street and Kinistino Street and finally to a large house next to the Savoy Hotel, where she employed four girls. By the end of 1913 she had saved enough money to be able to pay cash for the contents of a king-sized rooming house. At no time, she said, did the police ever bother her though she was acquainted with many of the members of the force. That she was able to expand and prosper during the Lancey term in office can be taken as an indication that a policy of controlled toleration was in operation in Edmonton. [12]

Any estimate of the number of brothels which existed in 1911 to service the 8,500 unwed Edmontonians has to be mainly conjecture. But from evidence which came out later it could hardly have been less than 50 and could quite easily have exceeded 100. That Lancey ran the kind of town Edmonton wanted him to run can hardly be doubted. But after two years on the job he decided to switch to a better post as a provincial liquor inspector. He resigned in March of 1911 and R.W. Ensor was brought in from Regina. Ensor's first action was to impose a blackout on all police news as he began to tighten up on law enforcement. He lasted six months and then the city invited Lancey back at a good raise in pay. It was a short honeymoon. The first trouble started when the ratepayers on Kinistino Avenue held an indignation meeting a month after Lancey returned. They petitioned City Hall to close down the Kinistino Street dance halls which, they said, turned into riots three or four times a week. [13] The union of Edmonton and Strathcona was going through and this entailed the expansion of the police force from 44 to 81. Gambling was getting out of hand and, while raids on gambling dives increased, convictions became more difficult to obtain. Then G.S. Armstrong was elected first mayor of the newly combined city, and a system of government by commissioners was adopted for the civic departments. Theoretically this took the police department out of politics, but that did not stop the aldermen from keeping their hands in.

Early in July of 1912 Detective Ernest Seymour became involved in a police station altercation with a local citizen he had arrested for being drunk and disorderly. The citizen was rather seriously roughed up and filed assault charges against Seymour. During a shouting match at the police station over the case one of the city aldermen charged that the police were allowing fifty-four brothels to run wide open and criticized the St. Regis Hotel in which the chief of police had a financial interest. At its next meeting the city council passed a resolution instructing Chief Lancey to suspend Seymour until after his trial. Lancey refused. The aldermen insisted by passing a second resolution. Again Lancey refused, and when Seymour came to trial he was acquitted.[14]   Lancey then resigned because, he said, he was tired of the police business and aldermanic interference and wanted to try something else. He got a homestead south of the city and took over the full-time management of the St. Regis Hotel.

With the appointment of Silas H. Carpenter to succeed Lancey the lid went on in Edmonton tighter than it ever had before. Carpenter had been a police inspector in Montreal and he had fifteen years' experience behind him when he took the job. He turned out to be a very straight-laced character indeed. He insisted that the hotels pay the salaries of the police stationed in bars and shook up the department by firing several of Lancey's officials, including Detective Seymour. He then sent his squad out on a series of raids on the brothels and drove many of the prostitutes out of the city. As a result of his efforts during the last three months of 1912, the jail was filled to overflowing. Year-end statistics showed 2,422 arrested on drunk charges and 58 as keepers of houses of ill repute, along with 150 as inmates and 130 as frequenters. In addition the new chief began to put the vagrancy statute to use and filed 195 of those charges. In the following year he not only kept the pressure on, he increased it. His force made 2,603 arrests for drunkenness and brought in 447 vagrants, 352 gamblers, 80 opium smokers, 48 brothel keepers, 35 inmates, and 152 frequenters. The best Lancey had managed, in comparison, was 1,000 drunks and 18 prostitutes in 1911.

When any police crackdown on prostitution occurs, it usually ends the co-operation of the brothels with the police. The madams and inmates stop pleading guilty and can only be convicted with evidence which will stand up in court. Gathering such evidence becomes the function of undercover men who visit the brothels, pay for the service with marked money, and trigger raids to catch the women with the incriminating currency. Chief Carpenter added ten of these agents to his detective department, and the photographer who took their group picture neatly summarized the general public's attitude toward all such hired informers with these cut lines: "Here are five city detectives and ten of the police department pimps whose activities often provoke the scornful comment of the magistrates when they appear in Court." [15]

Chief Carpenter might well have failed in his efforts to clean up Edmonton, but he was giving it his best effort when the props were pulled from under him and his world collapsed around his ears. Whether the main muscle in the pull was supplied by Alderman Joseph A. Clarke or W.J. McNamara will probably never be known, but reasoning after the fact clearly points to Clarke as the architect of the disaster. Bill McNamara was a successful real estate operator and promoter who in the fall of 1913 was smitten mildly by political fever. The disenchantment with the Carpenter crackdown had spread through the city until the mumblings of discontent reached City Hall. Most Edmontonians wanted a wide-open town, just as long as the worst excesses of being wide open were prevented. As Joe Clarke testified on his oath, he was never in favour of segregated prostitution but he was very much in favour of toleration.

Clarke was a graduate in law from Osgoode Hall in Toronto, where he had been a varsity football player. Instead of practising his profession upon graduation, he took off for the Klondike during the gold rush and spent the next ten years in the Yukon. He turned up in Edmonton in 1908, hung up his shingle, and was soon settled into the role of the Bob Edwards of Edmonton politics. In a long interview in the *Journal*, he described himself as a "radical conservative of socialist leanings", and as the former "stormy petrel of Yukon politics".[16]   Whatever else he was, Joe Clarke was no shrinking violet. He immediately ran for the city council and was elected alderman.

City council meetings in pre-war Edmonton were never noted for decorum, and the impugning of motives and the bandying of insults across the council chamber were regular features of the proceedings. Joe Clarke fitted perfectly into that environment. He was given to declaiming at the top of his voice, which he did not only at council meetings but at every public meeting he attended. When McNamara started muttering about running for mayor, Joe Clarke egged him on. McNamara also enlisted the support of the former policemen who had been fired by Carpenter, together with a couple of labour aldermen. Former Chief Lancey himself even got into the campaign behind McNamara. For a campaign in which the real issue, as Joe Clarke saw it, was an open versus a closed town, it was an incredibly dull one, because nobody ever mentioned that issue. Instead the candidates talked only about gas franchises, faulty civic engineering, low water pressure, and trouble with the electric generating system.[17]   In the back of McNamara's mind, however, was a gnawing gripe against the police department. He was an enthusiastic new owner of an automobile which he drove with considerable recklessness. He got enough traffic summonses to give him a persecution complex and the word got around that if he were elected he would fire the chief of police. McNamara pulled a first-class upset by winning the election. After he took office, information that Chief Carpenter's days were numbered became an open secret in City Hall.

Several disconnected events played into McNamara's hand. A justice of the Alberta Supreme Court severely chastised one Dan McGillis, whom he sentenced to eighteen months in prison for luring a young girl into prostitution under promise of marriage. In passing sentence he complained that Edmonton tolerated the existence of similar vice.[18]   Then a young girl was found in a hotel suffering from an overdose of cocaine after she had been seen in the company of two police constables. This was followed by statements from Mayor McNamara that two of the city's largest hotels were open houses of prostitution, that prostitutes and pimps were being blackmailed by the police, and that members of the force were willing to pay money to keep their jobs.

On January 21, the mayor appointed M.S. Booth, the manager of the Hudson's Bay store, as police commissioner. In an interview with the newspapers he "touched on the social question and stated that he did not think that this evil could be eliminated but would try to see to it that no men or madams were street walking or soliciting and that no men or women earned their living that way."

With Chief Carpenter marked for oblivion, the Edmonton branch of the Temperance and Moral Reform Society called an emergency meeting on January 26. They passed a strong resolution supporting the chief and included a statement that "social conditions" in Edmonton in 1914 were no worse than they were in the previous years. [19]

On February 1st, 1914, the mayor fired Chief Carpenter and sent the town into a turmoil. Then he fired the head of the morality squad. A huge mass meeting was called to protest the firing and it demanded that the city ask the attorney general to launch an investigation into the mayor's charges against the police department. On the mayor's deciding vote, the city council refused. Then a half-dozen former mayors got up a petition of 3,000 names asking for reconsideration. Council refused again and Joe Clarke's comment added insult to injury. He was not impressed by the former mayors, he said, because three of the them had instigated the taking into the city of areas of prostitution and now they were coming forward for political reasons to complain about prostitutes.

On February 2, A.C. Lancey became chief of police for the third time in five years. What happened during the next four months, which ended in the final firing of Lancey, depends on the weight to be attached to the evidence before an inquiry which undoubtedly established a Canadian record for plain and fancy perjury. Lancey's evidence is perhaps as credible as any. His story was that immediately upon his appointment he was invited to a meeting in Mayor McNamara's office in the Tegler Block which was attended by the mayor, Joe Clarke, and Aldermen Kinney, May, and East. His instructions were to let the whorehouses run as long as there were no complaints but to stage a big raid now and then to create a splash and to let the public know he was on the job. The aldermen denied attending any such meeting or being a party to any such orders. Chief Carpenter, however, said that when he first came to Edmonton Joe Clarke had come forward to explain the sort of place Edmonton was. Conditions there, Clarke had advised him, were far different from those in the east. Edmonton people were more free and easy and they wanted segregated areas of prostitution and open gambling under police control. "I told him that no chief of police had any legal right to permit any such thing," Carpenter said, and that was the end of that.[20]

Whether there was or was not any such meeting as Lancey reported, he did get on with his raids, the biggest of which was on Mamie Clarke's house across from the Pendennis Hotel. Twenty-eight girls and sixty-four men were found in the house. He also carried out smaller raids, but in the process Chief Lancey must have felt like a man in a trap. While the Mayor and Joe Clarke pushed him one way, his new immediate superior, Commissioner Booth, was pushing him another. The first official communication he received from Booth instructed him to take immediate steps to drive out all the pimps and prostitutes and close all the gambling joints and disorderly houses. Somewhat incredulous, Lancey took the letter to Booth to see if he really meant *all* houses of ill fame. Well, perhaps that would be too difficult, the Commissioner admitted. The real problem was not with the small places where there were only one or two girls working but with the bigger places. And certainly something would have to be done to run the women off the streets. Weeks later, when Booth again wrote to Lancey, he once more bore down hard in emphasizing houses with *more* than two prostitutes. In any event the conversation seemed to clear the air for Lancey, so under his guidance Edmonton reverted to the pre-Carpenter status quo of controlled prostitution.

With Lancey on the job, the word went out that Edmonton was back in business as a wide-open city and many of the girls who had left after the Carpenter crackdown returned. Several of the former Lancey lieutenants who had been fired by Carpenter were rehired, including Sergeant Seymour, whose blundering behaviour eventually cost Lancey his job. As the town opened up, the underworld scum quickly moved in to take advantage. The one who played the biggest role was William Wheeler, who was described by a friend as "a pimp, a tout, a gambler and a damned nuisance". Wheeler had wandered into Edmonton in 1910 and worked as a bartender for a year. Then he bought the Waverley Rooming House, and ran it as a notorious brothel until 1913. Next he took over the management of the Dominion Club on First Street adjacent to the Lewis Brothers' restaurant. He circulated the word that he was the official go-between for the police with the underworld and started to try to put the squeeze on the prostitutes for protection money.

Unhappily for Wheeler he ran into competition. A couple of liquor-store operators let it be known that the police wanted all the brothels to buy their liquor from them. Another pimp named Ora West claimed that he worked for the police magistrate and tried to talk a prominent madam out of $200. Then Walker Turner, who operated the Douglas Club, started canvassing the brothels with the proposition that only twenty-eight of them were going to be allowed to run and it would cost them $100 a month each, payable in advance. Still others went around claiming to be collectors for the chief of police, for Alderman Joe Clarke, or for members of the detective department. One girl swore she gave Tom Douglas of the Queen's Hotel $150 to give to Detective Coleman.

As spring came Commissioner Booth discovered that nothing much was being done to clean up the town. The reports from outside sleuths he had hired to spy on the police department were non-committal, so he went out to investigate conditions on his own. He found streetwalkers on every block. He watched them taking their pick-ups into brothels. He passed the addresses along to Lancey in the form of instructions to raid. Occasionally, the instructions were carried out. The only complete success Booth scored was in the crusade he launched against lace curtains on brothel windows. He complained to the Chief that pedestrians strolling along First Street and Jasper Avenue could watch through the lace curtains as the prostitutes served their customers. The lace curtains were all removed in favour of green blinds which shut off the public view of the interior of the brothels.[21]

For his part, Chief Lancey was having trouble getting his orders obeyed. Once he planned a raid on a gambling club and gave Detective Seymour orders to hit it between eleven o'clock and midnight. But Seymour said he had become preoccupied with two Negro streetwalkers from north of the C.N.R. tracks who were soliciting customers under false pretences. They were powdering their faces with flour, he said, in an effort to hide their colour, an outrageous subterfuge. He was determined to catch them in the act, so when he had spotted them he had given chase and didn't get around to the gambling raid until well after midnight, when the gamblers had all decamped. His next raid on the Dominion Club on First Street went off as planned, but it was in the planning, execution, and follow-up that everything went wrong.

The raid on the Dominion Club was straight out of Mack Sennett and the Keystone Cops. Detectives Seymour and Burbeck with a couple of helpers turned up at the club at 1 a.m. on Sunday morning, May 17, 1914.[22] The club was jammed to the rafters and all the crap tables, card tables, and gambling wheels were operating at capacity. Instead of surrounding the club the police simply broke in the front door. They made such a racket that they alerted the gamblers, who left by the back windows. In short order the crowd of 200 dwindled to 50. The police took the names of the inmates and, having forgotten to bring the patrol wagon, stood around in confusion for some time wondering what to do next. Along came Bill Wheeler, the self-styled fixer with a friendly suggestion. "Why," he asked, "spend the rest of the night hauling all the equipment down to the station as evidence?" He would be responsible for it and they could send around for it Monday at their convenience. He would even guarantee the keepers would all turn up in court and plead guilty. The detectives accepted the suggestion and went home. Fifteen minutes later the games were all back in full swing and continued without interruption for the rest of the weekend. Naturally the story of the raid got out and the police department became the city's biggest joke. The public was still laughing a week later when Commissioner Booth blew up in anger and fired Chief Lancey.[23] But not before another maladroit exploit by Detective Seymour.

The day before he was dismissed the chief handed Detective Seymour a list of 30 houses which Commissioner Booth had ordered him to close down.[24] Instead of staging the raids, however, Seymour took the list to Bill Wheeler. If the houses were to be closed anyway, Wheeler suggested that they ought to put the bite on the girls for some protection money before it was too late. He got into a taxi and started making the rounds. When he got back to Seymour he explained it had been a wasted effort, that "Joe had been around with the big mitt before I got there and the girls would not come through".

Seymour then gathered his forces together and went out and made some raids. When they turned up at Carmen Daily's at 630 Kinistino Street, she screamed foul at the top of her voice. Bill Wheeler had come to her with his demand of $100 protection and she had consulted one of the honest cops on the force, Detective Richard Fryant, who had been told to roust the streetwalkers but to leave the houses alone. She asked Fryant if there was going to be a segregated area on Kinistino Street, and would she be able to stay open by paying the $100? Fryant's advice was for her to ignore Wheeler and "if he bothers you again call me right away." She took Fryant's advice, and her name was at the very top of Seymour's list of brothels to be raided. "I should have paid the money and not listened to your advice," she told Fryant; "then I could have stayed open!"

The combination of the abortive gambling raid, the plague of streetwalkers, and the firing of Lancey provoked the biggest public meeting in Edmonton's history in the McDougall Methodist church.[25]   Minister after minister attacked the "social situation" in the most extravagant terms. Said the Reverend R.G. Stewart: "I was conversing with a man who lived in New York for many years who said that the worst parts of New York were rather tame compared with the conditions in Edmonton."

The Reverend Dr. J.H. Riddell said: "If the citizens can see the forms of vice flaunting themselves before the eyes of respectable people, surely the men who are paid to stop this sort of thing can see them also."

The meeting passed a resolution demanding that the attorney general launch an immediate inquiry into the Edmonton police department and all its works. This time the city council gave in and joined in the request for an investigation. The attorney general named Mr. Justice D.C. Scott to conduct the inquiry. It was the sort of circus that left few of the reputations of the principals unbesmirched.

The hearings opened on June 11, 1914, with O.M. Biggar as commission counsel. Such were the times that the probe had to fight for headline space every day. The first Turner Valley oil strike had turned all Alberta into an oil stock promotional madhouse. Mayor McNamara deserted the inquiry to rush to Calgary to buy up acreage with which to organize his own oil company. Then came the Crowsnest mine disaster in which 200 miners were buried alive in the Hillcrest mine. And in far off Sarajevo, Gavrilo Princip fired the bullet into Archduke Ferdinand that set off the First World War. But despite such competition for attention, the Scott inquiry played to a standing-room-only audience that included most of the leading madams of the town. Regardless of the competing news stories, the Scott inquiry got column after column of space every day.

During the two weeks of hearings, everybody contradicted everybody. Witnesses disappeared and were never heard of again. It was demonstrated beyond doubt that an embryo protection racket was being set up in Edmonton, though whether it involved the police department or not was uncertain. One detective reported turning in gambling and brothel locations repeatedly but none was raided. Another policeman was taken off the beat when he proved too energetic. When he complained, his colleagues told him he would be well advised to ignore the whole thing. The untenable position of Chief Lancey came out strongly in the testimony of Mrs. Jessie Bell, who only wanted to sell a house full of furniture and got caught up in a police inquiry. Mrs. Bell owned the furniture in a nineteen-room, men-only rooming house at 450 Kinistino Street next to the Savoy Hotel. It was a two-storey brick building with a store below and rooms above. When her newspaper advertisement appeared it caught the eye of Billie Morton, who sent a friend around to examine the furniture. His report was favourable so she made arrangements to buy out Mrs. Bell for her asking price. Word of the transaction quickly got back to Chief Lancey and he hit the roof.

"My God," he stormed, "we can't have a house like that at that location!" It would have been the biggest brothel in western Canada and there was no telling what kind of a scandal might erupt when the moral reformers got wind of it. So he sent word to Billie Morton that the deal had to be called off. But Billie had already made a deposit on the furnishings and said something about having to consult with her lawyer, Alderman Joe Clarke. That was all that had to be said to send poor Lancey scurrying for cover. "If that's it I wash my hands of the whole business, and poke my nose out of it," he said, and dropped the subject.

As for Joe Clarke, he was in and out of the inquiry like a jumping-jack. He had one courtroom manner, to shout his objections at the top of his voice. When prostitutes claimed that Clarke had acted for them, he rushed in with denials or explanations. In the Billie Morton deal he was able to show that he had not been involved in her negotiations and had not drawn up the lease. When it was whispered that he had deposited $10,000 in his wife's name recently, he turned up with bank statements to put the lie to the rumour.

One of the main things the inquiry did was reveal for Edmontonians how widely the brothels were spread over their city. At the request of Judge Scott, the city assessor produced a list of the property owners of the brothels raided over the previous two years. In 1912 a total of almost 100 houses were listed as having been raided. The 1914 list was down to 50 addresses, many of them duplicated from the previous list. The main concentrations were on Jasper Avenue and Kinistino Street. But Namayo, Clara, Fraser, Grierson, and Isabella were well represented. These were all in the Old Town area but the traffic spread far beyond these limits. The addresses hop-scotched westward onto Fourth, Fifth, Sixth, Eighth, Ninth, and Eleventh streets, and across the city to White Avenue.

What the actual count of operating brothels would have been was impossible to estimate, and Mr. Justice Scott did not try. Billie Morton, who had been in business longer in Edmonton than any of the other girls who testified, put the number at between 400 and 500. Mignon Douard, who operated several small establishments, put the figure at somewhere between 50 and 100. Another girl refused to hazard a guess but volunteered the opinion that there was too much competition along Kinistino Street to make it profitable for anybody.

Judge Scott brought down his report on July 23. [26] He found that the mayor and his cohorts had in fact determined to turn Edmonton into a wide-open city and had not been justified in the firing of Silas Carpenter, whose reputation alone seemed to emerge unscathed. The following day the Temperance and Moral Reform Society filled McDougall church with citizens who clamoured for the resignation of Mayor McNamara. The mayor, however, was off on his oil promoting. Joe Clarke turned up and fired off a tirade that all but disrupted the meeting. McNamara ignored the demand, but at the next meeting of the city council on August 6 he could not ignore Joe Clarke. Toward the end of the meeting, the McNamara-Clarke alliance blew up before the assembled aldermen with a force that threatened to destroy the council chamber itself. It began innocently enough, for such things were common in municipal politics — the mayor and the alderman simply halted proceedings temporarily while they exchanged insults.

"You," shouted Clarke, "are a liar and a perjurer."

"You tried to get control of the police department and I stopped you!" the mayor screamed back, apropos of nothing.

"That's a lie, a deliberate lie," Clarke replied. "You went onto the stand and swore to what was false and now you are making yourself into a perjurer."

"I said nothing of the sort," McNamara replied.

"You did and you are a deliberate, malicious liar," Clarke shouted back, "and I'll mop the earth with you."

The antagonists ran out of breath, or insults. Order was restored and the aldermen proceeded to complete most of their routine business. As adjournment was moved, McNamara arose and yelled at Clarke:

"You are a liar, Joe Clarke. You are a liar and a thief and a blackmailer! And you are a dirty coward as well! Now mop the floor with me!"

The fight was on and the aldermen and city officials scattered in all directions. The combatants pushed and shoved and wrestled each other for a couple of minutes and then the fists flew in earnest. Since McNamara was getting the worst of it, his chauffeur rushed to his defence. He grabbed Clarke by the throat and held him while McNamara beat a tattoo on Clarke's face. Clarke got free, shook off the chauffeur, and drove McNamara out of the council chamber and into the fire-escape room. Then they fought back into the council chamber, where the aldermen, who by now thoroughly disliked both men, pulled them apart. They moved out of the City Hall onto the street, where the fight broke out more violently than before. After ten minutes the general public took a hand and broke it up. Clarke was bleeding from one eye; his other eye was black and blue, and he had a cut on his cheek. McNamara had a blackened eye and badly bruised face.[27]

That was the political end for Mayor William J. McNamara. After he refused to resign, a private citizen sued on a technicality, and McNamara and one of the aldermen who had supported him were unseated. When he ran for re-election he was badly beaten. It looked for a while as if Joe Clarke had also been marked for oblivion. George Hill, the new chief selected to succeed Lancey, was a no-nonsense Scot who had been a police inspector in Edinburgh. The dust was not yet settled on the Scott report before Hill arrested Clarke on four charges of aiding and abetting the commission of criminal offences. The charges were based on a confession obtained from a burglar from Saskatoon, who claimed that Clarke had arranged with the Saskatoon police department to send three Saskatchewan thugs to Edmonton to start a crime wave there in order to discredit the new chief of police. [28]

Clarke was quickly brought to trial but was acquitted. His accuser changed his story, claiming to have fabricated it at the instigation of the Edmonton police in order to destroy Joe Clarke. The Saskatoon chief of detectives testified that the charges against Clarke were false. Some of the gloss was taken from Clarke's acquittal, however, when within a matter of weeks the Saskatoon detective was en route to the penitentiary for running a protection racket involving burglary and fabrication of evidence. Clarke's name disappeared from the newspapers and when he ran for re-election in December of 1915 the *Journal* devoted columns to the speeches of the other candidates and spared for Clarke but a single sentence — "Joe Clarke delivered his usual harangue."

Clarke was defeated and left politics, but not for long. Out of nowhere he emerged to run for mayor for the 1919-20 term and astounded everybody by winning the election. Some years later he served another couple of terms on the city council and was mayor again for three years in 1935, 1936, and 1937. When he died in 1941 at the age of seventy-one he was eulogized by the *Journal* as one of the city's greatest sports supporters. No mention was made of his early efforts to turn Edmonton into a wide-open town modelled on the authentic Klondike of his youth. Joe Clarke was the spiritual godfather of Edmonton's Klondike days and his name has been immortalized in the football stadium he was instrumental in obtaining for his adopted home town.

Long before his death, however, he came back to haunt Chief Hill. The Chief was barely rid of Joe Clarke when a problem far more serious than prostitution arose to confront him in the form of prohibition law enforcement. Until prohibition, the city police concentrated on drunks and left the enforcement of liquor licence laws to the provincial police. Indeed, there was so little co-operation between the two forces that a provincial inspector once got beaten up by a city policeman on duty in a bar, and the Edmonton police jailed the provincial inspector instead of his assailant.

With the coming of prohibition most of the steam went out of the Edmonton Temperance and Moral Reform Society. It had achieved legal prohibition, but as temperance seemed farther away than ever it concentrated all its efforts on getting the liquor act enforced. And it was on that question that Joe Clarke emerged once again as the indestructible nemesis of chiefs of police. When he was elected mayor in 1919 he immediately started to agitate for the abolition of the commissioner system. The reason the police were not enforcing the law against bootlegging, he said, was that the commissioner system removed them from the pressure of public opinion. When the commissioners defended their law enforcement record Joe Clarke rounded up a dozen clergymen and conducted them on a tour of Edmonton's blind pigs, where he demonstrated a complete lack of trouble in buying booze. The following year he was able to convince the legislature that it should change the Edmonton charter to provide for a police commission composed of the mayor and two aldermen. That was about as much of Joe Clarke as Chief Hill wanted; when the change was made, he resigned and took off for Vancouver.

To the old-time whores along Kinistino Street, history had come almost full circle. But not quite, for in common with the other red-light districts of the West, the onset of prohibition which closed the bars profoundly affected their trade. To stay in business they had to rely more and more on revenue from illegal booze, and the penalties for bootlegging were out of all proportion to profit for the amount of booze a brothel could sell. Besides, as elsewhere, the automobile and a loosening of moral restraints was introducing a heavy injection of unfair competition into their trade. Like a fading actress, Kinistino Street made a valiant attempt to recapture its past lustre. It never quite made it.

"To hell with Pearl Harbor — remember Pearl Miller!"

An anonymous English author in 1912 began an 88-page panegyric to Calgary with these words:

> Calgary is one of the figures in the foreground of a picture that appeals with almost irresistible force to the imagination of the Englishman. It stands as one of the great triumphs of the late nineteenth and early twentieth centuries; it is a city which has arisen in a night, but it rests on

124

long centuries of experience, and has arrived at full age at the moment of its birth. There has been no need to grope blindly through the long centuries seeking for improvement in evil conditions of life: progress has not been held in check by social forces that aim either at enslaving the worker or at taking sufficient of his increase to keep him poor and subservient all the days of his life. Calgary, for all that it looms so large in the history of the western prairie today, was unknown 30 years ago. Freedom as full as the Pilgrim Fathers knew when the "Mayflower" found safe harbourage at last, but redeemed from the trials and troubles that beset the old-time settlers; commercial and agricultural opportunities boundless in scope and infinite in possibilities, a full modern life in a bracing upland air and amid delightful natural surroundings — these are but some of the good things within Calgary's gift. The mere thought of them has the stimulus of a mountain breeze...[1]

And so on for another 30,000 words. It contained nary a hint that Calgary was in the process of becoming the booze, brothel, and gambling capital of the far western plains. Nor did it describe exactly the kind of place that greeted the eyes of the settlers as they stepped down from their C.P.R. daycoaches. Or their noses, either, if the wind happened to be in the right direction. The wind must have been right on the summer morning in 1910 when a trainful of immigrants stepped onto the Calgary station platform.

"The thing I remember most about my arrival in Calgary," one of them recalled years later, "was the smell. It was the horse-smellingest town I could ever remember!"

In the decade between 1900 and 1910 Calgary's human population skyrocketed from 4,000 to 40,000 and the horse population must at least have kept pace. Across the C.P.R. tracks on Eleventh Avenue was the biggest horse barn west of Winnipeg, perhaps even the biggest barn west of Toronto. It housed sixty teams of heavy draft horses which were used to haul freight for Pacific Cartage. The manure from the stable was piled at the north end of the barn and accumulated into a small mountain before being hauled away and dumped in some convenient hollow. Its after-a-rain fragrance was wafted stationward on the southeast morning breeze.

As the building boom rushed toward its peak in 1912, not even sixty teams working a twelve-hour day could keep up with the volume of freight the Canadian Pacific Railway was depositing in Calgary. Lumber and cement came in by the trainload. Yard engines hauled carloads of red brick from kilns on the western outskirts to be distributed by teams and wagons to the scores of downtown building sites on which eight- and ten-storey office buildings and warehouses were going up. Wagon trains brought in the limestone blocks being quarried on the Scarboro hill for the schools and public buildings, and for foundations in the ever-expanding residential areas. Dirt being hauled from the excavations coated the downtown area with a heavy veneer of dust during the dry spells, and turned the streets into quagmires when it rained. Within that downtown area there was a livery stable in every other block, fifteen of them in all, usually flanked by a blacksmith shop, of which there were a dozen.[2] The hotels were so numerous — ten of them in five blocks along Ninth Avenue — that the street became known throughout southern Alberta as "Whisky Row". If there was a mine strike impending, as there usually was, the fuel yards flanking the tracks west of the station stock piled huge mounds of coal. The coal piles gave off an odour all their own which somehow accentuated the piquancy of the aromas being wafted from the bars and stables. Afternoon gales which blew down from the north hill picked up the coal dust and deposited it on the new furniture in the mansions of the real estate promoters, which were going up all over "American Hill", a mile to the south of the tracks.

Like all the other prairie cities, pre-war Calgary went through an aberrant period when it tried to pave its streets with creosoted wooden blocks. Unhappily, the blocks heaved into blisters with the first spring thaw. There was the endless excavating, dirt hauling, and dust blowing attending the original block laying. Then, as the blocks were torn up and discarded, there was gravel hauling and macadamizing and surface oiling, all accomplished with horse-drawn dump wagons, water wagons, and oil sprayers. The alleys behind the livery stables were usually piled so high with manure that access was impeded, and the city fathers were continually complaining that the law against lane littering needed more enforcement. When the wind was blowing, and it usually was, Calgary was the dustiest and smelliest city between the Lakehead and the Pacific. On calm days it was only the smelliest. Then pedestrians on its main street were assaulted, seriatum, with the acrid odours emanating from saloons, greasy-spoon cafés, Chinese laundries, livery stables, and blacksmith shops; odours trapped and held by its unusually narrow streets.

When the pre-war boom got under way in 1905, downtown Calgary was a nondescript collection of two- and three-storey hotels and small frame cottages huddling on twenty-five-foot lots in a pie-shaped segment of land on the flood plain between the Bow and Elbow rivers. Because transportation was lacking, the working population tended to live as near as possible to their places of employment. Settlements had sprung up east of the confluence of the Bow and Elbow rivers around the Calgary Brewery and the Burns Packing Plant on the Brewery Flats. Similarly there were clutches of houses around the sawmills on the rivers, around the flour mills, and in Victoria Park between the railway freight yards and the race track.

The Calgary boom was the product of the C.P.R.'s great land promotion schemes which came in with the new century. The railway land department sent its agents scouring the American Great Plains States for potential settlers, and Americans by the tens of thousands poured into western Canada. Many of them headed directly for Calgary, where the C.P.R.'s Department of Natural Resources was located. Not only did armies of American farmers come in, but there were American businessmen, financiers, promoters, and investors in such numbers that the poshest residential area of the city became known as "American Hill". With the American influx came all the accoutrements of midwestern civilization. There were twenty-four American fraternal societies in business by 1908 along with twenty-five labour union locals affiliated with the American Federation of Labour.[3] There were also thirty Protestant churches into whose activities the Americans joined with enthusiasm. They tended to lean to the Baptist and Methodist faiths and were enthusiastic supporters of the Temperance and Moral Reform Society. There is no way of determining what proportion of Calgary's 44,000 citizens in the 1911 Census returns came from the United States. The census tabulated on the basis of racial origins; and, as many of the Americans were of British background, they undoubtedly were included among the 29,000 people identified as of British origin. The census actually listed only 4,000 Americans, but several pioneers of the era put the number as high as a third of the population.

Whatever their numbers the Americans, like the settlers from eastern Canada, were predominantly Protestant in religion and law-abiding by nature. Indeed, an overweening respect for law and order seemed to be the dominant characteristic of all the ethnic groups who came to Calgary. Among the hundreds of Italian workmen who did the hard manual work on the construction of the C.P.R.'s Ogden shops, crime of any kind was almost unknown. The large German colony which took over most of the Riverside area north of the Bow River was almost saintly in its compliance with the laws of the land. Despite its rapid expansion and unusually large floating population, Calgary was remarkably free from serious crime for the whole of its early history. The gun-toting tough guys who rode the American range had no counterparts among the cattle men of southern Alberta. Around Calgary even the Indians were peaceable and only the drunks were belligerent. It was, therefore, no accident that for the first quarter-century of its life Calgary got along with a police force that could only have been described as rudimentary. The duties of the force consisted almost entirely in maintaining order in the streets, a chore that consisted chiefly of breaking up drunken brawls and hauling the most aggressive off to jail. By mid 1906, when there was some public complaining about the police, Chief Tom English brushed it off with a "what do you expect" type of reply. He had, he said, a staff of seven to keep order night and day from Shagganappi Point to Brewery Flats and from the Bow to the Elbow. That area of about six square miles contained over 14,000 people, and until just recently Chief English had got by with a force half that size.[4]

Had it not been for the liquor problem, neither the Calgary police nor the Mounties would have had much work to do. When any law-breaking involving the criminal code did occur, the Calgary police usually handed it over to the Mounties for solution, and where possible they turned most of their prisoners over to the Mounties for incarceration. The Calgary jail was as close to being a three-room slum as the West contained. The heating system seldom worked; it was given a lick-and-promise cleaning periodically and its primary purpose seemed to be to serve as a deterrent to Calgary drunks. The mere thought of having to spend a night locked in it was enough to have stayed the arm of the most confirmed imbibers.

Things seem to have gotten out of hand for the first time in the spring of 1884 when the Mounties arrested two local prostitutes. Nina Dow and Nellie Swift were sentenced to six months in jail for being inmates of a house of ill fame, with commitment held up for twenty-four hours to permit the girls to get out of town.[5] Clearly prostitution was becoming an established Calgary industry even before the town had a population of 500. A similar sentence handed out to Maud Lewis that fall indicated, however, that the girls who were leading the C.P.R. construction crews westwards were finding the Calgary climate rather inhospitable. All that would change rapidly during the next decade.

Under the benign eye of Tom English, who became chief of police in 1891, Calgary developed into as wide-open a town as there was in the Canadian West. The city was mildly racked from time to time by minor gambling scandals, and by periodic outcries against drunkenness and prostitution. The chief greeted all such complaints with studied indifference. In 1906 he allowed, in response to protests, that there was less gambling and prostitution in Calgary than in any other city on the continent.

"There may be houses of prostitution in Calgary," he said, "but if there are I don't know where they are."

It took Chief English some weeks to live down his rash disclaimer. Former alderman W.G. Hunt, a pillar of the business world as well as of the Protestant Church, said that everybody knew there were places on Ninth Avenue where cards, whisky, and women were always on tap. A couple of weeks later the Reverend F.W. Patterson, in a sermon in the Baptist church, asked his worshippers to raise their hands if they believed there were houses of prostitution running wide open in Calgary. Half the hands in the congregation shot upward. It was not just a question of "believing" prostitution was rampant in Calgary.[6] The residents would have been incredibly naïve, and blind and deaf as well, not to know that the trade was flourishing. Sixth Avenue between the Mounted Police barracks and Fifth Street East had been largely taken over by houses of ill repute. And there were several places on Ninth Avenue which, from the casual way they were referred to in the newspapers, must have been notorious joints.

The *Calgary Herald*, in April 1907, carried a puzzling story about the misadventures of Carmen Hall, "a lady of leisure who lives at The Restaurant". On the night in question she had been drinking at the "chicken ranch on Ninth Avenue" and upon leaving cut across a vacant lot "next to the Japs" and fell into some weeds. In falling she had dropped $45 she had been carrying in her hand. When she arrived at the Star Restaurant she ran into "Slim" and told him about losing her money. If he would find it for her, she said, she would "make it right with him". So Slim wandered back toward the "Nagasaki", found the money, and headed for the nearest bar. Carmen went looking for Slim, found him, and demanded her money. When he denied having it she called in a friendly policeman who arrested Slim on a charge of theft. He was convicted and sent down for thirty days. The *Herald* said of Carmen, "She did not look her trade but told her story without hesitation."

A commonplace happening, surely, that scarcely deserved the attention of a police reporter even on a dull day. But its commonplace character is indicative of the Calgary attitude. Prostitutes were clearly common enough so that a reporter's glance revealed which of them "looked their trade" and which did not. Lack of identification of locations indicated all were well enough known to *Herald* readers not to need addresses.

The same awareness applied to the dozen or so brothels which operated in Riverside just below the old General Hospital, opposite St. George's Island. The newspapers frequently referred to the prostitutes of the area, but only as "women from across the Langevin Bridge". The area was just outside the city limits and hence came under the jurisdiction of the Mounties. What was needed, the Calgary aldermen insisted periodically, was better co-operation between the city police and the Mounties in combating "the social evil". There is no record of that co-operation ever having been achieved. In February 1907 a delegation from Riverside appeared before the city council to plead for help. Traffic to and from the brothels was so heavy at times that the peace and quiet of the neighbourhood was destroyed. Moreover, respectable citizens were frequently annoyed by men forcing their way into their houses looking for "women of ill fame". They had to keep their doors locked day and night to protect themselves.[7]

The aldermen listened sympathetically. Some even got into the discussion, if only to point out how difficult it was to get conviction against the nuisance when most of the houses were small-scale operations with only one or two inmates. The police, however, did take action to reduce the traffic congestion, but hardly in a way that

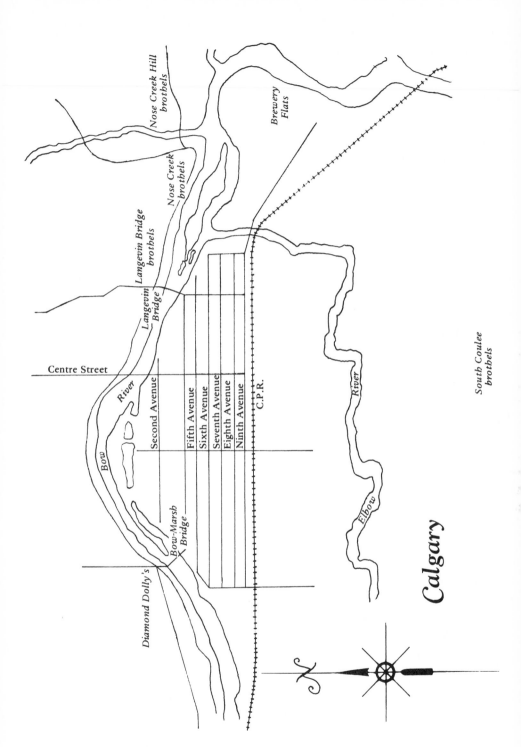

Calgary

would have helped the complaining citizens. Two weeks after the delegation's protest the *Herald* reported:

> Police have taken strenuous efforts to keep the ladies from across Langevin Bridge out of the city. Many of them have developed the habit of visiting with friends for long hours in different blocks in the city. The police will not allow this practice to continue. Frankie Day, found in the Ramsay Block with Cleve Boyd, was fined and ordered to return across the river.

Clearly this crackdown was of minimal assistance to the residents of Riverside, and could even be interpreted as a modicum of protection for the downtown girls from the effects of outside competition. In the months that followed, agitation against prostitution in Calgary itself mounted, led in the main by Aldermen Adoniram J. Samis, T.A.P. "Tappy" Frost, George E. Wood, and W.G. Hunt. All were pillars of the church and prominent business leaders, and they kept stirring up trouble for Chief English and his minions. "How can the police say there is no prostitution," Samis demanded, "when we continually see these women flaunting themselves in their silks and satins, driving around in hired liveries, and employing Chinese servants?"

Certainly when the fallen women went on shopping tours they went in a style that scandalized all the respectable ladies who crossed their paths. In September, Samis charged that Japanese, Negro, and white women were all operating houses of ill fame within four blocks of the Post Office.[8] A couple of weeks later he testified against a woman charged with keeping a house on Eighth Avenue East. Alderman Hunt came out with a charge that there were ten houses running wide open within a ten-minute walk of the police station on Seventh Avenue East. In the fall of 1907 the quartet was instrumental in organizing the Calgary Citizens Committee, which exerted enough pressure on the attorney general to get an official inquiry ordered into the Calgary police chief's department. Mr. Justice Charles A. Stuart was appointed to run the investigation.

When the lawyers started to prepare for the inquiry they were stymied at once because of lack of specific information. The charges were general in character as follows:

1. Bawdy-houses were allowed within the city limits with the knowledge and consent of the chief of police.
2. Criminal prosecutions were compromised and withdrawn with the knowledge and consent of the chief of police.
3. Intoxicating liquor was being sold in the city without licence with the knowledge and consent of the chief of police.
4. Insulting and abusive language was used in public places toward citizens by the chief of police.
5. The chief of police did not act in harmony with the members of the force whereby the interests of the city and justice have suffered.
6. Gambling was allowed by the chief of police.

It quickly became apparent to both the Citizens Committee and the lawyers that some concrete accusations had to be brought forward to get the inquiry rolling. So the committeemen undertook to go out and gather evidence while the sittings were delayed a few weeks. There was then set in motion a most uncommon comedy of errors.

George Wood, one of the moving spirits of the investigation, was a unique individual. He was an idealist and social reformer who backed his convictions with his own resources. A real estate promoter by profession, he was a dedicated welfare pioneer by avocation. At his home at 110 Second Avenue East he had established a rescue home for fallen women and homeless children. Over the years his clients multiplied to a point where he had to build a large red brick addition to his rather handsome frame house. His wife functioned as the matron and Wood himself was occasionally successful in convincing prostitutes that a return to respectability had something to recommend it. It was from these women that he obtained the addresses of the houses of ill fame which the others used for oratorical ammunition. However, the reformed young women had no burning desire to rush into court and bare their shame to the world as witnesses for the committee. So the committee was faced with the need to produce other witnesses with concrete evidence. Knowing prostitution was rampant was one thing; proving it in court was something else again.

The first step taken by the committee was to hire a Vancouver detective to make an undercover investigation. His name was W.H.

Walker and he turned out to be a total loss to his employers.[9] He later testified he was able to buy beer in Elsie Hall's at 522 Sixth Avenue East, at Flo Smith's at 511 Fifth Avenue East, and "at Tootsie's place". But all the girls he encountered were very ladylike and none solicited him.

When it became clear to the committee that Detective Walker was a bumbling incompetent, they were thrown back on their own resources. Samis located a couple of manual-labouring types from Riverside and with Wood and "Tappy" Frost they set out on an evidence-gathering excursion of their own. On cold January nights, "Tappy" Frost and George Wood huddled on the sidewalk while Charlie Chivers and Charlie Carter rang doorbells on Fifth Avenue East and Ninth Avenue East. From their testimony it was clear that both Charlies were more afraid of the madams than the madams were of them.[10]

When the doors opened, one or both would blurt out a request for beer. Clearly only idiots would be wandering around Calgary on below-zero nights looking for beer — idiots or men up to no good. As the suspicious madams wanted no part of either, they repulsed the efforts of the amateur sleuths. Here and there, however, one of them flung the door open for them to enter.

"I ain't got no beer, honey," one of the girls said and added, according to Chivers, "but if it's something else you want it will cost you five dollars."

The amateur hawkshaws fled in confusion. "I could tell from the way she spoke that she was not a virtuous woman," Chivers told the Stuart Commission. Two more improbable witnesses have seldom faced a royal commission. They forgot the most important details of their investigation and what they did remember was jumbled and confused. The moving spirits behind the investigation followed their secret agents to the stands and did little better. They were able to pinpoint the existence of prostitution but unhappily were utterly unable to present any evidence to substantiate their charges against Chief English. The four reformers all lived within a few blocks of the main Calgary brothel area between Fifth and Ninth avenues. Frost testified that the value of the property he owned had been seriously depreciated by the changing character of the area. And, of course, he and the others all had been solicited on the streets of the neighbourhood. The only witness the commission could find who could contribute much in the way of useful factual information was Minty Johnson, who operated the Red Barn Livery Stable on Seventh Avenue East. He knew most of the houses of ill fame on both sides of the river and indeed had a private telephone connection into one of the houses in the Nose Creek area. His was one of the first two-telephone establishments in Calgary and it was a facility highly prized by both the customers and the keepers of the bordellos.[11]

As if to salt the wounds of the Frost-Samis forces, the commission itself called three of the madams from Sixth Avenue East to testify to the respectability of their neighbourhood. Jessie Gay said that she had been a housekeeper in the Nose Creek area before moving to 620 Sixth Avenue. She denied ever selling liquor and said she lived off the income she received from property she owned in the United States. Ethel Clayton said she was buying her house, had a husband in Chicago who sent her $75 a month, and received $25 a month from some property she owned in Winnipeg. Flo Smith said she had property in Centralia, Grand Forks, and Seattle, Washington, as well as in Calgary. Her American investments brought in $250 a month which was deposited in a Seattle bank. She, like the others, never sold liquor and had seen no disorderly conduct in the neighbour-hood.[12]

The inquiry drifted away quickly into inconsequentials. Chief English himself boycotted it. In his report Judge Stuart lashed out at everybody involved except the lawyers. The proceedings, he said, reflected no credit on any of the participants. That houses of ill repute existed was apparent and he judged the police to be ineffi-cient in not knowing about them. He found the charges against the Chief were not proven but said it was regrettable that the Chief had chosen to absent himself from proceedings.[13] The Chief, with eighteen years of service behind him, clearly assumed that the Scotch verdict of the Stuart Commission left him in a completely impregnable position. Within eighteen months he was on the outside looking in. And it all happened, in Chief English's eyes, because he tried to enrich the Calgary treasury at the Alberta government's expense.

The streets around the railway stations in all the western cities were frequently infested with con-men, pickpockets, pimps, and other vermin preying on incoming immigrants and visiting settlers. Calgary was no exception. During Summer Fair time all the police departments worked together to give the unwary what protection they could. It was, for example, the practice for many years after the Calgary Stampede was inaugurated for the Winnipeg police to send Inspector James Melville of its bunco detail to Calgary to point out Winnipeg thieves to the Calgary police. In the days of Chief English, however, this kind of co-operation was just beginning, and each year when the Calgary Summer Fair opened, thieves were as thick as flies wherever strangers were likely to congregate. There was no way in which one police force could protect the gullible public from all the traps laid for them.

The commonest trap was for a shill to haunt Ninth Avenue disguised as a farm hand and strike up an acquaintanceship with likely-looking yokels. If the train from the north had recently arrived, he would claim kinship with any town on the line his prospect happened to hail from. "What a coincidence," he'd exclaim as an opening gambit, "I used to work there myself." On a particular occasion during Fair Week 1909, a shill collected a couple of well-heeled dupes from Red Deer and shepherded them into the alley at Ninth Avenue and Centre Street, where Big Bill Holmberg, Fred Hill, and W.D. Edwards of Edmonton were running a crooked roll-down ball game. The operator rolled a ball down an inclined board which had a number of holes at the low end. The players bet on the hole into which the ball would fall and the operator by controlling the roll of the ball could win at will. After the unlucky visitors had lost $230 they became suspicious that the game was crooked, and complained to the police, who arrested Hill, Holmberg, and Edwards. The latter, it turned out, was wanted by the Edmonton police, and the Calgary police already held a warrant for his arrest. Hill was released and given a floater out of town. Holmberg was released on bail and when he appeared in court the information against him was mysteriously defective.

The fraud charge against Edwards was laid under the criminal code, which made him liable on conviction to a jail sentence as well as a fine. Jail sentences were seldom imposed and if the culprit was fined the money would have gone automatically to the provincial treasury. Chief English, when he was laying information himself, was always careful to charge offenders under city by-laws so that the fines went to the city and were reflected in the profit-and-loss statements of his department. When he discovered that the Edwards charge was under the criminal code he took action to withdraw it and re-lay it under a city by-law. All this took time so the court was adjourned and reconvened several times while the red tape was untangled. Then Bill Edwards was whisked in, fined $100, and turned loose. The Chief ignored the Edmonton warrant for Edwards' arrest that was lying on his desk.

When the hearing had ended, the victims of the swindle asked about the promise that they would get their money back. They were told that if they wanted to press charges against Holmberg, they would have to wait around for a week for the trial. And, the magistrate warned them, they themselves might very well be charged with gambling and be liable under the city by-laws to fines of twenty dollars and costs because they too had been involved in an illegal enterprise. That was too much for the men from Red Deer and they shook themselves free of Calgary dust and Calgary justice.

It was also too much for the *Albertan*. The day after the trial it demanded to know, in a front-page editorial: "Do the courts control gamblers or do gamblers control the courts?"[14]

The paper printed a long report of the manoeuvring that went on between the police and the courts in the Edwards case, the foul-up in the charges against Holmberg, and the seeming police connivance in letting Edwards escape the Edmonton warrant. The city council, which had been growing increasingly restive with Chief English since the Stuart inquiry, seized upon the *Albertan* exposé as an excuse to get rid of the Chief. When he refused to resign as requested he was summarily fired in July 1909.[15]

As Calgary was outgrowing its police department it was also outgrowing its own boundaries, and the process of expansion caused a series of major disruptions within the red-light districts. Immediately after the Stuart inquiry, the women of ill repute disappeared from the houses on Sixth Avenue East, vanishing like lemmings into the tide of immigrants that was flooding over Calgary. Some of them began infiltrating the area west of Centre Street, which was beginning to change from residential to business occupancy. A good many moved into the Manchester area on the south city limits, where a new string of brothels was emerging in the vicinity of the Mountain Springs brewery in South Coulee. Mostly, however, the exodus was across the Langevin Bridge into a settlement which had been moving steadily eastward since the turn of the century.

The first recognized area of prostitution in Calgary was north of the old Bowmarsh Bridge in Hillhurst. It was here that Diamond Dolly settled and held sway as Calgary's queen of the fleshpots throughout the Edwardian era.

> I could never watch a Mae West movie without thinking about Diamond Dolly [a pioneer merchant recalled]. They were dead ringers for each other, except that Diamond Dolly was a brunette. They had the same mannerism, the same style, the same clothes, the same grand manner.
>
> There was a lot of interest in the horse Diamond Dolly used to drive. It was a big rangy dark bay, over 16 hands high, with a blaze face. It was the kind of a horse that really stood out in a crowd, as the saying goes. If you happened to look up the street and saw half a dozen buggies coming along you could tell Diamond Dolly's from all the rest a block away by that blaze faced horse of hers. Of course you could tell it by Diamond Dolly herself. She was the damndest woman for big hats with ostrich plumes on them. Mostly she rode around with the top of her buggy folded back and it was a wonder how she ever kept those big hats on in the wind that whistled down Eighth Avenue.
>
> We used to say you'd think she was a politician's wife the way she'd wave to all her friends and customers as she went by. Lots of times the fellows would sort of turn their heads and pretend they didn't see her. That didn't faze Dolly. Like as not she'd shout out — "Hey there George, how are you George? Where you been keepin' yerself lately?" — Whatever George it happened to be would give her a short hello and duck into the nearest store.
>
> She came by her name Diamond Dolly naturally. You might say she invented that saying — "Diamonds are a girl's best friend." She never went out without ten pounds of jewelry. The clerks in L.H. Doll's jewelry store said they could always tell when things were booming across the river, Dolly would be in for a new diamond ring. She used to tease hell out of clerks everywhere, particularly if they were kind of bashful. She called them by name, at the top of her voice and asked them when they were coming over to see her. When the clerks saw her coming they'd all run and hide. [16]

Who was Diamond Dolly? A most diligent search into the surviving records of the era has failed to turn up a single clue. She was
just Diamond Dolly, whose beginning — and end — are as clothed in
mystery as her real name.

An unidentified liveryman who stabled Diamond Dolly's horse
added a minor footnote to the evidence before Judge Stuart's investigation. There was a lot of gossip around the town about Chief
English's relationship with Diamond Dolly because he was seen
occasionally driving Diamond Dolly's horse around. Was the Chief
accepting favours from the town's leading madam? By no means,
said the liveryman. The horse belonged to him, not to Diamond
Dolly. She only rented it from him by the hour like everybody else,
including the Chief of Police.

When the area around the Bowmarsh Bridge became solidly
settled, Diamond Dolly moved to the Riverside Flats below the old
General Hospital in the lee of the Tom Campbell Hill. Soon there
were a dozen other houses in the general area. When the city
extended its boundaries to encompass it, the "sisterhood" moved
around the tip of the hill into the Nose Creek Valley just beyond the
Calgary city limits.

In the early days of settlement the valley of Nose Creek was one of
the most beautiful of prairie streams. Once it had been a mighty river
a half-mile wide and 100 feet deep. Now reduced to a babbling
brook, it meandered through a lush valley where the grass grew waist
high from its deep black loam. When the C.P.R. decided to build its
branch line to Edmonton in 1891, it took the path of least resistance
out of Calgary up the Nose Creek Valley. That was the end of the
beauty spot. First a brewery, then a packing plant, a cooperage, and
an incinerator discovered that the little stream would make a perfect
sewer for their wastes. Around these plants the usual clusters of
workmen's houses sprang up and it was at the southern edge of the
workmen's settlement that the whores from Riverside moved late in
the English regime.

To succeed Chief English, the Calgary city council promoted his
deputy, Thomas Mackie, whose problems with the social evil
mounted steadily with the flood of people into the city. How many
prostitutes prowled the downtown Calgary streets was never com-
puted, but they were at least sufficiently numerous to take care of

the immediate demand. Outside the city the brothels at Nose Creek employed upwards of 50 women and a similar number were engaged in the South Coulee red-light district. Chief Mackie, of course, was responsible only for the suppression of vice within the city. The Mounties had jurisdiction elsewhere.

Prostitution, however, was only a minor segment of Mackie's problem. His difficulties steadily multiplied as a result of the frantic rate of Calgary's growth. Its building permits doubled and redoubled by the year, from $2,400,000 in 1909 to $20,000,000 in 1912. During the summer the population of the city rose at better than 1,000 newcomers a month. The police force itself skyrocketed from eighteen men when Mackie took over from English to seventy when he quit two years later. The bigger the force got, the worse everything became. Mackie himself had come into the service when the policemen qualified by what was jocularly called "brute strength and ignorance". As with all other prairie police forces, the primary requirement for policemen in Calgary was physical strength and the size to go with it. Being able to read and write and willing to work a twelve-hour day seven days a week were also desirable, plus a reasonable leaning towards sobriety. Having qualified on all counts himself, Chief Mackie naturally adopted them in his own expansion program. Unhappily for him, Calgary was outgrowing such a rough and ready organization.

By-laws by the barrelful were going onto the books. Early closing laws were extended and refined. The kind of nuisances that small towns took for granted became verboten to the citizens of an urban metropolis. In almost a matter of months, a police force that had never been called on to do more than roust the drunks off the street and to try the locks on the doors of stores was forced to rush around in all directions. New sanitary regulations had to be enforced. Cows and pigs running loose had to be impounded. People accustomed to tossing trash in alleys had to be reprimanded. Boys riding bicycles on sidewalks became objects of attention. Chinese laundries had to be forced to stop dumping their tubs in ditches. The automobile was having such an impact that a whole new body of street regulations had to be enforced by a new breed of policeman — the traffic cop.

From the day he took over till the day he quit, Chief Mackie lived in the eye of the storm. Not only was he no administrative genius, but his department was directly controlled by the city council, whose aldermen were forever whipsawing him with demand for action and appeals for inaction. When the aldermen let up, the newspapers climbed on his back. The *Calgary Herald*, for example, in one of the few front-page editorials it ever ran, on November 6, 1911, demanded that the police enforce By-Law 822. This was the ordinance which forbade spitting on sidewalks. It was, as the *Herald* pointed out, pithy but all-embracing: "No person shall expectorate, spit or otherwise deposit saliva on any sidewalk in the City of Calgary, or in any public building."

And how were Calgarians observing that law? In the breach, said the *Herald*. Both sides of Centre Street between Ninth and Eighth streets were stamping grounds for loafers by the hundreds. Outside the Royal Hotel, where loafers congregated day and night, the streets were filthy beyond description. Scores of men on both streets were spitting tobacco juice on the sidewalks under the very eyes of the law. With the kind of force he had, Mackie could not possibly handle the volume of complaints that reached his desk. But he tried. His patrolmen were instructed to keep an eye peeled for illegal spitters and when they saw one to pounce. Perhaps a stiff fine or two would impress Calgarians with the need to improve their public manners and hone their social graces. The first tobacco juicer caught decorating the sidewalks proved to be the last one apprehended. He explained to the magistrate that he had only been cleaning his moustache, and when he was let off with a $1 fine the deterrent effect of police action on illegal tobacco spitters became completely nullified.

Chief Mackie clearly had trouble enough without the moral reformers also breathing down his neck. The scars from the farce of the Stuart Commission were still an impediment toward mounting any more all-out campaigns against booze and the social evil. But Chief Mackie felt the reformers' pressure none the less. It came mainly by indirection through their sermons. When the city annexed Nose Creek Flats Mackie announced on January 8, 1911, that he had ordered his department to clean out the prostitutes. He of course was confronted immediately by the problem of how to do the job. The law on prostitution was hazy, and successful morals prosecutions were hard to bring off. On January 27, however, the Chief was able to get a conviction that made headlines, and one which it was anticipated would send the ill-famers scurrying for cover. Maud

Rogers was fined $250 for keeping liquor for sale and $50 for keeping a house of ill fame. Three of her girls, Olive Regan, Blanche Douglas, and Louise Livingstone, were each assessed $35 for being inmates. These were the stiffest fines ever assessed in Calgary and they spread consternation through the brothel business, but not for long.

Several years previously a character known as "Klondike" Campbell built four large, three-storey houses in a coulee in Nose Creek Hill across the tracks from the Flats. When Mackie declared war on the brothels in the Flats, the women simply moved across the tracks into Campbell's coulee. "Stutterin' May" King not only moved out of the Flats to Nose Creek Hill, she moved her house with her. Its location at the bottom of the hill made it one of the most popular brothels at Nose Creek. The biggest place was just above May King's and was operated by Helen Hubert, who regularly employed six or seven girls. Lila Wilson and Madge Jennings leased the other Campbell houses, and seven or eight other brothels and a general store made up the settlement.

The Nose Creek Hill bordellos prospered mightily during the construction boom of 1912 and 1913 and both Helen Hubert and "Stutterin' May" King took steps to turn their houses into authentic palaces of joy. They brought in pianos and hired piano players. Thereafter Calgary nights were filled with music all summer long. When atmospheric conditions were right, the Nose Creek Hill coulee acted as a sound trap, and the music and laughter was carried as far south as Scotsman's Hill, a half-mile away. Indeed, an early resident of that hill swore that the lyrics as well as the music could both be heard distinctly when the wind was gently blowing from the north on a warm summer night.[17]

Residents of Brewery Flats, which flanked the south bank of the Bow River across from the brothels, got the benefit of the impromptu concerts regardless of the wind. On C.P.R. payday nights it was impossible to sleep through the din. The labourers working on construction of the Ogden shops got paid once a month and had long since adopted the coal miners' practice of making the day after payday an unproclaimed holiday. By pre-arrangement, the livery operators of Calgary brought all their democrats to the shops and had them lined up waiting when the workers came off work with their pay envelopes in their pockets. In a matter of minutes a dozen carriages would be loaded with a hundred labourers boisterously heading for the trail which would take them to the Nose Creek Hill.

"We could hear them coming a mile away," a resident of the Brewery Flats recalled. "You'd think an Italian Opera company was coming to town from the noise they made, but what they were singing none of us kids could understand. All we knew was that the settlement they were headed for was populated by 'bad' women and if we were ever caught sneaking over we'd get a hiding we would never forget. And I can remember how mad my father used to get as we sat around a mosquito smudge on the steps and listened to the uproar across the way. 'We'll get no sleep tonight, I can promise you that!' my father used to say as we went in to bed."

Neither did the partying labourers. Along toward morning they would start the return journey, somewhat more subdued vocally but still boisterous enough for the East Calgarians to be angered by singing that now had deteriorated into caterwauling. Back at Ogden, they would fall exhausted into their tents and sleep the clock around.

The imposing size of the Nose Creek Hill houses was in sharp contrast with the dismal appearance of those of the equally large red-light district in the South Coulee. It was located hard by the brewery in the Manchester district, which also contained a tannery, a tack factory, a cooperage, several blacksmith shops, and a brick plant. It was surrounded by the modest houses of the factory hands, ranging from neat cottages to mere shacks. The first brothel in the district was a made-over garage owned by a city alderman, and most of the others were slum-type houses, inside and out.

As long as the whorehouses were outside the Calgary city limits they were beyond the jurisdiction of the city police. But much of the nuisance created by both districts impinged on the Calgary citizenry, so they complained both to their own police and to the Mounties, who were clothed with authority over both districts. If nothing much was ever accomplished, it was not because the Mounties were completely out of sympathy with the complainers. In his *Annual Report* for 1909 Superintendent R.B. Deane had this to say:

> The social evil has been somewhat in evidence here as elsewhere recently. The Presbyterian and Methodist clergymen have said that the existence of a colony of sporting

women at Nose Creek was prejudicially affecting the morals and welfare of the Community at East Calgary and I promised to do what I could in this connection.

In company of Sergeant May I visited each house and saw the respective proprietresses and told them that they must choose some other locality to live in or they would get themselves into serious trouble. They all took the hint and departed, except one who sent a doctor to say she was too ill to move right then.

Needless to say, every house has since been re-occupied, the landlords and their agents saw to that. . . .

Superintendent Deane returned to the problems of Nose Creek in his report for the following year as follows:

On April 15 last a tragedy occurred in the "red light" district at Nose Creek which brought that community into prominence for the time being. A man named Joe More had some time previously brought to Calgary a girl named Rose Smith who had left her husband in Brooklyn. A couple of weeks before the tragedy More had beaten the girl, who left him and took up her abode at Nose Creek. She was afraid of the man and had repeatedly refused not only to return to live with him but to see him.

On this occasion the girl said he might be admitted to the house as she wanted to speak to him. The subject matter of their conversation can only be inferred, but the inevitable inference is that he requested her to return to him, and on her refusal shot her dead and then blew his own brains out.

Obviously this might have happened in a railway station, or an hotel, or in any other place where the man could obtain access to the woman whom he was determined to kill if she would not accede to his desires, and, so far as the "red light" district was concerned, the incident had no special significance whatever.

I mentioned in my report last year that, at the request of a deputation of East Calgary residents, I had promised to do what I could to suppress the "red light" district, then situated on Nose Creek Hill, which gave particular offence to the gentlemen in question.

Some of the speakers at our meeting expressed their

conviction that if the keepers and inmates of these houses were, on conviction, to be punished with imprisonment instead of by fine, the evil would soon be eradicated.

Some of the women moved away to other parts, but some of the houses remained open in spite of all my efforts to induce their occupants to leave.

In some cases I awarded imprisonment on conviction, and the number of houses slowly diminished. In the case of one house which continued to remain persistently open for business, I, in conjunction with Inspector Duffus, issued a warrant to search on July 25 last. The house in question was notoriously a house of ill-fame, owned by a woman named "Diamond Dolly", who found no difficulty in renting it at $125 per month.

Corporal Ryan and Constable Rosenkrantz, men of integrity and veracity, were detailed to execute the warrant. I am particular in giving these minute details because the final issue of this prosecution is of interest to any and every peace officer whose duty it may be to carry out the provisions of the vagrancy section of the Criminal Code, more particularly in the Calgary district.

Corporal Ryan and the constable were admitted to the house by the keeper thereof at about 5 A.M. on July 26 last. Corporal Ryan showed his warrant and asked if any man was in the house. She replied she did not know, gave him a lamp, and he went upstairs with the constable. In one room he found a woman in bed alone. In another room Constable Rosenkrantz found a man and a woman in bed together. As soon as he opened the door the woman asked whom he wanted. Instead of replying to her he called Corporal Ryan, who entered the room. As he did so the woman greeted him with the remark: "This sleeper has paid me."

In the subsequent hearing at the barracks, where Ray Mason was charged with being the keeper, and Lillie Smith and Myrtle Munford with being inmates of a house of ill-fame, the man who was found in bed with the woman deposed that she was not his wife, that the house had a bad reputation, and that Ray Mason acted as mistress of the house. He said that his companion was sick and that was why he stayed with her.

The defendants were represented by counsel, who made no defence of any kind, and the keeper of the house was sentenced to three months, and the two women inmates to one month's imprisonment in the Calgary guard-room.

Notice of appeal was given in the case of Ray Mason, but nothing was heard of it until the 17th September, when I received subpoenas for witnesses returnable on the 19th id. As Constable Rosenkrantz was by that time on detachment duty at Carbon, and the earliest mail could not reach him before noon of September 20, I so informed the crown prosecutor's partner.

I heard nothing more about the matter until the afternoon of September 20, when a lawyer's clerk brought me an order from the judge of the District Court quashing the conviction.

I have vainly endeavoured to procure a copy of the judgment herein, and can only quote a newspaper report which said "Judge Winter allowed the appeal and quashed the conviction, and in his judgment stated that he found no evidence which justified the conviction having being made."

The Moral Reform League must, therefore, understand that the suppression of the houses which they hold in particular abhorrence will in future be attended with more difficulty than ever; for when it becomes generally known that a man and a woman, who are not husband and wife, may with impunity meet and go to bed together in a house of assignation, so long as one poses as the patient and the other as the nurse, we may expect a widespread epidemic of a permanent nature.

As things turned out, Chief Mackie's raid on Nose Creek Flats was as much a Pyrrhic victory as Superintendent Deane's had been, but for different reasons. Chief Mackie's moment of glory was clouded almost at once by the emergence from nowhere of a private detective, William Grimsdale, to charge that Calgary police were doing everything in their power to make it a wide-open town. He had been employed as an undercover agent by the Provincial Liquor Law Enforcement Agency to gather evidence of liquor act violations in Calgary. He boasted of buying seventeen bottles of whisky illegally in the city and roasted the city police for lack of interest or co-operation in suppressing bootlegging and gambling joints.[18]

The following month the Women's Christian Temperance Union held its convention in Calgary with the Reverend J.G. Shearer as the keynote speaker. It was Dr. Shearer who had made the charges a couple of months earlier that led to the famous Winnipeg brothel inquiry. Dr. Shearer had found the lot of a royal commission witness a very trying one and to the surprise and disappointment of the convention turned out to be a very chastened fire-eater. Recalling Winnipeg, he said more could often be accomplished by quiet persuasion applied to governments than by public protests. He promised to take up the matter of the Calgary brothels with the Alberta government. Spring drifted into summer and Calgary boozeries and brothels slid back into the *status quo ante* the Maud Rogers prosecution. Then in November 1911 the Mounties swooped down on nine houses of ill fame on Nose Creek Hill in the biggest raid in the province's history.

The raid had followed hard on three other events that refocused attention on moral issues. The newspapers began to keep count of the cases in which the city police staged raids and then dropped the prosecution. On November 8 the police arrested Sam Amedia and charged him with keeping a house of ill fame at 631 Sixth Avenue East.[19] Three girls were arrested as inmates. It became the sixth case in recent months to be dropped after charges were laid. Considering the educational standards for policemen, the low esteem in which the job itself was held, the long hours and low pay, it is easy to understand how the mysteries of laying charges properly could easily and innocently have baffled the policemen making the arrests of the madams and their *filles de joie*. But the repetition of well-publicized raids followed by quietly dropped charges naturally aroused suspicion in a public which tended to lack faith in its police department in the first place.

The second disturbing event coming hard on the heels of the Amedia case was the conviction in Supreme Court of Roy and Ethel Beckman, who got five and three years respectively in the penitentiary for procuring a sixteen-year-old girl for immoral purposes. Then, on November 23, former Chief Tom English himself returned to the jousting with a front-page letter to the *Herald* in which he called for the removal of Chief Mackie on grounds of incompetence and for the establishment of an independent police commission composed of a judge, a magistrate, and the mayor of the city.

Chief Mackie rode the storm through the Christmas season but on January 15, 1912, he decided that he could stand the heckling and pressure no longer and threw in the towel. The city council took its time in choosing a successor and a month later announced the appointment of Alfred Cuddy, who was forty-nine years old and an inspector of the Toronto police force. As things turned out, he was also everything his predecessors had not been. He was a "professional" policeman in every sense of the word, and he tolled the bell for all the lovely Nells in the Calgary brothels. He undertook publicly to put them all out of business, and he meant it. That he largely failed can, of course, be taken for granted. But until he left the force seven years later to head the provincial government's Liquor Enforcement Department, he never stopped trying. Under Cuddy, Calgary ceased to be the most wide-open city in Alberta. It took most of the year to get his organization in shape and then he moved in on the brothels. The days of toleration and token raids were at an end. When Chief Cuddy's men raided the brothels it was for the purpose of putting them out of business permanently.

On October 25, 1912, the Chief sent his force on a drive through the South Coulee and it emerged with 56 women in custody. The next day the first offenders among the keepers of houses of ill fame each paid fines of $198 and costs; second offenders were assessed $248, and the inmates $10 each. The newspapers reported that more than $4,000 in fines was collected, an indication that better than a dozen brothels were involved in the raid. It was an occasion which brought out the purplest prose in the pen of the *Albertan*'s police reporter. About the inmates of "the gilded palaces of hollow laughter" he wrote:

> Rouge paint and powder could not conceal the unmistakeable traces of dissipation. That sin had collected at least part of its wages was apparent to even the most casual observer. The sunken eyes, some of them brilliant from belladonna, and hollow cheeks told a story of riotous living that could not be denied.
>
> The trial was held in camera and while it was going on a

crowd of male acquaintances of the women loitered in the corridors. The majority were of the "pink cuff" type of "secretaries" or "macs" who exist on the earnings of the unfortunate women. After the payment of the fines the unfortunates made their way back to the dens of vice in The Coulee where they will ply their wretched vocation without molestation until the next raid is ordered.

There were *Albertan* readers among the Local Council of Women who promptly whipped up a resolution calling for jail sentences for prostitutes to end the social evil in Calgary.[20] Chief Cuddy heartily approved but pointed to an insurmountable difficulty — no jail. The Mounted Police had limited accommodation for women prisoners in their guardhouse when it was not already full of men; but the old Calgary jail was barely suitable for housing animals, let alone human beings. The Salvation Army and the Presbyterian Church operated rescue homes for women. But entry in both cases was voluntary and there were few takers for either charity. Far from discouraged, the women amended their resolution and sent it off to Edmonton to urge the Alberta government to erect a women's prison. The following year Calgary built a new jail for Chief Cuddy.

As a wielder of new brooms, Chief Cuddy swept the Calgary tenderloins with dedication and vigour. Within a year he was claiming complete success in putting the South Coulee out of business, although he had to admit that many of its denizens had taken up residence in the downtown core. But sweep the city clean he never did. Nose Creek Hill survived largely intact until circumstances, as much as police action, undermined its viability. The most important factor was the First World War.

While permanent barracks were being erected, the army took over several downtown stores and turned them into residential quarters for its volunteers. As long as both the bars and the barracks were in the downtown area the women could not afford to be too far away. The Nose Creek Hill brothels were too remote to compete effectively with the downtown whores for the army trade. Gradually the Nose Creek houses emptied and those which were not torn down burned down. The whole area reverted to the city for taxes and the Coulee itself disappeared when Calgary turned it into a garbage dump after the Second World War. But while it lasted it was not only a brothel area that employed upwards of fifty girls in a dozen houses; it was a mecca for Calgarians by the hundreds on their Sunday afternoon strolls.

All that remains of the Nose Creek Hill brothels is a photograph in the Glenbow collection taken in 1910 by Thomas Wilson, and the taking itself provides a sidelight on the times. Wilson, the teenage son of the famous Banff pioneer explorer and outfitter, was attending business college in Calgary. On a bright Sunday afternoon he took his camera and went for a walk when "going for a walk" often meant covering several miles. His stroll took him out Ninth Avenue East, across the C.P.R. bridge to where he discovered the settlement on Nose Creek Hill. Wilson cocked his camera and as he climbed the hill behind the houses took a picture of the settlement, completely unaware of the nature of the place. Along the hill were scores of other Calgarians who had walked out from the city and were picnicking, resting, sleeping, or just sitting on the hill looking down into the settlement where a couple of dozen men were strolling around talking to the girls.

Wilson walked to the far end of the ridge and decided to come back through the settlement, shooting pictures as he went. He concluded from the number of girls around the houses that he had blundered into a girls' college of some kind and when he got close to one of the groups he asked them to pose for a picture. They refused his request with language that sent him fleeing from the scene in red-necked embarrassment.[21]

A Calgary police sergeant whose duties frequently took him into the brothel areas thought Wilson lucky to have emerged with a whole skin.

"These houses were always a popular attraction for Calgary's curiosity seekers," he said. "It was a popular pastime for them to walk out to South Coulee or Nose Creek on a Sunday afternoon and bait the girls. But the girls gave as good as they got. Some of them were pretty athletic and would collect a pile of stones near where they were standing. Then when the gawkers came along they would shout: 'Aw ye - - - - - - cheap skates if you don't want to - - - - -, - -!' With that they would let fly with their rocks and many a smart aleck went home from a stroll through one of those districts with a sore head he hadn't bargained for."

Showing off Calgary's brothels to the visiting firemen was an entertainment highly esteemed by the populace as long as the houses existed. During the 1920s the girls on Sixth Avenue, on Ninth Avenue, and in the re-established South Coulee brothels quit throwing rocks in favour of making obscene gestures at Sunday strollers who resisted the invitations extended to them from behind the lace curtains on the front-room windows.[22]

As long as Cuddy ran the police department, however, there was no brazenly uninhibited solicitation, indoors or out. In 1912 he convicted 116 operators of houses of ill fame and 267 inmates. Thereafter the figures declined as he began charging the customers found in the brothels as well as the keepers and inmates. By 1916 a change in vice patterns could be discerned from the statistics. There were 90 keepers arrested but only 47 inmates along with 31 pimps — an indication that the women were moving from the brothels to individual enterprise and using procurers to drum up trade.

In his drive to uplift Calgary morals, Chief Cuddy got tremendous assistance, as he always emphasized, from prohibition. He pointed out that the abolition of the bars was serving as a preventative for every type of crime. Arrests for drunkenness dropped by 85 per cent from 1,743 in 1914 to under 200 in 1917. In addition to cutting the strength of his force by a third Cuddy was able to put the men on an eight-hour day and give them two days off a month. It was a far cry from the days of Chief English, when the force had worked twelve hours a day, seven days a week.[23]

Yet in Calgary, as elsewhere, the more proficient the force became, the more tolerant its criminal investigation division grew toward the houses of ill repute, despite Chief Cuddy. The morality squad was charged with enforcement of both the liquor and the morality laws and tended to stay out of other police work. Similarly detectives in other branches intentionally kept clear of the morality field because many of them used information supplied by the women of the houses to solve crimes. The petty crooks, safe crackers, burglars, and common thieves all seemed to develop homing instincts that brought them quickly to the houses of ill fame as soon as they had made an important score. It was not uncommon for them to impress the lights of their evenings with a display of purloined baubles. Many a solid reputation of a city detective had its origin in tips whispered into his ear by a prostitute who wanted to keep in well with the gendarmerie. So while Chief Cuddy and his hard-nosed morality squad were cracking down on the houses of ill fame, the rank and file of the department tended to take a more detached view of prostitution. [24]

The women of ill repute managed to survive both Chief Cuddy and the First World War and were ready for business when the flow of immigrants resumed after the war. But it was a different Calgary to which the new settlers came and a far cry from the wide-open town of the English-Mackie years. Gone were all the bars from Eighth and Ninth avenues, though the city remained a mild refuge for the gambling fraternity. Poker playing was still a popular male pastime and the police had great difficulty making gaming-house charges stick unless they had positive proof that a rake-off was being taken.

By 1921, the brothels had largely been re-established along Ninth Avenue and Sixth Avenue East. The switch in emphasis from sex to liquor made the prostitutes vulnerable to a change in morality squad tactics. After prohibition it was comparatively easy to catch the whores with illegal booze in their possession, and the fines for keeping liquor for sale were far greater than those imposed for prostitution. For the brothel operators, the cost of doing business rose sharply and so did the risk of being caught and heavily fined. As public support of prohibition faded, so did public respect for the police, who still had to enforce the law. The respectable businessmen who had once tarried in the downtown bars at lunch and after work began to patronize regular bootleggers, some of whom were also prostitutes. If these women managed to restrict their clientele and live quietly in the west end, they were seldom bothered by the police. But east of Centre Street was still the teeming slum and hence an area in which circumspection was not usually a characteristic of the patrons of the palaces of pleasure. The drunks became more numerous, noisier, and more troublesome as the years passed, and the police stepped up their efforts against the bootlegging madams. They did so within a community which utterly refused to co-operate.

"There were a couple of places on Ninth Avenue East, real dives, that we wanted to catch with a stock of liquor that would put a severe crimp in their operations," a veteran of the morality squad recalled. "The C.P.R. used to keep its empty freight cars stored on the siding adjacent to Ninth Avenue and not move them for days. So we decided to hide in the freight car opposite these houses and keep watch for the bootlegger making his deliveries. We never caught him. As soon as we got into those box cars, somebody would phone the C.P.R. yard office and pretty soon we'd feel an engine hooking on to pull the cars away. If they got hooked up before we could get the door open and jump out, they'd haul us clear out to the Ogden yards."[25]

Ninth Avenue was the point from which Pearl Miller launched herself into a twenty-five-year reign as Calgary's most famous prostitute. A squat, homely woman given to outlandish use of rouge and make-up, she turned up in Calgary from the interior of British Columbia and worked on Sixth Avenue until she moved into her own house at 526 Ninth Avenue East in 1926 and lived there until 1929. Some time during that period she established a liaison with the son of one of Calgary's most prominent lawyers. He is reported to have walked out on his family to set Pearl Miller up in a fieldstone house on the Macleod Trail south of the Calgary city limits in 1929. The house quickly became the most famous brothel in Calgary but, unlike the houses from which Pearl had graduated, catered to as high-class a trade as it could attract. Oil men en route to Turner Valley and back regularly dropped in for a drink, sex, and quite often a game of bridge with Pearl and her inamorato.

Pearl Miller so prospered catering to the carriage trade that she decided she could do even better with a better location. In 1935 she bought a house at 1813 Ninth Street West on the fringe of Mount Royal, Calgary's poshest residential district. It too was a great life while it lasted and Pearl made it last until 1939 when, as a result of police pressure following persistent complaints from the neighbours, she moved back to 526 Ninth Avenue, where she spent the war years. In 1950, after almost thirty years in the profession, Pearl called it quits, retired, and moved back to her house in Mount Royal. There she became infected with the Pentecostal religion and was soon making regular excursions down to her old Ninth Avenue haunts, not to return to her former profession but to try to rescue the women who were following in her trade. If she happened to be in the neighbourhood after a police raid on one of the brothels, she'd wander up to the jail, pass the time with the jailers, and try to get at the girls while they were in a receptive mood to be reformed.

Pearl Miller died full of years in 1957 in the sure knowledge that she had become a Calgary legend about whom the natives wove their favourite fantasies, and told their biggest lies. The biggest of all was the one long current among members of the Calgary Highlanders, told about members of the Princess Pats and vice versa. Here it is:

> The Pats were camped next to an American outfit before D
> Day and one day the Americans, who were great on
> slogans, tacked one up in the sergeants' mess which read:
> "Remember Pearl Harbor!"
> The Pats went back to their outfit and had a sign painted
> to express their own feelings. It read:
> "To hell with Pearl Harbor
> Remember Pearl Miller!"

The story is obviously a fabrication, though Calgarians can be found who will swear they were there when it happened and saw the sign. Yet the story really ought to be true of a city where the most famous woman in its entire history was the keeper of a common bawdy-house.

Lethbridge and Drumheller: Something more than a House

Isolated as Lethbridge and Drumheller were in remote corners of the Alberta boondocks, it was inevitable that their brothels would develop life styles of their own, in legend if not in fact. What other community, for example, could claim that its gaggle of whorehouses doubled as cultural centres, as Lethbridge's did during the expiring years of Victoria's reign? There, after savouring the primary pleasures of the joints, a young cow hand from the Rio Grande could relax with a good book, and, if necessary, be taught to read by a

155

former schoolteacher turned prostitute. Or he could lean back and enjoy a piano solo by one of the talented bawds, or learn the latest dance steps from a new girl from Wichita via Great Falls, Montana. He might even be instructed in how to spot a crooked card dealer in a poker game, by a girl who had been a faro dealer in Fort Benton. And after a cowboy had blown what was left of his wad in a Round Street gambling joint he might seek shelter from the weather in a bagnio on "The Point" and not be turned away.[1]

The unique character claimed for the Lethbridge brothels was attributed by surviving customers to the cow-hand influence rather than to the coal miners whose industry gave birth to the town. The claim, however, cannot be sustained when tested against the experience of Drumheller, another mining town. Drumheller might never have called its brothels cultural centres, but they were certainly community centres without which its Chamber of Commerce, service clubs, and miners' unions would have been hard put to find congenial surroundings for their meetings. Nevertheless the Lethbridge claims have a certain specious appeal as legends, if not as history.

As a long-retired cow hand recalled it:

When I was a boy growing up in Lethbridge, this was the cattle shipping point for the last great open range that extended from Macleod to Maple Creek. The spring round-ups would extend for hundreds of miles. When the round-up was over the cowboys would be paid off and they went looking for entertainment with pockets full of money.

Cow hands are not like miners. If you have ever been in a mining town on pay day you've seen the miners rushing for the whore houses like an army on the attack. You could often see them lined up outside the front door waiting their turns and they'd be in and out of the joint in a matter of minutes. The cowboys were different. After weeks or even months of nothing but cows, horses and other riders for company, they wanted to enjoy the pleasure of female companionship, to sit and relax and have a drink and listen to talk. Most of all they wanted to take their time doing everything, to string out the enjoyment of whatever they were doing. Because they were never tight with their money the cow hands were given special treatment, and the Lethbridge places that catered to them seemed to be able to attract higher class girls than those at Macleod, or in the Crow's Nest Pass, for example.

As the witness was an old cow hand himself, he was probably prejudiced. Yet others with memories of the early days also insist that Lethbridge brothels were a cut above those at Macleod or Calgary. Certainly, they were palaces of joy in more than the usual sense of the term. The presence of a customer with a good singing voice could trigger a night-long song fest around the piano in which both the inmates and customers joined. Some of the first phonographs in Lethbridge were imported by the madams, and the earliest complaints against the brothels were not about the trade itself but about the boisterous carolling of the customers.

An early resident recalled:

In the early days when I was growing up I don't remember any agitation against the houses on The Point. We lived a block away and I can never remember my mother getting on her high horse about the houses, or their inmates. When you saw the girls on the street you couldn't tell them from anybody else when I was young. They looked just like school teachers, or milliners, or housewives.

Most families kept a cow in those days and we had to take turns driving ours down the coulee past The Point to the Belly River for water. The grass was long in the coulee in summer and we would dawdle on the way up because it was a long climb. The girls would often be out picking flowers or just sitting on the grass and sometimes working around in the gardens of the houses closest to the coulee. I got to know some of them pretty well and on a hot day they often invited me into the kitchen for a glass of lemonade. Sometimes the girls would be sitting around the table playing cards, or just talking. Sometimes they'd be sewing, or doing fancy work. Some of the houses had Chinese house-boys who seemed to do all the chores like washing dishes and waiting on table and serving drinks.

One thing I never forgot was the fancy furniture in one of those houses. It even had a grand piano with a fancy silk shawl draped over the top. It took up most of the living room. Us kids all liked to run messages for the people on

The Point. They always gave us good tips and they sure
were friendly people. They weren't the same kind of
women when I was a boy as the rough characters who came
in later.

It was coal, however, and not cattle that brought the railway to
southern Alberta and turned Lethbridge into a cattle-shipping point.
Prior to the arrival of the railways, the pioneer settlers of southern
Alberta drew their supplies from and had contact with the outside
world only through Fort Benton, Montana. An immense trade was
done in goods that moved up the Missouri River to Fort Benton and
thence by wagon train into Canada by way of Fort Whoop-up, Fort
Macleod, and Fort Walsh. The rich deposits of coal on the Belly
River were known from the first days of Fort Whoop-up. Nicholas
Sheran gave up mule-skinning for coal mining and developed the
mine that supplied the coal which the wagon trains took back to
Fort Benton from Canada.[2]

As the Canadian Pacific Railway pushed west, word of the existence of the coal beds reached the east and Sir Alexander Galt himself came out to investigate. Galt then retained William Stafford to
make a detailed investigation and as a result formed the Northwest
Coal and Navigation Company with £50,000 in capital. It imported
miners to develop the deposits along the Belly River flats, established a settlement of "Coalbanks" on the site, and built a narrow-
gauge railway from what had become Lethbridge to Dunmore south
of Medicine Hat in 1885. It was then in the coal business to stay and
was soon importing miners from Pennsylvania, Nova Scotia, and
far-off Hungary.[3]

By 1890, the mines were pouring out 1,000 tons of coal a day to
power the C.P.R. between Calgary and Regina. The company then
pushed the construction of a narrow-gauge railway line to Great
Falls, Montana, to supply fuel to a new smelter there. Between 1885
and 1890 Lethbridge was the boomingest settlement in the West.
The coal company moved out of the river bed up to the high tableland through which the Belly River flowed. It sank three separate
shafts to replace the horizontal tunnels it had driven in from the level
of the river bed. It was making plans to employ a force of 1,500 men
and in November 1890 recorded a payroll of $55,000. Miners, who

were paid eighty cents a ton for their production, were earning $140 a month.⁴

But burgeoning Lethbridge was also beset with such growing pains that the N.W.M.P. stopped trying to police it from Fort Macleod and established a branch at Lethbridge. The importation of the Hungarian miners gave the Mounties a special problem when the miners quickly found a way around the rigid but largely unenforceable liquor laws of the Territories. As Superintendent R.B. Deane reported in 1887:⁵

> Hop beer is extensively brewed and sold here. So long as it is not adulterated it is not unpalatable, and one would certainly judge it to be harmless. It has, moreover, the advantage of keeping the money in the country.
>
> The Hungarians consume large quantities of it. When they lay themselves out for a day's enjoyment they empty several dozen bottles ($1.50 per dozen) into a tub, sit around and drink and soak their bread in the mixture. On the Sunday of the riot a number of them had been thus drinking in one of their houses the greater part of the day, with the result that by evening many of them were undeniably drunk.
>
> Taken in moderation, this beer is certainly harmless, and it is puzzling to know how a man can swallow enough to get drunk on. Given, however, a man of the required capacity, who deliberately sits down to consume two or three dozen bottles in an evening, it is to the interest of saloon keepers not to serve him beyond a certain point. Two or three Hungarian miners think nothing of drinking sixty or seventy bottles between them in an evening.

Despite the occasional violent accompaniments, the boozing of the Hungarian miners was something the Mounties in southern Alberta could cope with. The Indians were something else. As Superintendent Deane commented in 1887:

> The Indians that have come this way from the Blood Reserve have, on the whole, behaved themselves well. Some few come to work, and work well. Others bring their

women for immoral purposes, and these I have made a
point of sending away as soon as I know of their arrival and
business.[6]

Three years later, Superintendent Deane was still complaining
about the Indians who were using their wives and daughters as
prostitutes:

> The principal trouble with them is in connection with their
> women. For instance, an Indian comes here with his family
> and says he has got work ... He then establishes his women
> kind in the river bottom and thither go all sorts and condi-
> tions of men, not unfrequently provided with whisky
> which answers their purpose better than the cash value
> thereof.[7]

The general attitude of the Mounties toward prostitution was
summarized quite clearly by Deane in an aside in his report. "The
next best thing to abating it is to have it under control." With that
the burghers of Lethbridge found themselves in general agreement
and for the next decade managed to resist all the efforts of uplifters.
Then, as the pressure of the Temperance and Moral Reform Society
became irresistible, a great clean-up campaign was launched under a
new chief of police. It lasted only a few months. The town gradually
drifted back into segregated prostitution, which became a Lethbridge hallmark and its main tourist attraction, between 1920 and
1942.

The first Lethbridge brothels were the teepees the Indians pitched
on the Belly River flats 300 feet below the flatland on which the city
itself was eventually located. However, as the Galt mansion and the
rather elaborate houses of the mine manager and the foremen were
also built on the flats, the Mounties tended to run the Indians off
into the adjacent coulees and away from the settlement. The first
permanent brothels were built in the coulees on the west side of the
river by women who came in from Medicine Hat and Great Falls with
the railway. As employment in the mines expanded, Lethbridge,
except for the prostitutes, grew almost as a town without women.
While a few of the European miners brought wives and children with
them, most of the first settlers were single. The result, according to
legend, was that the river-bottom brothels did a roaring business

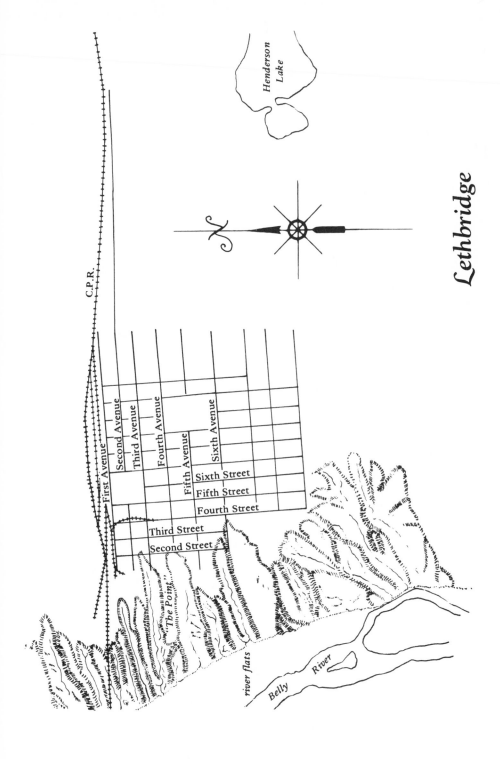

Lethbridge

Henderson Lake

C.P.R.

N

First Avenue
Second Avenue
Third Avenue
Fourth Avenue
Fifth Avenue
Sixth Avenue

Sixth Street
Fifth Street
Fourth Street
Third Street
Second Street

"The Point"

river flats

Belly River

until the coal company began opening up its pits on the area above the river valley.

Two factors combined to put the town of Lethbridge on the tableland high above the river and on the east bank. The railway ended on the east side of the deep Belly River valley, and the best seams of coal were located on the east side of the river. When the coal company built a huge bunkhouse on the flats above the river to serve its single miners, the other miners gradually moved into lodgings close to the upper pit heads.

As their clients moved away, the madams also moved to the top of the hill and established an enclave of brothels on a triangular spit of land on the extreme west side of the settlement. It was flanked on the north by a huge coulee that extended from the river clear up to the back door of the Lethbridge Hotel on Round Street, which later became Fifth Street South. On the south another deep coulee extended from the river almost to Fourth Street. The widest point of this triangle was at Second Street between Third and Fourth avenues.

By 1890 there were six brothels and the coal company dormitory within the triangle which was famous throughout southern Alberta as "The Point".[8] Its gaudily painted two- and three-storey frame houses became the town's most prominent landmark. They could be spotted miles away from almost any direction, day or night. Across the river the prairie was wide open to the Rocky Mountains. When the C.P.R. took over the railway lines and converted them into its Crow's Nest Pass branch, the brothels were the first sight of Lethbridge that travellers got as they crossed the famous high-level bridge. Winter or summer, the friendly lights of The Point were beacons for late-arriving travellers from the west, the north, and the south.

When the cow hands were in town the houses on The Point went on round-the-clock shifts. This caused the matron of the nearby isolation hospital to complain that her patients were being kept awake by the sounds of revelry being wafted eastward, and by the whooping and hollering of the revellers as they careened off Fifth Street onto Third Avenue headed for The Point.[9] The brothels that stayed on the river flats survived as sort of minor-league farms for the *casas di malaffare* at The Point. Girls who ran afoul of the law in Lethbridge, or fell out of favour otherwise, gravitated to The

Bottoms. Other newly arriving girls found employment in The Bottoms while they were negotiating their way into the plusher establishments in the upper town.

Finding satisfactory employment in Lethbridge was more difficult for new prostitutes than it was elsewhere. Once a girl was settled on The Point she tended to stay put. Working conditions were good. From the beginning the police saw to it that no pimps moved in to knock the girls around.[10] Their customers were generous and usually pleasant and girls with an idea of picking up a husband found suitors plentiful.

A factor limiting employment on The Point was the cramped terrain which restricted the number of houses the area could accommodate. As the town grew toward city status, the trade gradually expanded eastward into houses along Second and Third streets as they were vacated by prospering business and professional men moving into more commodious quarters to the southeast. The railway tracks, the station, and the railway shops were the first northern boundary of the city, and the first business development hugged the south side of the tracks. To the north the settlement of Staffordville clustered around the pit head of Number 3 mine. Because of the overwhelming predominance of men, First Avenue and Second Avenue were given over largely to lodging houses. Fifth Street developed as the main business thoroughfare, though several two-storey business buildings were going up across the square from the station on Third Avenue. There was at least one hotel, one livery stable, and a poolroom in each block in the downtown core. Until the mines were affected by a depression in 1894 the influx of miners made the town the most cosmopolitan in Alberta. The "No Mail Today" sign which was hung frequently in the post office was in eight different languages — French, German, Slavic, Hungarian, a dialect of Hungarian, Danish, Italian, and Chinese.[11]

The steam went out of the Lethbridge boom in the mid nineties as coal mines were developed in the Crow's Nest Pass and Banff areas, and the population changed with the economy. Many of the Central European miners drifted westward and their places were taken by an influx of middle-class settlers from Ontario and the United States. Polyglot Lethbridge was gradually transformed into Anglo-Saxon Lethbridge. By the turn of the century the moral climate of frontier Lethbridge was beginning to chill. It was a change that was accentuated by the arrival of a steady stream of stiff-necked Mormons, Baptists, and Mennonites.

Upon its incorporation as a town in 1891, Lethbridge outfitted itself with the usual complement of licensing regulations with which to hector its citizens. It also hired Corporal Lewis away from the Mounted Police as combined police chief and licence inspector, in charge of just about everything. He issued licences of all kinds, collected fees, ran the pound, chased dogs and stray cows, policed the garbage dump, and tried to keep the wide-open gambling under some sort of control. Looking over his shoulder as he went about his work was a gradually expanding army of moral uplifters centring in the Protestant churches.

At the head of the forces of righteousness was the Reverend Charles McKillop, the leading Presbyterian of the district. Enforcement of the law against prostitution was a responsibility of the North West Mounted Police. But getting the Mounties to take action against the houses on The Point seemed beyond even the persuasive powers of Dr. McKillop. So in 1898 the reformers convinced the town council it should have its own by-law. The councillors passed By-Law 94, which provided that no person within the town limits could "keep a bawdy house, house of ill-fame or disorderly house" on pain of a fine of fifty dollars or thirty days in jail. It further provided that "anyone not being a bona fide resident of a bawdy house" found on the premises would be liable to a twenty-dollar fine or ten days. It did not define what constituted being a "bona fide resident of a bawdy house".[12]

Once safely enacted, By-Law 94 was filed carefully and ignored. From his combination jail and licence office at the corner of Second Avenue and Fourth Street, Corporal Lewis could look down Fourth Street to the corner of Fourth Avenue, where "Swede" Alice was operating the largest brothel in town. Located as it was two blocks east of the entrance to The Point, it was strategically placed to catch both the impatient and the misdirected. A half a block away, but just out of sight, was Cowboy Jack's, an equally imposing structure which catered mainly to the cattlemen and was Lethbridge's most famous bordello.[13] Cowboy Jack was a woman whose real name is lost to history, and not even the oldsters who remember her place could suggest how she acquired the masculine nickname. They only recall that there was either an irrigation ditch or a horse trough in front of her place into which drunken cowboys were frequently deposited by playful friends.

The cowboys' playfulness frequently got out of hand, and by 1899 the *Lethbridge News* was agitating for the stationing of more Mounties in the town. It naturally blamed the rowdiness on the "foreigners".[14]   At the next annual meeting of the town the Reverend Charles McKillop arose to demand that the town constable take action to see that the bars closed at 11 p.m. instead of staying open until all hours in violation of licence regulations. That, said the constable, was not his job. It was up to the territorial liquor inspector. Well, said the reverend clergyman, what about the Chinese laundries that were operating on Sunday, the drunks and rowdies on the streets, and the stores staying open after hours? Corporal Lewis said the hell with it, and quit.

The town ran through several replacements for Corporal Lewis as its population grew from 1,500 in 1895 to 3,000 in 1903. In the summer of 1903 the first step was taken to enforce By-Law 94, although, through the years, the houses on The Point had been raided periodically and minor fines had been imposed, for disorderliness more than for anything else. However, the existence of brothels outside the segregated area at The Point was beginning to create public uneasiness. The *Lethbridge News* report of the town council meeting of August 6, 1903, said:

> The question of getting rid of houses of questionable character was brought up and it was unanimously decided that it was about time something was done. Their continuation in the present location was the cause of serious deterioration in the value of other property and a source of danger as recent fires have testified. The sentiment of the town was that they should be put out.
>
> It was ordered that the inspector be instructed to give notice to all occupants of houses of ill repute that after September 1, By-Law 94 will be strictly enforced. This By-Law provides for a fine of $50 or 30 days for keeping a house of this description. Also [the *News* added warningly] for fining or imprisoning of frequenters.

At the meeting of the town council a month later, the *News* reported:

Representation were made on behalf of certain persons who have been requested to leave their present quarters, asking that no action be taken until October 1, as they were expecting to secure property outside the town and expected to move out by that date. Council decided that it could not give formal consent to the request but it was understood that acquiescence would be given.

The madam in question built a handsome new house well outside the eastern town limits near Henderson Lake, where she prospered mightily with a sort of halfway house for farmers coming into Lethbridge from the east. The house was still doing business twenty years later and it is generally believed to have burned down during the depression.

The episode raised an interesting question. How does a community run people out of town who are property owners and taxpayers? It does not, of course; so the houses on The Point which were owned by the madams continued in business, albeit in a somewhat more restrained fashion than before. The council, however, kept up appearances. In July 1904 it replaced By-Law 94 with By-Law 195, which was identical in form except that all the penalties were doubled. By this time Lethbridge was beginning to think about moving from town to city status. It expanded its police force to three men and seems to have made a mild attempt in 1904 and 1905 to bring prostitution under control. On June 19, 1905, the *News* contained this curious letter to the editor:

> Who was the town councillor who on Tuesday last, in the afternoon, acted as house agent for a Jap of the female persuasion, and did he find her a house? Our former councils have put their feet down firmly on the brothel traffic. What will the present council say about their member's behavior?
>
> [signed] One who knows.

Three weeks later the *News* provided a partial answer: "The Yellow Peril has been averted in Lethbridge! The oriental lady (?) who took business premises here sometime ago has been requested to move on."

Where she moved to was probably across the river to the old

brothel area in the coulees where the Japanese prostitutes were concentrated. As an old-timer recalled: "The Japs were favorites with the Fifth Street gamblers. You'd often hear them throw down their cards in disgust and say, 'I'm going over to the Japs and change my luck.' " In Calgary and Edmonton it was the Negro prostitutes to whom the unlucky gamblers repaired.

The mild police pressure applied in 1905 and 1906 did water down the ministerial agitation. The city's population was again expanding rapidly with the development of irrigation and the settlement of the farm lands in the neighbourhood. While the influx naturally brought in the usual quota of women of ill repute, the police tended to divert them into the Belly River flats, where they had only the tolerant Mounties to worry about. Within the city itself, wide-open gambling supplanted prostitution as the dominating concern of the forces of righteousness. The *Lethbridge Herald* thundered periodically against the gambling evil but the police, like the public, had long since become reconciled to living with a problem they could not eradicate. It was an attitude which prevailed toward prostitution as well when Joe Gillespie, a retired Mounted Police sergeant, was made chief of police in 1905. He was barely settled in his office before Dr. W.S. Galbraith was elected mayor at the head of a reform ticket. An implacable foe of prostitution, Dr. Galbraith nudged the council into putting up a $250 slush fund for the suppression of all forms of vice and immorality.[15]

The police and licence departments still operated as a unit and, as it had done from its inception, the Lethbridge council expected its police department to operate at a profit. So there were periodic raids of the houses on The Point and nominal fines were assessed to balance the budget. This seemed to satisfy Dr. Galbraith and keep the department on the right side of the ledger. But events were building which would ultimately bring the whole system clattering down. The first seeds of the destruction of their way of life were sown by the women of The Point. Being hived away by themselves was all right when business was booming. But in the quiet stretches between the miners' paydays, cowboy invasions, and local celebrations, life in the brothels tended to pall on the inmates. To lift the flagging spirits of their help the Lethbridge madams took to plying them with little surprises. After a good weekend, for example, Ethel Fuller or May Howard might drop into one of the Fourth Avenue millinery stores and order new hats for all her girls. The next time it might be a fancy waist, or ornamental combs, or pieces of costume jewelery. Such patronage was as much appreciated by the merchants as the gifts were by the girls. But the practice posed a problem. What good was the new finery to the girls unless they had some place to wear it? [16]

Soon Lethbridge was being treated day and night to the sight of the *filles de joie* in all their finery parading along Fifth Street and Third Avenue. And finery it was, since, except for the money the ambitious were saving for brothels of their own, most of the girls' earnings were spent on clothes. They could afford the finest, and they went abroad attired in the gaudy best Lethbridge or Sears-Roebuck in Great Falls could offer. Naturally the resentment of the ladies of the town mushroomed. Soon their own shopping excursions were followed by irate protests to their pastors at having to rub elbows in the stores "with *them*".

In the spring of 1909 the Temperance and Moral Reform Society, which was by now a force in Lethbridge, was moved to action. It circulated a petition with the following preamble:

> To the Mayor and Aldermen of the City of Lethbridge
> Gentleman: —
>   We the undersigned residents of this city wish to present to your notice the following petition: —
>
> Whereas it is a matter of common knowledge that certain houses of ill-fame are said to exist in our city notably in the vicinity of the Isolation Hospital and Galt Hospital such a state of affairs we consider to be a disgrace to our city.
>
> Therefore we would hereby petition you to do all in your power toward closing up such houses and suppressing the social evil to the full extent of your legal power.

The petition was signed by all the leading citizens of the town.

Dr. Galbraith, the former mayor, was spokesman for the group before council and he made a passionate plea on behalf of respectable Lethbridge to have the women run out of town. It was wrong to call prostitution a necessary evil, he said. It was not necessary; and it was untrue that segregated prostitution prevented the spread of disease. The so-called medical supervision of the brothels was a farce. So was the effectiveness of police supervision. In any event the existence of the brothels on The Point was a menace to business, a nuisance to the nearby hotels, and a disgrace to the respectable people trying to raise their families in the neighbourhood. The petitioners applauded Dr. Galbraith and then took their seats to fix baleful eyes upon their elected representatives as they confronted the great moral issue before them.[17] Drafting a motion to reject the petition without antagonizing the petitioners was not easy. Here is the first draft: "That the council receive the petition from the residents re houses of ill-fame and regret to say that they cannot at present see any way to interfere with the conditions and in no way countenance the present location; that they will see if something can be done to remove them from their present position."

That motion was lost and the aldermen tried again with this one: "That the council receive the petition of the Moral Reform League and regret to say they cannot suggest any remedy at present for the state of affairs supposed to exist, but that the matter will have consideration in due course." It was carried by three to two.

True to its word, the council did consider the matter in due course. It sent Joe Gillespie to call on all the brothels with the orders that from now on "landladies and girls are forbidden to appear on the streets of Lethbridge except on Tuesdays and Fridays between two and five o'clock in the afternoons."[18]

Chief Gillespie, by the end of 1909, headed a police department of nine men and two detectives. He assumed, no doubt, that it would be good public relations if he and Detectives Pat Egan and L. Silliker assumed direct responsibility for supervising the brothel business. Any one of them would have been enough to put the fear of the law into the most brazen brothel keeper. Detective Silliker was 6'6", weighed 275 pounds, and had the strength to go with the frame. Detective Egan was a graduate of the Klondike school of law enforcement which operated on the principle that no suspect of a crime had any rights a law-enforcement officer necessarily had to respect. Most of the morality work fell to Egan. He set up a regular system to insure that all the women had health examinations weekly. Those who failed their exams were run out of town.

The one aspect of prostitution about which Chief Gillespie was wariest was the intrusion of procurers into the trade. Procurers who blew into town with their women were cooled off in the police cells while they waited for the next train out. If they came back they had either Silliker or Egan to confront, and the legendary Egan was nobody to trifle with. He was reputed to have once shot the heels off a football player who refused to obey instructions to get out of town. But Gillespie was more of a father-figure to the whores than a cop to be feared. His sympathies were all with them and he was clearly distressed by the way in which society handled its prostitute problem. The following year, at the tail end of another Temperance and Moral Reform uprising, he allowed his humanity to boil over in public. [19]

"We have been having a very difficult spring," he said. "For weeks the city has been overrun with drifters of the worst kind and we have had a difficult time keeping them on the move. We have been plagued with tinhorns and hangers-on of unfortunate women who we have run out of town as soon as they arrive."

"Several unfortunate women drifted into town and took up abode in cheap rooming houses. When we got on to them we ordered them out of town. But all these unfortunates had been driven out of other cities. What good does it do for one city to drive these poor women into another city only for them to be driven out again? The system is wrong. Some day I hope to see . . . an effort made by every city to look after its own unfortunates instead of hounding them from one city to another."

Chief Gillespie's concern was in sharpest contrast with the attitude of the Temperance and Moral Reform leaguers who were in full cry again in the spring of 1910.[20] The Reverend T.P. Perry kicked off the crusade at a "clean-up-our-city" meeting in the Wesley Methodist church. A meeting of the Knox Presbyterian Men's Club then heard lengthy harangues about the "social evil" and unanimously passed the following resolution:

1. The meeting urges the city council to do away with the Red Light district and the evils of prostitution as a menace and a disgrace.
2. That the police be given hearty support in suppressing all houses of prostitution.
3. That all possible help be given to the unfortunate women toward the leading of a pure and virtuous life.

The delegation that carried this epistle to the city council was headed by the Reverend Alex Gordon for the Presbyterians, the Reverend Perry for the Methodists, and the Reverend A.J. Prosser for the Baptists.

The spokesmen blasted the city for allowing the brothels to be located in the poorest district of the city. As if the poor people didn't have enough trouble, they had to live in the midst of segregated brothels. Why, the Reverend Perry wanted to know, did they always inflict segregated brothels on the poor? If they were determined to retain the system, why not locate the houses in the better-class districts among the well-to-do? Besides, he said, it was impossible to cater to the spiritual needs of the women as long as they were herded together in a segregated district.

E.A. Cunningham, a local merchant, took a different line. It was he said, bad for business to tolerate prostitution. Young men who came under the evil influence of these women stole money from their employers to satisfy their base desires.

The members of council gave as much as they took.

"Why do you people keep coming before us empty handed?" Mayor Ian Adams wanted to know. "Suppose we close down these houses. What is to become of these unfortunate women? Now if you people would come here and say that you wanted to build a home for these women so that they could be restored to respectable society, I am sure we would all support you. But where is your Christianity when you come forward only with the request that we push the women farther down the path to ruin?"

Alderman Bowman defended the Lethbridge system as the best in the country. It was up to the churches, he said, to put out a helping hand to the women. It was up to the clergy to combat the causes of prostitution. It was cruel simply to be content to drive the women out of town. Alderman Frayne said any attempt to get rid of prostitution by closing the segregated area could not succeed. The women would be scattered throughout the city, and it was a well-known fact that the problem was worse where there was no segregation.

The clergymen launched an immediate counterattack. Mr. Perry said that he had the word of the resident captain of the Salvation Army that the women were beyond redemption. He saw the problem as a very simple one. The council could order the women to reform or oust them from the city if they refused. The Reverend Prosser came to Perry's support with all oratorical guns blazing. Summaries of his speech that survive can give no adequate picture of this sacrosanct zealot's attitude. But one can easily picture him as a Biblical prophet calling down fire and brimstone on Sodom and Gomorrah at The Point, or as a Puritan divine preparing to whip a harlot into outer darkness.

"How dare you try to foist the responsibility onto us?" he thundered. "We are under no responsibility to do anything! It is up to you to enforce the law for you have no right under the law to permit a segregated area of houses of ill fame to exist! You say things will be worse if the houses are closed. I say close these houses and drive these evil women from our city, and then if you are correct, the law can be changed!"

Once again the council stood firm against the demands of the moral reformers. Mayor Adams, however, did work out a compromise plan which he hoped would ease the problem. They would force the madams to paint their houses in more subdued colours. The streets leading into The Point would be better lighted. A policeman would be placed on patrol in the area. No more houses would be permitted to go into business and no more prostitutes would be permitted to come into Lethbridge.[21]

The Reverend Prosser had only contempt for the proposals. Some months later he enlisted a policeman for a guide and made a tour of The Point. They located six houses, in which there were twenty-two inmates, six servant women, six Chinese servants, and four Negresses. "All the inmates," he said, "were from outside Lethbridge, all were the most hardened types and, 'to top it all,' most of them were aliens!" "Enforce the law! Drive them out of the city!" thundered the Reverend Prosser. He pointed out in passing that there had not been a single prosecution of an inmate for two years.[22]

As Mayor Adams had noted the previous year, the Lethbridge Temperance and Moral Reform officials were not notably flowing with Christian forgiveness.

Curiously enough it was not prostitution but booze that temporarily ended segregated prostitution and speeded the doom of The Point. By 1912 Lethbridge had become a city of almost 10,000 and the body politic was turning its attention from booze and prostitution. It was in the throes of installing and expanding sewer and water systems, planting trees like mad, paving streets here and there, extending its boundaries, and trying desperately to go as deeply into debt as it could to finance all this expansion. Besides, the reverend clergy were also expanding their services with fancy new churches in the newer residential districts far removed from The Point. In any event, the moral reformers seemed to run out of steam after the 1910 confrontation, and both The Point and the houses on Third Street and on First Avenue ran, more or less, wide openly. Into this scene in 1912 stepped Inspector Robert Nimmons of the Alberta Liquor Licence Board to lay charges against the brothels under the Liquor Act. When Lulu Hill was fined $100 for selling liquor illegally in her brothel, Nimmons noted for the press that this made $2,500 in liquor fines that had been collected in the previous six months. He pointed out that his enforcement of the liquor laws was largely undertaken without the co-operation of the city police, and as a result of complaints over increasing rowdiness in the abodes of the demimondaines.[23]

The *Lethbridge Herald*, which was then being published next door to The Point, bestirred itself editorially to demand to know what was going on in The Point. "Where," it asked, "are the police when teen-aged boys are permitted to buy liquor illegally, and carouse around the streets?"

Chief Gillespie's answer was to raid The Point, and "five soiled doves from the Tenderloin", as the *Herald* described them, were charged with selling liquor to minors. The offenders were identified as May Howard, Daisy Martin, Ethel Parker, Corrine Lewis, and Rose Russell. When the case came to trial, however, Ethel Parker was the only one prosecuted.

In the meantime, the newspaper agitation about drunken teen-agers continued to a point where Frankie Berry, one of The Point's "soiled doves", took pen in hand for a blistering reply to the *Herald* editor. Not only were the boys not getting booze in the brothels, but they were not even permitted in them, she wrote. What they were doing was getting tanked up outside the area with booze supplied by respectable Lethbridge citizens, and then coming into The Point, whooping and hollering like a bunch of young Indians, and creating a disturbance when they were prevented from entering the brothels.[24] There must have been sound basis for Frankie's protest because the case against Ethel Parker was dismissed for lack of convincing proof when it came to trial.

The uproar over the teen-agers brought a long-simmering feud within the police department to a head. By 1912, Chief Gillespie had headed the force for seven years, which was well above the average tenure of chiefs of police in Alberta in that era. His two trusty lieutenants, Egan and Silliker, went to the Police and Licence Committee with charges against Gillespie. He replied with countercharges against them. On August 1, the city council in secret session suspended Chief Gillespie and fired Egan and Silliker. Then it held another meeting, re-instated both detectives, and then suspended them along with the Chief and asked for a judicial inquiry into the police department.

While the auditors went to work on the police station books, the court clerk resigned. Judge Roland Winters was named to conduct the investigation into a number of charges against Gillespie, including taking money from bawdy-house keepers, being drunk on duty, drinking in bars, and using obscene language in public.

Into Judge Winter's court that summer trooped a half-dozen madams to testify about contributions they made to the Chief. Two members of his staff testified they had gone collecting for the Chief. But collecting for what? It was quickly revealed that Gillespie had been using the brothel owners to finance charity for which there was no other source of funds. According to Sergeant Bill Lamb, who later became the Lethbridge truant officer, Chief Gillespie had reduced charitable solicitation to a simple system. When some hardship case came up, he would send Lamb around with a note to selected brothels for donations. Thus when an aged man suffering from an incurable disease turned up, the residents of the *lupanars* contributed twenty dollars to finance his journey home. Similarly, young women in trouble often were rescued by the generosity of the brothel owners who were tapped by Chief Gillespie. [25]

The generosity of the whores of the West was more than a legend; it was a well-documented fact. A pioneer C.P.R. company doctor recalled that in times of disaster it was always the local prostitutes who were first on hand to succour the sufferers or the survivors. It was an era when whole towns frequently were wiped out by fire, when train wrecks happened almost on schedule, between such monumental calamities as the Frank Slide of 1903 and the Hillcrest mine disaster of 1914. Whether it was to shelter orphans, nurse the wounded, or donate money, the authorities recognized that when the crunch came they could always count on the bordello residents. Thus in Lethbridge, when the Salvation Army was confronted with a special sort of crisis, the Chief himself escorted the Sally Ann lady around to the brothels for donations. Ethel Parker and May Howard, who ran houses at The Point, testified to making a number of donations. Helen Howard, who ran a brothel at 218 First Avenue, a block east of the brewery, confirmed making payments but insisted that she had never paid anything for Chief Gillespie himself. [26]

Clearly the madams knew the Chief well and liked him. He frequently dropped in for a drink with them and they were obviously most reluctant to incriminate him. Gillespie, however, had been a very poor bookeeper. Whenever anybody came in to take out a licence or pay a fine, the money was dropped in the drawer of his desk. The auditor found discrepancies in his petty cash records.

In his report, Judge Winters largely exonerated Gillespie of the charges against him. He did find that the Chief had taken money from the brothel keepers although he had solicited them for charitable donations. The judge urged that

> the police be instructed that under no circumstances are they to apply to keepers of houses of ill-fame for pecuniary or other donations to charitable causes. Such a proceeding savours of blackmail and opens the door for unscrupulous officers to obtain money for his private ends. [27]

The city council on September 16 fired Gillespie with one month's pay and dumped Silliker and Egan on the spot, for what reason no one took the trouble to explain.

Chief Gillespie's immediate successor, William Davis, lasted less than a year. During that time he conducted a series of raids which closed The Point forever but, in scattering its denizens all over the city, made the problem very much worse. By the end of The First World War, Lethbridge had grown tired of prostitution without segregation. Dr. James Lovering, who had been chairman of the police committee when Davis closed The Point, stated publicly that he had come to the conclusion that a system of limited toleration of prostitution in segregated areas was best. [28] With the closing of The

Point there had been a serious rise in venereal disease and requests for abortions. Dr. Lovering recommended strict medical supervision of the segregated brothels. Letters to the editor began to appear in support of segregation. A resident of the north side protested that "after the moral reformers closed the segregated area we are all living in it."

It was under Chief James Harris, who had a brief fling at the job in 1920, that Pat Egan returned to the force. *De facto* segregation had already re-established itself in Lethbridge as the prostitutes took over Third Street and First Avenue. Egan restored the trade to the *status quo ante* William Davis. He re-established and rigidly enforced a system of regularly scheduled medical inspections, ordered the women off the streets, laid down strict rules of decorum for the operation of the houses, and ushered in the golden age of prostitution in Lethbridge. [29]

The extension in the 1920s of the business district southward from the railway tracks along Fourth, Fifth, Sixth, and Seventh streets and on Third and Fourth avenues eastward tended to cut Third Street off from the main residential areas. The effect was to remove a prime cause of complaint from the moral reformers about The Point — that the trade was carried on in full view of the respectable population. In the 1920s and 1930s Third Street, Lethbridge, became to southern Alberta what Annabella Street was for Manitoba, a magnet for all single settlers off on a spree.

A veteran policeman who came to the Lethbridge force while Pat Egan was still there recalled growing up in Lethbridge and delivering papers to the houses on Third Street in the late 1920s.

> I had the best route in town and made twice as much money as any of the other carriers. It was a rather peculiar route because I never knew how many papers I'd sell. If I was making deliveries when a house was full I might sell as many as a dozen papers. Often one of the girls would meet me at the door and take a bundle of papers and sell them for me. She seldom sold them for the regular nickel, however, sometimes she would sell them for a quarter a piece.

Years later, when he became a member of the police force, his path crossed those of the women from the brothels who had made the conversion to respectable society. Their secret was safe with him. Fond memories of his boyhood experience as a newsboy on Third Street made it so.[30]

Third Street itself survived until 1942 when, like other segregated areas across the prairies, it succumbed to the pressures of wartime, never to arise again. Third Street, however, never developed the character The Point had had and that fact alone demolishes the legend that it was the cowboys who converted the brothels into cultural centres. Cattlemen still abounded in southern Alberta long after houses on The Point were torn down or burned down. But they made no lasting character imprint on Third Street. On the other hand, it could hardly have been coincidence that the miners of Drumheller turned the brothels they patronized into establishments similar to those which the miners of Lethbridge had patronized on The Point.

Because it was the last-born of the prairie cities, Drumheller perhaps could have been expected to develop many of the characteristics of a youngest child of a large family. Certainly it was the wildest town on the prairies, and one in which politics, crime, vice, and business were linked in Chicago-type relationships. In Drumheller a town policeman shot a prisoner in a jail cell in 1926 and was acquitted. It was the only city in Alberta in which the Ku Klux Klan got a foothold, in 1927, drawing strongly for support from the Anglo-Saxons in the population. So wide open was gambling in the town that it attracted the malign interest of a specialist in card marking. When his manipulations were exposed by the editor of the *Drumheller Mail*, an attempt was made on the editor's life.[31]

Until coal was discovered in commercial quantities and the first big mine opened in 1911, Drumheller was not even a good-sized village. Then one mine quickly led to a dozen others. The railways came in and transformed the town overnight into a transportation, commercial, and distribution centre. The population of the immediate Drumheller district expanded from nearly nothing to upwards of 12,000 within five years. Drumheller itself never got much above small-town size though it did achieve the legal status of a city. The 1921 Census gave it barely 2,000 in population, which was made up mostly of railroaders, mine-operating personnel as distinct from coal miners, and the owners and employees of the hotels, all-night restaurants, gambling joints, general stores, poolrooms, and brothels. In short, it was the shopping centre and fun capital of the Red Deer River Valley.

On one count Drumheller was fortunate in being born late. The previous decade of mass migration had brought in large numbers of coal miners from eastern Europe, the English midlands, the eastern United States, and the Maritimes. So there were lots of experienced miners in the West, though many of them chose to go homesteading or to settle into better jobs in the cities and towns. The collapse of the construction boom in 1913, however, threw thousands of unemployed onto the labour market and the Drumheller mines were able to staff up from a wide choice of applicants. Mostly they chose Poles, Ukrainians, and Hungarians for the bull work underground, and English midlanders and Americans for the shift-boss and straw-boss jobs. In doing so they laid the foundation for years of industrial strife between the "white men" and the despised "bohunks" in the pits and in the mineworkers' union.

The ratio of males to females in the Drumheller valley in the period between 1912 and 1919 was probably higher than in any other district in the West at that time. The overwhelming proportion of the miners were single, and lived mainly in rough company dormitories or in rougher shacks clustered around the pit heads that dotted the valley for a distance of a dozen miles. As the mine operators' main concern was to keep the men digging steadily at the coal faces, they actively discouraged establishment of boozeries within walking distance of the mines. As a result, the miners stayed close to their diggings between paydays. On paydays, they stormed into the gambling joints, bars or bootleggers, and brothels of Drumheller.

In none of this was Drumheller different from other mining towns in Alberta or British Columbia. What made it unique were the uncommon qualities of two of the valley's most famous madams, Fanny Ramsley and Mary Roper. By the time they got to Drumheller after the outbreak of The First World War, both women were well past the age of active participation in their trade. They were, however, women of considerable competence, for they brought sufficient resources to Drumheller to erect houses that would have been ornaments to much larger communities.

Mary Roper's place was at Rosedale along the road where the penitentiary now stands. She drew her custom not only from the Rosedale miners but from employees of the Wayne and East Coulee mines as well. Her house, like Fanny's, was as much a community centre as a brothel. It contained a very large living room with a piano, and on quiet nights between paydays the miners could sit around, play cards, or dance as the spirit moved them. Paydays at Mary's was something else again. Ordinarily she kept five or six regular girls in her place but on paydays it was usual for her to bring out from five to ten extra helpers from Drumheller.

When the use of extra help was mentioned, it naturally raised a question about how the brothels in Drumheller itself were able to release their girls on payday to help out with the rush at Mary's. An old time Drumhellerite offered the following explanation:

> The big problem at both places was in keeping the girls from running off and marrying the customers. Among the early settlers there was not all that much prejudice against taking prostitutes as wives. As a matter of plain truth, women out of brothels who married those miners or homesteaders got all the worst of it. Look at it this way. They lived lives of reasonable comfort; the whore houses were certainly not palaces by any means but most of them were at least a long cut above the kind of shacks the homesteaders and miners lived in. For another thing, the girls had plenty of time to themselves. They could sit around and do fancy work, or read, or tend a garden, or keep chickens or even fool around making fancy cookies. And they could dress in the finest clothes any store in Drumheller could stock.
>
> Now look at it from the miner's point of view, or the homesteader's because one was as bad as the other. They lived mostly in miserable shacks they had built themselves. They cooked their own meals, made their own beds, if they were ever made, and lived lives of deadly and unnatural loneliness. Just to have somebody besides another miner around to talk to, or fight with, would have been worth any price at times.
>
> There you have the woman's side and the man's side. Now why on earth would any self-respecting whore change her place for that of a wife of a miner or homesteader? They had to be out of their minds! They would be giving up a life of ease and comfort for lives of deprivation and hardship you could hardly describe. My God, most of

those homesteaders' houses would have made inferior pig
sties. And those miners' shacks! They'd give you claustro-
phobia just looking at them from outside. What in the
name of God did either of them have to offer? Nothing but
lives of drudgery. But those damn fool women took up the
offers often enough that they kept the average age of the
women in the brothels at well below 25 years. At least
that's my guess. And they also kept Fanny and Mary
forever on the lookout for new girls. I don't know, but my
guess is that this was the way things were in all the other
red light districts of the West.

Which brings me back to the question of the part time
help. My guess is that they were simply Drumheller housewives going back to work in the brothels to make a few
extra dollars to buy shoes or something for their kids.

Regardless of where the extra girls came from, there was seldom a
large enough staff to keep up with the demand at Mary's when the
mines were going full blast. The line-up outside Mary's door usually
began to form early on payday afternoons and there are Drumheller
legends that Mary was still working on a backlog of day-shifters
when the night shift came to call.

Both Fanny's and Mary's places were built on the same general
plan, though Mary's was somewhat larger. The living room might
well have been a dance hall originally for it was at least thirty feet
square and took up almost half the floor space of the house. The rest
was taken up by half a dozen bedrooms on two sides of the dance
hall, separated from it by a corridor. Fanny's house was located in a
coulee a third of a mile or so east of the bottom of the south hill, and
by reason of its location drew a somewhat different clientele than
Mary's place.

Fanny employed a coloured cook named Mamie Carter who was
not only the best cook in the valley but a talented pianist as well.
When the mine operators, the miners' union, the Legion, or the Elks
were having a convention or get-together of any kind, they would
inevitably arrange for a dinner and a night of fun at Fanny's. Fanny
herself would preside at the bar. Mamie would fix the meal, play the
piano for the dancing, and fill the house with music during the
lengthy intermissions.

As with Mary's, Fanny's place was used as a community club by the miners in their off hours. Neither place worried about liquor laws before or during prohibition and always had drinks available for their customers. Because the main gambling joint in the Alexander Hotel catered to the "white" trade, many miners preferred to do their poker-playing at Fanny's or Mary's. There they could at least be sure that the cards that were costing them their pay were unmarked and honestly dealt.

Because both brothels were outside the Drumheller town limits, neither Mary nor Fanny had any trouble with the local police, and the Mounties or provincial liquor police raided them only following serious complaints. The pattern which the proceedings followed created suspicions in Drumheller that some of the complaints against the brothels might well have come from hard-up defence lawyers. The brothels would be raided, and the madams would appear in court, plead not guilty, and be convicted and fined. Then the lawyers would appeal the conviction and win a reversal when the case came before a higher-court judge.

"The judge knew better than to let a conviction stand against Fanny," a cynical old-timer recalled. "If he did she would never have allowed him in her place again, which meant banishment for life to the downtown hotels!"

Despite such vicissitudes as venal lawyers, strong-arm thugs, and prolonged mine strikes, Mary and Fanny demonstrated great staying qualities in Drumheller. They came in with the boom and were still there when the icy hand of the depression fastened itself on Drumheller and the West. When business dropped off to near nothing at the outbreak of the war, both women closed their houses and were swallowed up by the silences of time.

Requiem
for an Era

Despite periodic eruptions of moral indignation on the subject of prostitution, the fundamental and enduring concern of the Temperance and Moral Reform Society was the liquor problem. For generations drunkenness had been a blot on the social fabric of North America and vigorous campaigns for the total prohibition of beverage alcohol were going strong in Massachusetts in the 1820s. The movement spread into Canada and there were Canadian Temperance societies in existence when the West entered Confederation.

182

As one historian has said, "Prohibition and Temperance sentiment as a social force entered the Northwest Territories in the intellectual and spiritual baggage of successive waves of immigrants who flooded into the west between 1870 and 1915."[1] There is little question that it was the intense concern of the Protestant clergymen about the social wreckage caused by excessive boozing that directed their attention to the "social evil" of prostitution.

The western Canada to which the settlers came was a hard-working country where the young blades established their manhood by demonstrating an ability to lift the heaviest weight, pull the heaviest load, ride the wildest horse or break the roughest team, work the longest hours, strike the hardest blow, or, most important, drink the most whisky. The highest compliment one man could pay another was to concede that he held his liquor like a man, or to recognize that he could drink another under the table. Bellying up to the bar was a preferred preliminary to almost every type of male activity. All manner of community affairs started and finished with booze. A water bucket filled with whisky, which was drunk "straight" from a tin dipper at the end of each inning, could turn a neighbourhood baseball game into a free-for-all brawl.

When workers habitually headed into the nearest saloon with their month's wages on payday, hunger and privation for wives and children commonly resulted. In the aftermath of payday debauches, terrorized wives and children ran to their neighbours or their pastor for protection from berserk husbands. It was small wonder that the incoming clergymen mounted temperance crusades upon their arrival in the West.

As a general rule the brothels were regarded more as adjuncts to the liquor trade than as independently functioning instruments of Satan. Without the aphrodisiacal impact of whisky on the moral fibre of Canadian manhood it was believed the brothels and their inmates would cease to be a problem to anybody. If the liquor traffic could be abolished, all other social problems would disappear with it. It was the credo of the proliferating temperance organizations that crimes of passion and violence, crimes against property and morality, the loss of womanly virtue, and the destruction of family life could all be blamed on alcohol. Ergo, wipe out the liquor traffic and the slate would be left clean.[2]

Yet, despite the preference elsewhere for total prohibition campaigns, the first western temperance drive mounted in Winnipeg in 1883 had minimal objectives. With a population of less than 15,000, Winnipeg probably had more liquor outlets *per capita* than any other city in Canada, if figures quoted by the moral reformers are at all accurate. The bars attached to hotels were permitted to sell liquor by the glass and by the bottle. Grocery stores were permitted to sell bottled booze, if they had a licence. As there was nothing to prevent a customer from cracking his bottle open in the store and passing it around, worse debauchery frequently occurred in the grocery stores than in the saloons.

While Dr. Silcox was launching his crusade against the Winnipeg brothels, other Protestant ministers were getting ready for what would become a thirty-year offensive against the demon rum. The Reverend D.M. Gordon of the Presbyterian Church, the Reverend A.A. Cameron of the Baptists, the Reverend J.E. Starr for the Methodists, and Archbishop Pinkham for the Anglicans became the leaders of the newly organized Manitoba Branch of the Dominion Temperance Alliance. Their demands upon the provincial government were modest in the extreme. The Reverend Cameron said that there was a licensed bar for every 300 people in Winnipeg and he urged that the ratio be reduced to a bar for every 500. That would still leave Winnipeg with 60 licensed premises, he claimed (the arithmetic was his). The Reverend Dr. Gordon urged a tightening up on the definitions of both bars and groceries. To qualify as hotels, premises then had to have ten rooms. Some of the rooms were no bigger than closets and such hotels were rendezvous for tramps, gamblers, and thieves. He urged an upgrading in size, quality, and number of bedrooms hotels needed for a licence. The delegation also wanted the licence fees raised from $100 to $500 a year.

Here the delegates encountered a basic western problem. Winnipeg, like all the emerging towns of the West, desperately needed hotel and rooming-house accommodation for the incoming settlers. There is no evidence that running a hotel was a direct route to riches on the prairies, perhaps because hotel keepers too often drank up most of their profits. But the Bonifaces all insisted that they could not exist without their liquor profits. If regulations became too severe the small hotels, which had the cheapest rooms, would be run out of business. The same result would follow an increase in the licence fee beyond what the traffic would bear. The politicians, sensitive as they were to the realities of life, moved a great deal more slowly and not nearly as far as the clergy desired. The result was that the organized Temperance forces gradually evolved into organized prohibition forces.

Outside Manitoba, in the Northwest Territories, where prohibition of a sort was the rule, anti-prohibition sentiment was being built up. In the newly developing towns, the law was regarded as far too stringent for white men and justifiable only for Indians. When Joseph Royal became lieutenant-governor of the Territories in 1888 he immediately loosened the system so that anybody — except Indians, of course — who applied to a member of the Territories Council could get a permit to import and possess alcoholic beverages. Imports of whisky into the Territories, which had amounted to only 21,637 gallons in 1887, rose to 151,628 gallons in 1889, which worked out to around ten gallons a year for each adult white male in the Territories.

Anti-prohibition sentiment, however, was confined mainly to the cities and towns. The settlers coming in to take up homesteads were overwhelmingly temperance-orientated. Thus, while Joe Royal was loosening the regulations, the clergy were being nudged from their mild temperance stance to the advocacy of total prohibition by incoming homesteaders from Ontario and the United States.

Ten years after the Silcox crusade, the prohibition zealots were in full cry in Ontario and in the United States and the echoes were reverberating across the western plains. With the ending of prohibition in the Territories in 1892 and the institution of licensed premises, public drunkenness increased. And as it came at a time of economic depression, the prohibitionists were able to draw stark parallels between booze and economic deprivation. Drunkenness in moderation might well have been a luxury the new country could afford in times of prosperity. But in the years of adversity before 1900, booze became a sort of final straw in the load of adversity that the weather, crop failures, and economic stagnation imposed upon the settlers. Everybody needed all the income they could get just to survive.

The newly settled farmers were confronted with problems they had never anticipated — lack of boxcars in which to ship out their crops, an elevator system that cheated them on grades and quantities, the periodic disappearances of grain buyers. When they got cash for their crops, too much of what they got was frequently left in the bars in the towns. Much of the farm anger which was generated by a host of other causes came into sharpest focus in the areas of the final disaster — the city boozeries in which the settlers tried to drown their sorrows. When too much of the urban workers' pay disappeared behind the bars on paydays, the "ban the bar" movement began to make sense to the urban workers who patronized them as well as to the farmers.

As the times were becoming favourable for prohibitionist campaigning, the Protestant churches worked both sides of the street. Thus speakers of the Total Abstinence League, often reformed drunkards, toured the country preaching the wisdom of voluntarily taking the pledge to give up liquor. In Alberta the Anti-Treating League became quite active among the weaker-willed. They did not need to swear off, just take a pledge neither to accept free drinks nor to buy treats for friends. The Women's Christian Temperance Union and the Royal Templars of Temperance, however, were noncompromisers with "distilled damnation". They were for total prohibition by law of beverage alcohol, a position into which even the mildest temperance advocates were driven by the obfuscation and double dealing of the provincial governments in the face of the overwhelming support that gradually developed for the "dry" forces.

In a real sense, the periodic outbursts against prostitution in Winnipeg, Brandon, Regina, Saskatoon, Edmonton, Calgary, and Lethbridge in the period between 1905 and 1915 were but temporary diversions from the great prohibition crusade. In the end, it swept everything before it. As a wartime measure, Saskatchewan shut down the bars in 1915 and established government stores or "dispensaries" where whisky was sold by the bottle. Saskatchewan's example set off the wildest political campaign in Alberta's history. The liquor question was debated up and down the province with huge parades and public meetings that attracted crowds of 10,000. When the plebiscite vote was counted on July 21, 1915, prohibition carried by 47,000 to 28,000. Manitoba followed with a referendum on March 13, 1916, that was carried by 50,484 to 26,502. Then Saskatchewan went to the polls to decide whether or not to retain its liquor stores and voted them out by 95,249 to 23,666. Surely one of the greatest ironies in Canadian history must be the way in which the total victory of prohibition was frittered away, and with the frittering went western Canadian faith in morality legislation.

Every claim which the moral reformers made for prohibition turned out to be true.[3] It did reduce alcoholic consumption, perhaps by as much as eighty per cent. It did immediately improve the economic status of the working class. It did very substantially improve industrial efficiency by reducing absenteeism. It did reduce drunkenness and rowdiness in the streets. It did result in a marked reduction in all other forms of crime. One set of statistics is enough to demonstrate the striking change in conditions. In 1914 the city of Calgary had a police department of 63 constables, who made over 2,550 arrests for drunkenness and vagrancy. By 1918 the force was down to only 28 constables, who managed only 183 arrests for liquor offences. In that year Chief Alfred Cuddy was able to report that "the abolition of the bar continues to serve as a preventative for every type of crime." His assessment of the situation could have been echoed by every police department in the West. In the end it was prohibition and its subsequent withering away that created conditions which spelled the ultimate demise of segregated prostitution as a viable social institution on the prairies.

There was never a time, of course, when prohibition was acceptable to the whole population. The law was barely on the books before a wide-ranging conspiracy developed to supply the still substantial public appetite for booze. In the beginning the main thirst quenchers were the doctors and druggists, for medicinal alcohol was still obtainable under a doctor's prescription. In addition to straight whisky, the drugstores also laid in shelves full of new-fangled patent medicines for customers who could not afford doctors' prescriptions. Such old stand-bys as Peruna, Burdicks Blood Bitters, Ayers Sarsaparilla, Hostelters Bitters, and Lydia Pinkham's Compound became best-sellers. The most potent, Hostelters Bitters, was forty-six per cent alcohol and Lydia Pinkham's Compound contained almost five times as much alcohol as did beer. The virtues of them all, along with Tanlac and Dr. Smather's Asprolax, were trumpeted in newspaper advertisements with testimonials from happy imbibers.

Nevertheless, despite the leakage in the prohibition dikes, the volume of alcoholic consumption dropped almost to nothing. The issuance of 140,000 prescriptions a year by Edmonton doctors seems an imposing statistic. But since the orders were mainly for eight-ounce bottles, it works out to less than a bottle of whisky per capita for the residents of the area. The prohibition law, however, began to run into very heavy weather with the return of the troops from overseas in 1919. They came home with man-sized appetites they had developed in the pubs of England and the bistros of France. The enactment of the prohibition law while they were abroad fighting for King and Country became a rankling grievance that led to counterattacks from the war veterans. As that was the sort of argument for which the liquor interests were prepared to supply unlimited backing, it was not long before "Moderation Leagues" sprang up in all the provinces to advocate legalizing the sale of booze in one form or another. But, instead of yielding to the wets, the governments went on intensified drives to block the loopholes.

Until the temporary federal Order-in-Council of March 1918 prohibiting the inter-provincial movement of liquor, prohibition enforcement on the prairies was a complete shambles. Before that it was illegal to consume beverage alcohol; but it was legal to import and export it. So anybody who developed a thirst could send to Ontario and have all the booze he wanted delivered to him by parcel post or railway express. For some reason that remains unclear, huge liquor warehouses were established in Saskatchewan which did a land-office business diluting straight grain alcohol, spiking it with flavouring, bottling it under counterfeit brand labels, and exporting it to the United States as Scotch whisky.[4]

The Dominion ukase against interprovincial trade expired on December 31, 1919. Three years after the first prohibition votes, the temperance sentiment was still so strong in both Saskatchewan and Alberta that the voters gave substantial affirmative majorities to plebiscites on whether to bar importation of alcohol into their provinces. That, in the eyes of the reformers, should have resolved the question. It did nothing of the sort. They had neglected to mention exports. So there was nothing to prevent the well-stocked warehouses from continuing in the export business. It was a simple matter for thirsting Albertans to have their booze shipped to a British Columbia point where they could pick it up and bring it home.

In Manitoba the joy-juice flowed in from Ontario, regardless of the law. And as time passed the law against importation was honoured more in the breach than the observance. In the Winnipeg Grain Exchange, the vessel brokers who chartered lake steamers to the grain trade brought the stuff in by the case and sometimes by the ton. One broker habitually kept his vault filled with Johnny Walker and Canadian Club. After-the-market drinking became such an institution that it set off a boom in the plate glass business. To avoid staining their varnished desks the brokers covered them with custom-styled plate glass tops. One of the first electric refrigerators in the city was installed in a vessel broker's office for the storage of mix and the making of ice. Elsewhere it was the first morning duty of the office boys to check on the soda and ginger-ale supply and to ice the water coolers. Senior members of the city detective department soon discovered the superior quality of Grain Exchange booze and were frequent, but friendly, visitors to the brokerage offices.[5]

It took seven years of prohibition to change the public's mind. But change it did. Alberta and Manitoba in 1922 and Saskatchewan in 1924 opted for a return to legalized booze, but only if it were doled out from government stores. Suggestions for the re-opening of the bars, or even for the serving of wine with meals in restaurants, were snowed under.

The final overthrow of prohibition came not so much from argument or agitation as from the quiet erosion of public opinion. The bootleggers and blind pigs replaced the hotel bars as the prime object of public disaffection. The demonstrable difficulty of law enforcement encouraged the bootleggers to more open operation. In Saskatoon, during the heat of the summer, the druggists kept beer on ice in washtubs for their thirsty patrons.[6]

From time to time carloads of whisky were seized on railway sidings, rum runners were ambushed, and illicit stills were captured. In the reports of these events the value of the booze involved was always featured in headlines. Prior to prohibition, it was the general practice of bars and liquor dealers to improve their profit margins by wholesale adulteration. When the Saskatchewan government took possession of the dealers' stocks in 1916, chemical analysis disclosed just how universal the practice was of watering the stock and fortifying it with wood alcohol.[7] The bootleggers and home brewers carried on where the licensed dealers left off. The hospitals therefore were called upon to handle an increasing traffic in poisoned patients, some of whom became blind or died.

As the enforcement agencies demonstrated their inability to cope with the illicit whisky trade, people who had favoured prohibition began to search for alternatives. When prohibition was sweeping the country, scarcely a voice was raised in favour of the wet cause. Of the prairie daily newspapers, only the *Edmonton Journal* took a strong stand against prohibition. As the difficulties mounted, there was a noticeable edging away from the bandwagon. If sale of whisky by the governments under the most rigid regulation was the only way to banish the bootleggers as the bars had been banished, then public sentiment veered toward government liquor stores.

Yet, as the liquor interests pressed their counterattack, the unity of purpose among the clergy which had carried the day for prohibition seemed to evaporate. It may very well be that other social malaise besides boozing and wenching had become more compelling of attention. Such clerical leaders as J.S. Woodsworth, A.E. Smith, Salem Bland, William Ivens, William Irvine, D.S. Hamilton, and others became more interested in social causes than in moral reform. When the brewers got agitation going to bring back beer by the glass they found the big guns of their opponents spiked and the prohibition camp all but deserted.

The seven-year drought profoundly changed the lives of the women of ill repute in all the prairie cities, though the changes took better than twenty years to run their course. The transition from private enterprise to government monopoly of liquor sales had a most deleterious direct effect on the economics of brothel operation. When whisky sold for one dollar a bottle, it was not uncommon for a madam to dispense a preliminary drink or two with the compliments of the house. With whisky at four dollars a bottle, such hospitality became too expensive for the average brothel, even though the scale of fees had moved upward with wartime inflation. So they were forced to sell liquor as a sideline, and as bootleggers they became the objects of the attention of the liquor-law enforcers as well as of the morality squads.

A second unfavourable development was the sharp decline in male numerical superiority. More than 50,000 Canadians died during the First World War. Many of those who enlisted from western Canada and survived the fighting never returned. By 1921 the male preponderance was down to 100,000 and the more even balance in male-female numbers naturally caused a sharp drop in the demand for the services of the prostitutes.[8]

Perhaps most important of all the changing mores was the revolution in drinking patterns which prohibition brought about. The men who had tarried at the bars during lunch or after work began frequenting bootleggers in nearby downtown apartment blocks. There was a gradual movement of the whores out of the brothels in the old segregated areas into their own apartments, where they combined bootlegging and prostitution. As the drinkers had once developed "favourite" bars they now acquired "favourite" bootleggers, who as often as not were prostitutes on the side, but circumspect and discreet bootlegger-prostitutes. Even after government liquor stores were approved deep-dyed public prohibitionist sentiment still abounded. It was reflected in quick complaints to the morality squads if the voices emanating from next door or across the street were too frequently hilarious.

The need for the brothels to sell booze as well as sex became a fatal handicap for segregated areas. The big brothels were easy targets for morality squads. The fact that brothels were raided for booze regularly tended to scare much of the trade away.

Finally the automobile and the changing moral values of the 1920s brought so many willing amateurs into the business that the red-light districts fell on hard times from that cause alone. Yet they all survived, after a fashion, until the Great Depression turned the sin streets into ghost streets.

In Winnipeg a large manufacturing plant stands on Annabella Street hard by the C.P.R. spur track that serves a string of other warehouses in the area. One afternoon in the autumn of 1938 the plant manager was idly watching his workers heading for the Higgins Avenue streetcar when he noticed a couple of girls coming down Annabella from Higgins, carrying brown paper lunch bags. They walked under the subway and along another block and entered one of the Annabella Street brothels.

Could it be, he wondered, that the depression had reached a stage where the Annabella Street whores were reduced to walking to work carrying their lunches? He embarked on a girl-watching stint, off and on, for the next several weeks. One day he intercepted one of the girls to satisfy his curiosity. Was she, he asked, actually a prostitute going to work?

"Oh sure," said the girl, somewhat defensively, "what's it to you?"

"Oh nothing," he replied. "I was just curious because I always understood you girls all lived there full time."

"We used to, or rather some of the other girls used to and some still do. But I am on relief and the relief departments will pay $1.50 a week for a room for me but they won't pay for rooms on Annabella Street. So I've got a room over on Lily Street and walk back and forth. But it ain't really worth it any more. It just gives me a place to hang out and I've got nothing else to do."

Some time during the next decade she and the sisterhood disappeared from Annabella Street, and from all the other red-light streets of the prairie cities. But illicit sex is still for sale in 1971 and booze still lubricates the process of negotiation. The younger and fancier whores now sip their beer in the taverns or their cokes in the cocktail lounges waiting for prospective customers, who are numerous enough to make the waiting game worth while. The older, less attractive bawds walk the streets near the skid-row beer parlours under the casually benign eyes of the policemen on the beat. An octogenarian walking down Ninth Avenue East in Calgary or central Main Street in Winnipeg in 1971 might well shake his head once or twice and imagine he was back where he had come in sixty years ago. If he happened to be around when the drunks lurched from the boozeries at closing time, he would be sure of it. And he would be sure as well that alcoholism on the prairies is far worse than it was when the moral reform movement was at its peak. There is one vital and substantial difference today — there isn't an old-fashioned moral reformer anywhere on the horizon who has the slightest interest in trying to change the world or its inhabitants.

Appendix

Extracts from a double-column editorial in the *Macleod Gazette*, March 16, 1886:

According to Mr. Trivett's statement one not acquainted with the facts might easily imagine there is a market for girls going on at full blast at Macleod. One might also imagine an auctioneer introducing the various victims, dwelling on their merits and extolling the article he had for sale for the most grossly immoral purposes. We can imagine their horror struck faces as they listen in fancy to the "going, going, third and last time, are you ready — gone!" Another pure-minded Indian maiden sacrificed at the altar of human depravity for a small consideration of dollars and cents.

It is needless to say no such thing is going on. We do not argue that there are not many cases where white men do keep Indian women. We may show our depravity when we say we do not see anything wrong in this. In the great majority of cases the primitive bonds of matrimony were entered into long before the civilizing influence of white women was felt. In the great majority of these cases the white men have honourably clung to their bargain and have provided for their Indian wives according to the best of their ability.

It is stated that these women are taken from the camp, kept a certain time and then abandoned to become common prostitutes around the town. But only one side is shown. Nothing is said of the fact that many of these women were prostitutes before they went to live with the white men and in many cases the overtures for this so-called immorality comes from the Indians, or from the women themselves. Mr. Trivett neglected to say there are scores of Indians on the reserve, on which he is a missionary, who practice the revolting and unnatural crime of peddling their women around the towns and settlements.

There is another light from which to view this question. If Mr. Trivett had referred to it, it would have shown a greater desire on his part to deal fairly and impartially with this matter. We refer to the Indian marriage custom. Among the Indians there is no marriage ceremony. If an Indian fancies a lady friend he simply has an interview with the old man and after a little lively barter secures his prize in consideration of his giving two or three horses for her, according to her beauty, and carries her home. According to the law of the Indians, and according to the law laid down by the Government, it is a legal marriage. A white man can marry an Indian in the same way and it has been held in the North West as a legal marriage.

Footnotes

The booze-brothel syndrome of urban pioneers

1. Grant MacEwan, *Between the Red and the Rockies*, Toronto, 1952, pp. 83—93.
2. *Macleod Gazette*, Sept. 19, 1884.
3. M.C. Urquhart and K.A.H. Buckley (eds.), *Historical Statistics of Canada*, Toronto, 1965, p. 29.
4. J.W. Dafoe, *Clifford Sifton in Relation to His Times*, Toronto, 1931, p. 317.
5. J.B. Hedges, *Building the Canadian West*, Toronto, 1939, pp. 114, 165; Douglas Hill, *The Opening of the Canadian West*, London, 1967, p. 261.

6. Unpublished manuscript, in Glenbow-Alberta Institute, Calgary.
7. *Debates, House of Commons, 1881*, pp. 1,327.
8. *Manitoba Free Press*, July 5, 1904.
9. W.L. Morton, *Manitoba: a History*, Toronto, 1957, p. 166 et seq.
10. Ibid., pp. 190-1.
11. Joseph Kinsey Howard, *Strange Empire*, New York, 1952, p. 234; G.F.G. Stanley, *The Birth of Western Canada*, Toronto, 1960, p. 167.
12. Hedges, op. cit., pp. 127–68.
13. George Stevens, *The Canadian National Railways*, Toronto, 1960, p. 55.
14. *Census, 1911*; Eileen Garland, *Trails and Crossroads to Killarney*, Altona, Man., 1967, p. 162.
15. *Edmonton Journal*, Jan. 5, 1908.
16. Ibid., Oct. 8, 1907, and July 23, 1912.
17. *Calgary Herald*, July 2, 1907.
18. J.S. Woodsworth, *Social Surveys in Canada*, Toronto, 1914.
19. J.S. Woodsworth, *My Neighbor*, Toronto, 1911.
20. Royal Commission on Vice, Winnipeg, 1910.
21. *Calgary Herald*, July 16, 1909.
22. Howard, op. cit., pp. 265, 342.
23. *The Globe*, Toronto, Jan. 30, Feb. 24, and June 4, 1886.
24. *Edmonton Bulletin*, March 28, 1908.
25. Oral reports to the author.
26. *The Big Valley Story*, a pamphlet, Edmonton, 1967.
27. See personal recollection of the author in *The Boy from Winnipeg*, Toronto, 1970. Also *Edmonton Journal*, July 22, 1912.
28. *Lethbridge Herald*, June 8, 1909.
29. *Medicine Hat News*, April 14, 1904.
30. Oral report to the author.
31. *Medicine Hat News*, July 5, 1906.
32. *Saskatoon Phoenix*, Feb. 3, 1910.
33. Oral report to the author.
34. Royal Commission on Vice, Winnipeg, 1910.
35. Oral report to the author.
36. Royal Commission on Vice, Winnipeg, 1910.
37. Oral report to the author.
38. *Regina Leader*, Nov. 14, 1909.
39. Oral report to the author.
40. *Edmonton Journal*, Dec. 4, 1909.

There was no street like Annabella Street . . .

1. W.L. Morton, *Manitoba: a History*, Toronto, 1957, p. 172.
2. *Census, 1901*.
3. J.J. Hargrave, *Red River*, Montreal, 1871, pp. 260–74.
4. Ibid.

5. Morton, op. cit., p. 171.

6. Alexander Begg, *Ten Years in Winnipeg*, Winnipeg, 1879.

7. *Winnipeg Times*, April 1—30, 1883.

8. *Medicine Hat Times*, April 14, 1904.

9. *Census, 1901.*

10. *Census, 1901.*

11. Hope Ross, *Biography of Dr. F.B. DuVal*, a pamphlet.

12. *Manitoba Free Press*, and *Winnipeg Telegram*, Nov. 18, 1903, et seq.

13. Ibid.

14. *Manitoba Free Press*, Aug., 1904.

15. *Manitoba Free Press*, Jan. 9, 1904.

16. Royal Commission on Vice, 1910; Henderson City Directories, 1910 to 1940.

17. Winnipeg City Council, Minutes, July 1905.

18. *Manitoba Free Press*, Jan. 5, 1905.

19. Winnipeg City Council, Minutes, January 1906.

20. *Manitoba Free Press* and *Winnipeg Telegram*, Jan. 21, 1907.

21. Royal Commission on Vice, 1910.

22. Ibid.

23. Ibid.

24. Ibid.

25. Ibid.

26. Ibid.

27. Ibid.

28. Ibid.

29. Ibid.

30. Ibid.

31. Oral reports to the author.

32. Oral reports to the author.

... except Regina's River Street, which was in Moose Jaw.

1. Edward McCourt, *Saskatchewan*, Toronto, 1968, p. 84.

2. J.W. Powers, *History of Regina*, a pamphlet.

3. Ibid.

4. Ibid.

5. Earl C. Drake, *Regina, the Queen City*, Toronto, 1955, p. 22.

6. *Regina Standard*, Feb. 19, 1897.

7. *Regina Leader*, July 26, 1883.

8. McCourt, op. cit., p. 87.

9. J.S. Woodsworth, *Social Surveys in Canada*, chapter on Regina.

10. *Regina Leader*, June 1, 1904.

11. *Brandon Weekly Sun*, May 17, 1905.

12. *Saskatoon Star*, May 31, 1912.

13. *Regina Leader*, Dec. 23, 1913; Drake, op. cit., Toronto, 1955.

14. *Regina Leader*, June 28 and Sept. 26, 1921.
15. Oral report to the author.
16. Oral report to the author.
17. Oral report to the author.
18. J. Hawkes, *Saskatchewan and Its People*, vol. III, Regina, p. 1930.
19. *Moose Jaw Times*, June 1, 1906.
20. Oral report to the author.
21. Report of Bence Commission.
22. Ibid.
23. *Moose Jaw Times*, Feb. 18 and 19, 1924.
24. Oral reports to the author.
25. Ibid.

Saskatoon — where everything was handy to the station

1. Testimony, Scott Commission, Edmonton, 1914.
2. Testimony, Royal Commission on Vice, Winnipeg, 1910.
3. *Narrative of Saskatoon*, a pamphlet, p. 15.
4. Eric Knowles, *The Saskatoon Story*, a pamphlet, 1952, p. 17.
5. *Winnipeg Times*, March 1883.
6. Knowles, op. cit., pp. 52—62.
7. Ibid., pp. 62—4.
8. H.J. Archer, *Historic Saskatoon*, Toronto, 1949, p. 30.
9. *Saskatoon Phoenix*, June 7, 1909.
10. Oral reports to the author.
11. *Saskatoon Star*, July 20, 1912.
12. Ibid., Jan. 28, 1910.
13. *Saskatoon Phoenix*, Jan. 28, 1910.
14. *Saskatoon Star*, March 24, April 1, 1912.
15. Ibid., Aug. 6, 1912.
16. Ibid.
17. Ibid., Aug. 10, 1912.
18. *Edmonton Bulletin*, Dec. 21, 1914, and Jan. 27, 1915.
19. *Saskatoon Star* and *Saskatoon Phoenix*, Feb., March, and April, 1915.
20. Ibid.
21. Oral report to the author.
22. Ibid.

The saga of Joe Clarke — radical conservative with socialist leanings

1. *Edmonton Bulletin*, Oct. 24, 1888.
2. Ibid.
3. North West Mounted Police, Annual Reports, 1888—95.
4. *Macleod Gazette*, Feb. 16, 1886; *Regina Leader*, May 18, 1904.

5. *Edmonton Journal*, Dec. 11, 1907.
6. *Edmonton Bulletin*, March 31, 1908.
7. *Edmonton Journal*, Oct. 31, 1908.
8. Ibid.
9. *Edmonton Bulletin*, Dec. 31, 1908.
10. *Edmonton Journal*, Dec. 4, 1909.
11. Edmonton Police Department, Annual Report, 1911.
12. *Edmonton Bulletin*, June 12, 1914.
13. *Edmonton Journal*, Oct. 13, 1911.
14. *Edmonton Bulletin*, Aug. 9, 1912.
15. Photographic Catalogue, Alberta Archives, Edmonton.
16. *Edmonton Journal*, Oct. 16, 1908.
17. *Edmonton Journal* and *Edmonton Bulletin*, November and December, 1913.
18. Ibid., Jan. 14, 1914.
19. Ibid., Jan. 27, 1914.
20. Testimony, Scott Commission, June 12, 1914, et seq.
21. Ibid.
22. *Edmonton Bulletin*, May 19, 1914.
23. *Edmonton Journal*, May 25, 1914.
24. Scott Commission.
25. *Edmonton Journal*, May 26, 1914.
26. *Official Gazette*, Edmonton, July 23, 1914, pp. 303—6.
27. *Edmonton Bulletin*, Aug. 7, 1914.
28. *Edmonton Bulletin* and *Edmonton Journal*, Dec. 22, 1914, and Jan. 28, 1915.

"To hell with Pearl Harbor — remember Pearl Miller!"

1. *Calgary*, The Twentieth Century Cities series, London, 1912.
2. Henderson City Directories.
3. Ibid.
4. *Calgary Herald*, Oct. 17—19, 1906.
5. N.W.M.P., Annual Report, 1884.
6. *Calgary Herald*, Oct. 29, 1906.
7. Ibid., Feb. 26, 1907.
8. Ibid., Sept. 24, 1907.
9. Ibid., Jan. 11, 1908.
10. Newspaper reports on Stuart Commission testimony, January 1908.
11. Ibid.
12. Ibid.
13. Stuart Commission *Report*, Jan. 28, 1908.
14. *Albertan*, July 15, 1909.
15. Ibid., July 16, 1909.
16. Oral report to the author.

17. Ibid.
18. *News-Telegram*, Feb. 1–8, 1911.
19. *Albertan*, Nov. 15, 1911.
20. Ibid., Jan. 6, 1913.
21. Oral report to the author.
22. Ibid.
23. Calgary Police Department, Annual Report, 1917.
24. Oral report to the author.
25. Ibid.

Lethbridge and Drumheller: something more than a house

1. Oral report to the author.
2. *Short History of Lethbridge*, a pamphlet.
3. Ibid.
4. Ibid.
5. North West Mounted Police, Annual Report, 1887.
6. Ibid.
7. Ibid., 1890.
8. Oral report to the author.
9. *Lethbridge Herald*, March 5, 1909.
10. Ibid., May 4, 1910.
11. N.W.M.P., Annual Report.
12. Minutes, Lethbridge City Council.
13. Oral report to the author.
14. *Lethbridge News*, Dec. 7, 1899.
15. *Lethbridge Herald*, Sept. 5, 1907.
16. Oral report to the author.
17. *Lethbridge Herald*, April 20, 1909. Minutes, Lethbridge City Council, same date.
18. *Lethbridge Herald*, May 18, 1909.
19. Ibid., May 4, 1910.
20. Ibid., March 30, 1910.
21. Ibid., July 11, 1910.
22. Ibid., July 11, 1910.
23. Ibid., June 12, 1912.
24. Ibid., June 14, 1912.
25. Testimony before Winters inquiry, August 1912.
26. Ibid.
27. *Lethbridge Herald*, Sept. 11, 1912.
28. Ibid., Dec. 8, 1919.
29. Oral report to the author.
30. Ibid.
31. Ibid.

Requiem for an era

1. R.I. McLean, *Temperance and Prohibition in Alberta*, unpublished M.A. thesis, 1969.
2. See 1876 resolution, Nova Scotia Legislature; R. E. Spence, *Prohibition in Canada*, Toronto, 1919.
3. *Canadian Annual Review*, for 1918, 1919, and 1920, contains extensive reviews of statistical results of prohibition.
4. Royal Commission on Customs and Excise, 1928. *Interim Report 310*, pp. 50—6.
5. Oral report to the author.
6. *Calgary Albertan*, Jan. 1, 1916.
7. *Census*, 1921.

Index

Adams, Ian, 171, 172
Albertan, 137, 148, 149
Alcohol, in the West: associated with prostitution, 14, 49, 173, 183; bootlegging, 49, 55, 74, 75, 78–9, 152–3, 173, 185; control of sale and enforcement of liquor laws, 59–60, 67–8, 133, 146–7, 185, 190; drinking problem of Indians, 4, 185; drinking problem of R.C.M.P., 3, 4–5, 65; drinking problem of the public, 128, 159, 182, 192; as part of frontier life, 183;

revolution in drinking patterns, 191. *See also* Prohibition
Amedia, Sam, 147
Anderson, Lila, 47, 54
Arbuthnot, John, 35, 36, 37
Armstrong, G.S., 111
Ashdown, James, 43

Ballachey, Lawyer, 15
Battleford, 7, 59
Bauman, Ruby, 106

203

Beale, Billy, 104—6
Beaman, John, 47
Beckman, Roy and Ethel, 147
Belanger, Babe, 92—4
Bell, Mrs. Jessie, 119
Bence, A.F., 81, 82, 83
Berry, E.G., 74
Berry, Frankie, 173
Biggar, O.M., 118
Bland, Salem, 190
Booth, M.S., 113—14, 115, 116, 117
Bowman, Alderman, 171
Boyd, Cleve, 132
Brandon, 60, 66, 68—70, 186
Breckenridge, Louise, 79—80
Bruton, Martin, 74
Burbeck, Detective, 117
Burns, J.F., 65

Cairney, Constable, 100
Caldwell, Alderman, 69
Calgary, 7, 8, 10, 12, 18, 20, 21, 22, 23—4,
   27, 66, 101, 124—54, 186, 187;
   "American Hill", 126, 127; Bowmarsh
   Bridge, 138, 139; Brewery Flats, 127,
   128, 142, 143; early history, 125—8;
   Langevin Bridge, 15, 130, 132, 137; Nose
   Creek Hill, 142—6; population, 9, 125,
   127, 140; Riverside, 128, 130, 132, 134,
   139
Calgary Citizens Committee, 132, 133
Calgary Herald, 14—15, 20, 129, 130, 132,
   141, 147
Cameron, A.A., 184
Campbell, "Klondike", 142
Canadian Northern Railway, 7, 101, 103
Canadian Pacific Railway, 3, 6, 34, 43, 46,
   59, 75, 126, 127, 152—3, 162
Carmichael, J.A., 63
Carpenter, Silas H., 111, 112, 113,
   114—15, 120
Carter, Charlie, 134
Carter, Mamie, 180
Caulder, Alderman, 81, 82
Chivers, Charlie, 134
Chudek, Mrs., 10
Clark, A.J., 15
Clarke, Joe, 95, 112—13, 114—15, 116,
   117, 119—20, 121, 122, 123
Clarke, Mamie, 115
Clarke, S.J., 3—4
Clayton, Ethel, 135
Coleman, Detective, 116
Copeland, Maud, 15
Corbett, Griffith Owen, 28
Cowboy Jack, 164

Crime in Western Canada, 39, 78; arrests
   and convictions, 43—4, 107, 111—12,
   151, 187; drug abuse, 80—1, 85, 112, 113;
   gambling, 12, 72, 77, 111, 115, 117, 133,
   136—7, 164, 167. See also Alcohol, in the
   West; Prostitution
Cuddy, Alfred, 148, 149, 151, 152, 187
Cudlip, Constable, 100
Cunningham, E.A., 171
Curney, Gertie, 56—7

Daily, Carmen, 117—18
Daly, T. Mayne, 12, 44
Davin, Nicholas Flood, 61, 62, 64, 65, 66,
   73
Davis, William, 175, 176
Day, Frankie, 132
Deane, R. Burton, 17, 22, 143—6, 159—60
Denny, Captain, 4
Dewdney, Edward, 58—9
Diamond Dolly, 138—9, 145
Douard, Mignon, 120
Douglas, Blanche, 142
Douglas, Tom, 116
Dow, Nina, 129
Drake, Earl, 61
Drumheller, 155, 156, 177—81; early
   history, 177—8
Drumheller Mail, 177
Duffus, Inspector, 145
Dunning, William, 95, 96
DuVal, Frederick B., 35, 36, 37, 42

East, Alderman, 114
Edmonton, 8, 9, 12, 24, 27, 74, 95,
   99—123, 186; early history, 101, 103—4,
   107; merger with Strathcona, 101,
   110—11; Norwood, 104; Old Town, 104,
   107, 109, 120; population, 9, 101
Edmonton Bulletin, 100
Edmonton Journal, 15, 106, 112, 122, 190
Edwards, William D., 136, 137
Egan, Pat, 169, 170, 174, 175, 176
Emmering, George, 28
English, Tom, 128, 129, 132, 133, 134,
   135, 136—7, 139, 147—8, 152
Ensor, R.W., 110
Evans, Sanford, 54—5, 56

Finlay, Reverend, 68—9
Fleming, J.W., 69
Fogy, Constable, 4
Fort Macleod, 2, 3, 13, 59, 158, 159
Frayne, Alderman, 171
Frost, T.A.P., 132, 134, 135
Fryant, Richard, 118

Fuller, Ethel, 167
Fyvie, John, 85

Galbraith, W.S., 167, 168, 169
Galt, Alexander, 158
Gammie, George, 18
Gay, Jessie, 135
Gillespie, Joe, 167, 169, 170, 173, 174, 175
Gordon, Alex, 171
Gordon, Charles W., 41
Gordon, D.M., 184
Grand Trunk Pacific Railway, 91, 103
Gray, Constable, 96
Griffith, Sergeant, 106
Grimsdale, William, 146

Habourg, Annie, 60
Hall, Carmen, 129—30
Hall, Elsie, 134
Hall, Eva, 15
Hamilton, D.S., 190
Hannfin, Constable, 4
Harcourt, Alderman, 69
Harris, James, 176
Harwood, R.J., 67
Heaton, Frank, 95, 96
Herchimer, Colonel, 65
Hill, Fred, 136
Hill, George, 121—2, 123
Hill, Lulu, 173
Holmberg, Big Bill, 136, 137
Housing shortage and overcrowding, 9, 10, 94, 184
Howard, Helen, 175
Howard, May, 167, 173, 175
Hubert, Helen, 142
Hunt, W.G., 129, 132

Immigration, into Western Canada, 1—2, 3, 6—7, 32—3, 104, 127—8, 178
Ingram, J.S., 29
Irvine, William, 190
Ivens, William, 190

Jack, Captain, 4
Jennings, Madge, 142
Johnson, Minty, 135
Johnson, W.P., 79, 81, 82, 83, 84—5

Kerby, G.W., 20
King, May, 142
Kinney, Alderman, 114
Knight, Miss, 83—4
Kozuchar, M. and P., 10

Lake, J.N., 88, 89

Lamb, Bill, 174
Lancey, A.C., 107, 108, 110—19 *passim*, 121
Lethbridge, 12, 17, 66, 101, 155—77; early history, 158—9, 163—4, 173; population, 165, 172; "The Point", 156—77 *passim*
Lethbridge Herald, 173
Lethbridge News, 165, 166
Lewis, Corporal, 164, 165
Lewis, Corrine, 173
Lewis, Maud, 129
Livingstone, J.A., 88
Livingstone, Louise, 142
Lovering, James, 175, 176
Loyal Orange Lodge, 6, 33

McCarthy, John, 74—5
McDiarmid, Principal, 68
Macdonald, Frank, 44
Macdonald, John A., 4
McEachern, Alderman, 70
McElhaney, Adjutant, 20, 51, 52, 54
McGillis, Dan, 113
McKenney, Henry, 28
Mackie, Thomas, 139, 140—1, 142, 146, 148, 152
McKillop, Charles, 164, 165
McLeod, Colonel, 4
Macleod Gazette, 13, 193
McLorg, E.A.C., 96
McNamara, William J., 112, 113, 114, 115, 118, 120, 121
McRae, John, 35—6, 37—8, 39—40, 42, 44, 46, 47, 48
Manitoba College, 29
Manitoba Free Press, 40, 42, 61
Markwick, G.H., 16, 18
Marshall, Mrs. E.E., 108—9
Martin, Daisy, 173
Martin, E.D., 36, 55
Mason, Ray, 145, 146
Maxwell, Louise, 72
May, Alderman, 114
May, Sergeant, 144
Medicine Hat, 16, 18, 30, 89, 101
Melville, James, 136
Miller, Pearl, 21, 153—4
Minto, Lord, 41
Moose Jaw, 12, 66, 75—86, 89; contrasted with Regina, 76; early history, 75—6, 80
Moosomin, 59, 65
Moral crusades, 13, 14, 19; Calgary, 132—3, 134, 141, 146, 149; Lethbridge, 168—9, 170—2; Regina, 63; Winnipeg, 29—30, 35, 36—7. *See also* Temperance and Moral Reform Society

More, Joe, 144
Morton, Billie, 110, 119, 120
Munford, Myrtle, 145

Nimmons, Robert, 173
Norris, Amy, 54
North Battleford, 8
North West Mounted Police. *See* Royal
    Canadian Mounted Police
Northwest Territories, 6, 58, 59, 60, 62, 66,
    183; prohibition and importing of liquor
    in, 59–60, 65, 159, 185
Nor'Wester, 28

O'Connor, Lena, 96
Oliver, Frank, 100
O'Neil, Jack, 4
O'Neil, Mrs. Jack, 4

Palmer, Blanche, 15
Parker, Ethel, 173, 174, 175
Patterson, Corporal, 4
Patterson, F.W., 129
Penchant, Alice, 54
Perry, T.P., 170, 171, 172
Pinkham, Archbishop, 184
Police departments, municipal: attitudes
    and policies toward prostitutes, 15, 16,
    18–19, 27, 35–6, 44, 50, 54, 73, 96, 99,
    107, 110, 129, 167, 169–70, 175–6;
    Calgary, 128–51 *passim*, 187; complaints
    against and inquiries into, 74, 81–2,
    83–4, 95–7, 106, 113, 135, 147–8, 165,
    174, 175; difficulty of obtaining convic-
    tions, 41–2, 42–3, 73, 141, 146; Edmon-
    ton, 104–23 *passim*; lack of co-operation
    with R.C.M.P. and provincial police,
    80–1, 95, 130, 173; Lethbridge, 164–76
    passim; "licensing" of prostitutes by small
    fines, 19, 31, 69, 165, 174–5; Moose Jaw,
    79, 80–5; raids on brothels, 31, 39–40,
    41–2, 48, 49, 72–3, 79, 94–5, 106,
    111–12, 115, 116–18, 130–2, 145–6,
    147–9, 167; Regina, 67, 72–4; reliance
    on information from prostitutes, 21, 108,
    112, 151; Saskatoon, 94–7; Winnipeg,
    22–56 *passim*
Pow, Mah, 80–1
Prohibition: anti-prohibition sentiment,
    185, 188; attempt to form Temperance
    colony, 88–90; effect upon prostitution
    and crime, 123, 151; ending of, 78, 185,
    189; enforcement of, 80, 81, 188–90; in
    Northwest Territories, 59–60, 65, 185;
    temperance crusades, 27, 35, 88, 122–3,
    182–6

Prosser, A.J., 171, 172
Prostitution: and alcohol, 49, 69, 95, 99,
    123, 152–3, 173, 183, 190, 191; atti-
    tudes toward, 13–14, 15, 16, 150–1,
    157, 165–7, 168–9, 170–2; Brandon,
    68–70, 186; Calgary, 12, 20, 21, 23–4,
    124–54 *passim*; complaints of citizens,
    23, 47, 50–1, 130–2; decline of, 57, 123,
    177, 191–2; description of brothels, 22,
    51, 56–7, 179, 180; description of prosti-
    tute's life, 178–81; Drumheller, 155–81;
    Edmonton, 12, 23, 24, 99–123 *passim*; of
    Indians, 4, 12–13, 17, 159–60, 194; issue
    of segregated areas, 31, 42, 69, 168–9;
    Lethbridge, 12, 17, 155–77 *passim*;
    medical supervision of, 31, 48, 168–9,
    176; Moose Jaw, 12, 76, 77–80, 85–6;
    motivation to become prostitute, 19, 24;
    number of brothels and prostitutes, 12,
    110, 139–40; reformation and rescue
    attempts, 20, 24, 29–30, 51–2, 109, 133,
    149, 153; Regina, 12, 23, 62–75 *passim*,
    76; related to real estate development, 22,
    34, 47; Saskatoon, 87, 91–8 *passim*; Win-
    nipeg, 6, 12, 21, 22, 23, 26–57 *passim*,
    69, 70, 191–2

Ramsley, Fanny, 178, 179, 180, 181
Red River Settlement, 5, 6, 32
Reeves, Detective, 96
Regan, Olive, 142
Regina, 7, 8, 10, 12, 27, 58–75, 76, 85, 92,
    101, 186; contrasted with Moose Jaw, 76;
    early history, 58–61, 66; Germantown,
    10–11, 67, 70, 73, 75, 76; population,
    61, 66, 68
Regina Leader, 61, 62–3, 65, 66, 70–2, 73,
    74
Regina Standard, 63
Reynolds, Jack, 72
Riddell, J.H., 118
Riel, Louis, 5, 6
Robbins, Constable, 4
Robson, H.A., 54, 55, 56
Rodgers, Hattie, 15
Rogers, Maud, 141–2, 147
Roper, Mary, 178, 179, 180, 181
Rosenkrantz, Constable, 145, 146
Royal, Joseph, 185
Royal Canadian Mounted Police (North
    West Mounted Police to 1904, Royal
    North West Mounted Police to 1920), 17,
    59, 61, 62, 66, 67, 72, 91, 92, 94, 97, 99,
    140, 149, 159, 165, 167, 181; drinking
    problem in the Force, 3–5, 65, 100; en-

forcement of liquor laws, 60, 65, 80, 159; lack of co-operation with local police, 80—1, 95, 130; policy toward prostitution, 15, 16, 18, 63, 64, 101, 143, 160, 164; and problem of prostitution of Indians, 12, 159—60; sexual activities of members of the Force, 3—5, 100
Russell, Rose, 173
Ryan, Corporal, 145
Ryan, Sergeant, 4

Salvation Army, 20, 51, 52, 63, 149, 171, 175
Samis, Adoniram J., 132, 134, 135
Sandercock, John, 44
Sanders, W.D., 79
Saskatchewan Provincial Police, 80
Saskatoon, 7, 8, 27, 85, 87—98, 186; as an attempt at a Temperance colony, 88—90; early history, 90, 94; Riversdale, 91
Saskatoon Phoenix, 94, 95, 97
Saskatoon Star, 94, 97
Saunders, Martha, 15
Schultz, John, 28
Scott, D.C., 118, 120
Settlement, of Western Canada, 1—3, 6, 7
Seymour, Ernest, 111, 115, 116—17, 118
Sharpe, Thomas, 37, 43
Shearer, J.G., 52—3, 54
Sheran, Nicholas, 158
Silcox, J.B., 29—30, 31, 184
Silliker, L., 169, 170, 174, 175
Simmons, Mrs., 69
Simser, Constable, 82
Soo Line, 75, 85
Smith, Flo, 134, 135
Smith, Lillie, 145
Smith, Rose, 144
Springer, William, 95, 96, 97
Stafford, William, 158
Stanton, Mr., 64
Starr, J.E., 184
Stewart, James, 28
Stewart, R.G., 118
Strathcona, 101, 110
Stuart, Charles A., 132, 134, 135, 137, 141
Stuart, Helen, 15
Stuart, Marie, 15
Stuart, Sergeant, 96
"Swede" Alice, 164
Swift, Nellie, 129

Taylor, William, 72
Temperance Colonization Society, 88, 89, 90

Temperance and Moral Reform Society, 14, 52, 68, 102, 114, 120, 123, 127, 160, 168, 170, 172, 182
Thomas, C., 15
Thomas, Constable, 100
Thornton, Lulu, 44
Townsend, Tony, 79, 83, 84
Trant, William, 73
Trivett, Samuel, 12—13, 193, 194
Turner, Josephine, 72
Turner, Walker, 116

Underwood, Gertie, 63

Vennette, Doris, 40—1

Walker, C.P., 43
Walker, W.H., 133—4
Walsh, Major, 62
Waugh, R.D., 56
Webb, Nellie, 99—101, 102
Webster, Emelia, 72
Webster, Jack, 72
West, Ora, 116
Wheeler, William, 115—16, 117, 118
Wickson, A.W., 36
Wilson, Lila, 142
Wilson, Rosie, 95
Wilson, Thomas, 150
Winder, Captain, 4
Winnipeg, 5, 6, 7, 8, 10—11, 12, 26—57, 58, 61, 62, 64, 65, 66, 89, 90, 183—4, 186, 191—2; Colony Creek, 29, 31, 34; early history, 26—8, 32—4, 38, 43; population, 32, 38, 50; Sabbatarian nature of, 5, 33
Winnipeg Grain Exchange, 38, 189
Winnipeg Sun, 62, 64, 65
Winnipeg Telegram, 10, 55
Winnipeg Times, 29, 30, 31
Winter, Judge, 146
Winters, Roland, 174, 175
Wood, C.A., 72
Wood, George E., 132, 133, 134
Wood, Mr. Justice, 31
Woods, Minnie, 41, 44, 46, 47, 56
Woodsworth, J.S., 10, 11, 23, 66, 75, 190

Y.M.C.A., 29
Y.W.C.A., 24, 108, 109

Zeats, Theodore, 67, 72, 73, 74